THE LIVES
AND DEATHS
OF JUBRAIL DABDOUB

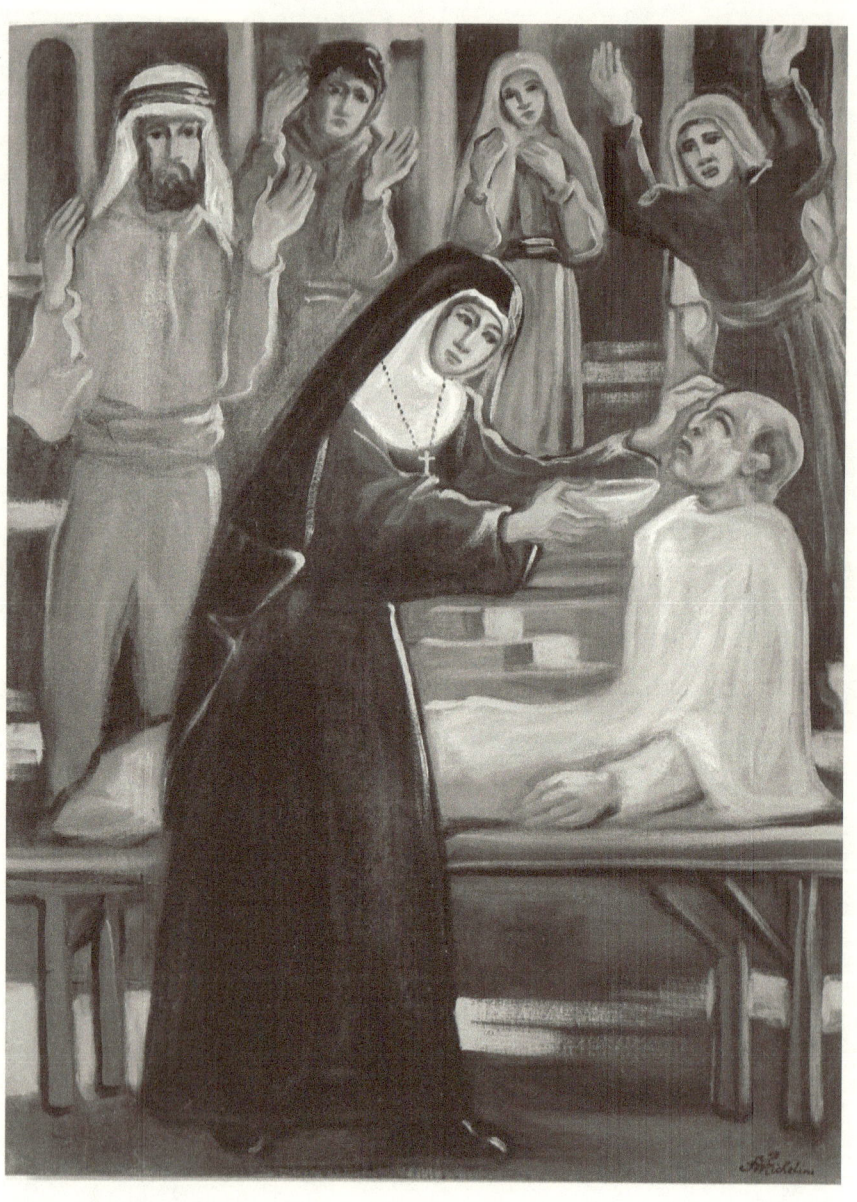

The Lives
and Deaths
of Jubrail Dabdoub

OR, HOW THE BETHLEHEMITES
DISCOVERED AMERKA

Jacob Norris

STANFORD UNIVERSITY PRESS
STANFORD, CALIFORNIA

Stanford University Press
Stanford, California
© 2023 by Jacob Norris. All rights reserved.

No part of this book may be reproduced or transmitted in any form or by any means, electronic or mechanical, including photocopying and recording, or in any information storage or retrieval system without the prior written permission of Stanford University Press.

Printed in the United States of America on acid-free, archival-quality paper
Library of Congress Cataloging-in-Publication Data
Names: Norris, Jacob, author.
Title: The lives and deaths of Jubrail Dabdoub : or, how the Bethlehemites discovered Amerka / Jacob Norris.
Other titles: How the Bethlehemites discovered Amerka | Worlding the Middle East.
Description: Stanford, California : Stanford University Press, [2023] | Series: Worlding the Middle East | Includes bibliographical references and index.
Identifiers: LCCN 2022022359 (print) | LCCN 2022022360 (ebook) | ISBN 9781503633285 (cloth) | ISBN 9781503633759 (paperback) | ISBN 9781503633766 (epub)
Subjects: LCSH: Dabdoub, Jubrail, 1860-1931. | Dabdoub, Jubrail, 1860-1931—Travel. | Merchants—West Bank—Bethlehem—Biography. | Palestinian Arabs—West Bank—Bethlehem—Biography. | Palestinian Arabs—Travel—History—19th century. | Bethlehem—History—19th century.
Classification: LCC DS125.3.D23 N67 2023 (print) | LCC DS125.3.D23 (ebook) | DDC 305.892/74056942092 [B]—dc23/eng/20220628
LC record available at https://lccn.loc.gov/2022022359
LC ebook record available at https://lccn.loc.gov/2022022360

Cover design: Susan Zucker
Cover illustration: View of Bethlehem, 1877. iStock | duncan1890
Typeset by Elliott Beard in Arno Pro 11/14

CONTENTS

Note on Translation and Transliteration		vii
Dabdoub Family Tree		ix
Introduction		1

PART I

1	Of a Land Called Amerka, or How Ammo Hanna Was Saved by al-Khadr	17
2	Of the Hallowed Ridge, or How Jubrail Learned to Profit from Christmas	23
3	Of the Toils of Yousef and Rosa, or How the Bethlehemites Acquired Their Names	29
4	In Which Bethlehem Gets a New Street	38
5	Of Unruly Markets and Underwater Ships	48
6	Of Sunken Eyes in a Casket, or How Bethlehem Came to Be Covered in Dust	54
7	Of Mechanical Wonders on Near and Distant Shores	59

PART II

8	In Search of Amerka	79
9	Of Troubles on the Trocadéro	89
10	Of the Decline of Hosh Dabdoub, or How Jubrail's Schooling Came in Useful	98
11	Of a Street Named Rosario	104
12	By the Truth of al-Khadr, I Went and Came Back!	111
13	Of White Cities and Bronze Medals	116
14	Of Fertility Potions and the Dizzying Heights of Success	127

PART III

15	Of Weeping Icons, Ghostly Armies, and Visions of the Virgin	143
16	Of the Enchanted Palaces of Bethlehem	149
17	Of Hyenas, Serpents, and French Philanthropists	157
18	Of the Resurrection of Jubrail Dabdoub	166

Epilogue	173
Author's Commentary	183
Acknowledgments	203
Glossary of Arabic Terms	205
Notes	207

NOTE ON TRANSLATION AND TRANSLITERATION

UNLESS OTHERWISE STATED, ALL TRANSLATIONS from original texts are the author's.

In the main text, Arabic words are rendered in the Latin script without diacritical marks for ease of reading. Colloquial forms of Arabic, local to the Bethlehem area, are preferred throughout. Where Bethlehemites have adopted their own spellings for names and places in the Latin script, these are generally preserved. This means the same name is occasionally spelled differently—for example, Isa and Issa—according to individual usage.

In the introduction, author's commentary, and notes section, quotations and citations from written Arabic works are transliterated using the system of diacritical marks adopted by the *International Journal of Middle East Studies* (*IJMES*).

A glossary of Arabic terms commonly used in the main text is provided at the back of the book.

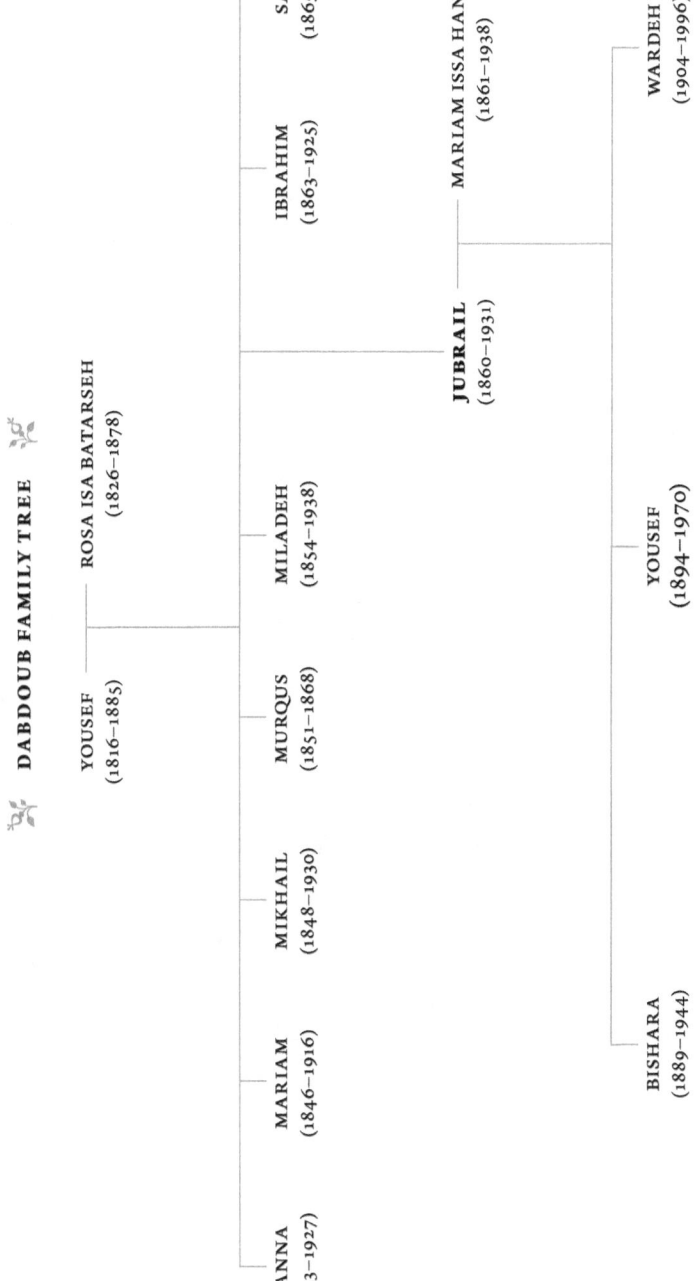

THE LIVES
AND DEATHS
OF JUBRAIL DABDOUB

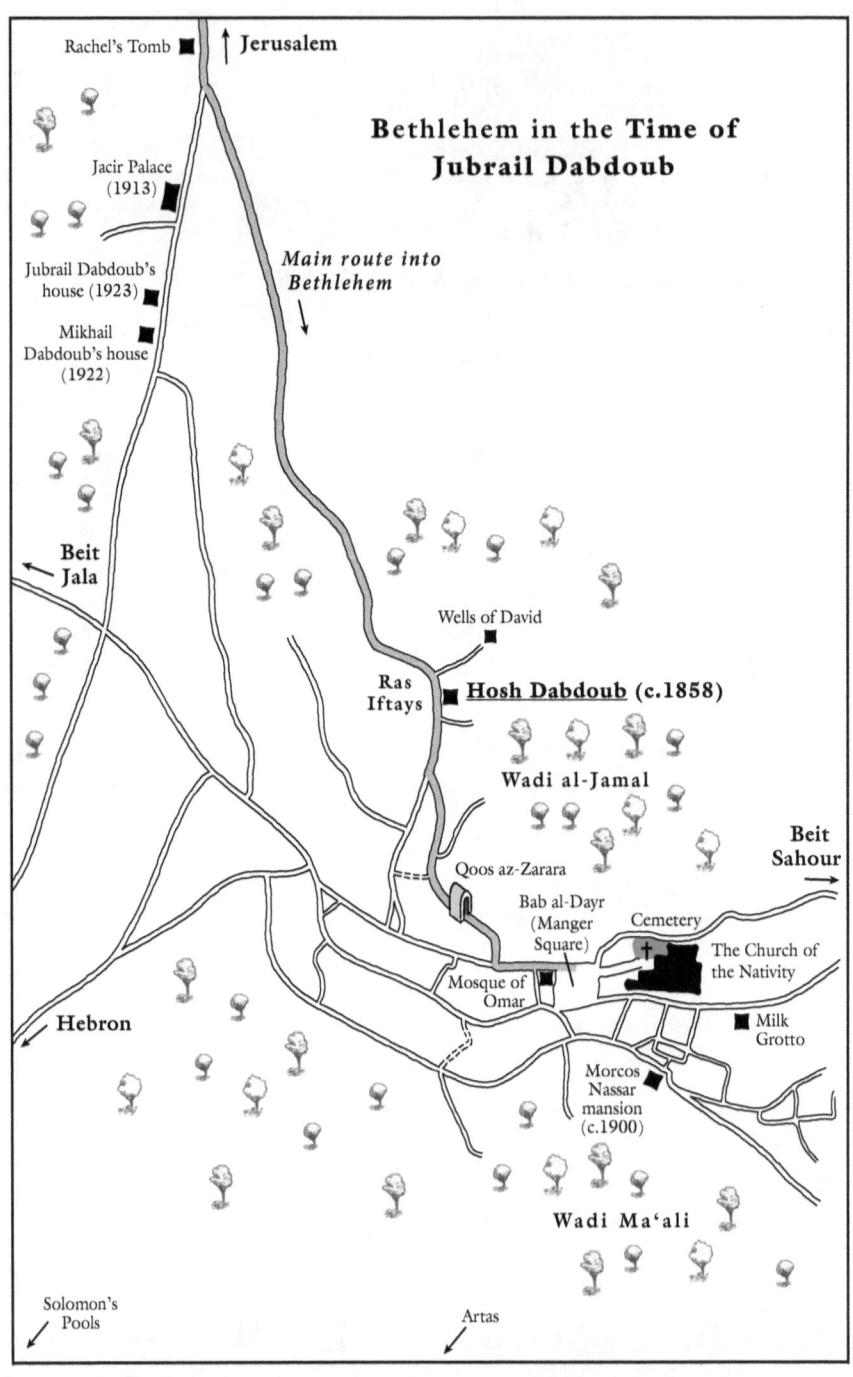

INTRODUCTION

IN THE LAST DECADES OF the nineteenth century, something miraculous happened in Bethlehem, something so extraordinary that it might be necessary to diverge from the impartial tones usually favored by historians. This is the story of how the Bethlehemites discovered Amerka, an Arabic term that came to refer not only to the Americas but more or less anywhere across the oceans. It is the story of young men setting off on the backs of donkeys with suitcases full of crosses and rosaries, returning a year later with those same suitcases stuffed with French francs, Philippine pesos, or Salvadoran colones; of strange inventions that befuddled and bewitched the Bethlehemites in equal measure; of the saints who accompanied them on their journeys to their ends of the earth and did their best to protect them from raging storms and the vagaries of tropical disease; of shimmering pink palaces that sprang up overnight upon the migrants' return; and of mysterious nuns giving sight to the blind and resurrecting the dead.

To tell such a tale is to delve into the realm of the fantastical, the improbable, and the absurd—realms in which the historian rarely sets foot. No doubt Bethlehem's age of miracles could be explained in terms of migrants following rational self-interest, of Palestine's incorporation into the capitalist world market, of a reformist Ottoman state, of the commoditization of religion, and so on and so forth. But how much of the story would we miss if we limited ourselves to such logical explanation? How much would we grasp of the fear and excitement of young travelers as they traversed the vast expanse of the Indian Ocean for the first time? How much would we tap into their sense of confusion and wonder as they witnessed the demonstration of electricity at a world's fair, or as they set foot on the jungle-clad shores of northern Honduras with only a trunk full of Holy Land trinkets for company? And would we feel the curiosity of townsfolk back in Bethlehem when those travelers returned, dressed in strange clothes and carrying exotic objects, to tell embellished tales of heroic voyages?

It was in May of 2015 that I realized this book would be about the life (and deaths) of Jubrail Dabdoub. Palestinian media was awash with news of Pope Francis's canonization of two women, Marie-Alphonsine and Mariam Baouardy. They were being celebrated as "the first Palestinian Catholic saints," the ceremony duly attended by President Mahmoud Abbas, the Latin patriarch of Jerusalem, and an eager crowd of over two thousand Middle Eastern Christians.

My interest was immediately piqued. Both these women had lived in Bethlehem during the late nineteenth century, placing them firmly in the world I was researching. As I sifted through online accounts of their lives, I came across a reference that stopped me in my tracks. There it was, written on the web pages of the Sisters of the Holy Rosary: among Marie-Alphonsine's many reported miracles was the salvation of a man named Jubrail Dabdoub, brought back to life after having been pronounced dead from typhoid fever in Bethlehem in 1909.

It was one of those moments of blissful serendipity historians experience all too rarely. For years I had been researching the merchants of Bethlehem, attempting to understand how their global journeys had transformed Bethlehem from rural backwater into one of Palestine's wealthiest—and certainly most globally connected—towns. Among these wandering merchants, Jubrail Dabdoub was already on my radar. Born in 1860, he was of the "pioneer" generation, which played a significant role in the establishment of new trading bases around the world. I had first encountered him in the National Archives of the Philippines, appearing in 1881 as the earliest immigrant among a new wave of Syrian and Palestinian migrants on the islands. Later I had spotted him among the exhibitors at the Chicago World's Fair of 1893, where he was awarded a Medal of Honor for his efforts. Back in Bethlehem, I had interviewed descendants of his siblings and visited houses he lived in. But the Dabdoub family was just one of dozens I had been tracing, each with its own set of family members strung out across multiple continents, each playing their role in Bethlehem's astonishingly rapid transformation. Trying to condense such an unruly cast of characters into a coherent narrative seemed like an impossible task.

It was in that one moment, as I browsed through the web pages of the Rosary Sisters, that Jubrail presented himself as the protagonist of this story. There he was in Bethlehem in 1909, being resurrected by a local nun, an illustration of the miraculous deed thrown in for good measure. Before long I had tracked down Marie-Alphonsine's notebooks in the Rosary Sisters' convent in Beit Hanina, where the nun's own description of Jubrail's salvation was still preserved in the original handwritten Arabic. Her notebooks became an entry point into a different type of historical experience—one I had been largely oblivious to in my pursuit of the Bethlehem merchants up to that point. Jubrail's unexpected appearance in Marie-Alphonsine's world of healing and piety revealed just how grounded these hard-nosed businessmen were in a more localized social landscape that embraced miracles as part of everyday life. The more I explored this world, the more I realized that the Bethlehemites viewed their economic success as a product of saintly interventions stemming from their own piety. As Jubrail himself put it in a letter to a cousin in Bolivia, "I offer my prayers to God Almighty to facilitate the smooth running of your mercantile affairs."[1] Travel, profit, faith, and magic, it transpires, were inextricably intertwined.

Out of these early strands of research, the book has evolved into a project of creative historical writing. More specifically, it stands as an experiment in "magical realist" historical prose. What most struck me about Marie-Alphonsine's description of the miracle was its mundaneness. There were no rapturous descriptions of sudden heavenly brilliance. Marie-Alphonsine had simply dipped her rosary beads in water and sprinkled some drops on Jubrail's face, reciting the Hail Mary as she did so. The tone was matter-of-fact, without the slightest hint that anything unexpected had occurred. There was no question the Virgin Mary had made an appearance, but she is described among an earthly cast of characters. "Slowly he came back to life," Marie-Alphonsine writes, "through the intercession of the Lady of the Rosary, whose rosary I had put in the glass of water."[2] Never does she use the word miracle.

Over time I came to appreciate how the wider Bethlehemite community tended to share Marie-Alphonsine's lack of surprise when it came to encounters with the spirit world. Interviews carried out in the mid-1930s with Bethlehemites who had experienced Marie-Alphonsine's miracles, including Jubrail's own family, reveal an acceptance of the nun's ability to communicate with the Virgin Mary: "His wife and son are still alive. In their eyes Mother Mary Alphonsus is a great saint."[3] Likewise, in the memoirs of Jubrail's cousin Ibrahim Yuhanna Dabdoub, success as a merchant is continually explained as a product of divine intervention and saintly appearances, particularly those of Saint George, or al-Khadr, in his local guise.[4] When matched against the bewildering experience of encountering faraway cultures, landscapes, and technologies for the first time, it becomes apparent that it was not saintly intrusions or ghostly presences that constituted the fantastical in nineteenth-century Bethlehem. Rather, it was the town's abrupt exposure to global capitalism and the absurdities of European colonialism.

These configurations resonate closely with classic traits in magical realist fiction. From its earliest literary incarnations in Latin America (to which the majority of Bethlehemite merchants traveled), magical realism viewed the world turned upside down, depicting a series of surreal, unexpected juxtapositions as a critique of contemporary society. It is no coincidence the genre was quickly adapted to other literary contexts in the Global South from the 1960s onward. Magical realist prose seemed particularly adept at capturing the arresting experience of a sudden and intensive exposure to the violence of European colonial subjugation and the traumas of postcolonial nation-state building. Writers around the world, from India to West Africa, embraced a style of writing that deliberately recast these forms of modernity as defying logical explanation, serving to collapse colonial binaries of rational/irrational and allowing the text to "see with a third eye."[5] Consider Salim Barakat's 1985 Arabic novel *Fuqaha' al-zalām* (The sages of darkness), in which the character Bikas (and later, his son), goes from birth to old age in a single day, serving as a commentary on the harrowing experience of Kurdish communities under both Arab Syrian and Turkish nation building. "How can I explain something I have no control over?" Bikas mutters to his brothers when he reaches the age of thirty by early afternoon. "I'm just as dumbfounded as you. I see you other people every hour, growing with me year after year, in an acceleration that mixes up my fixed understanding of things I knew before I came."[6]

It is this subversive reversal of the natural and the supernatural that renders magical realism a useful stylistic guide in writing the history of Bethlehem's global circulations. In some ways, Bethlehemites were beneficiaries, not victims, of European colonial networks in the late nineteenth century, as they tapped into the technologies of steam travel and the "liberalization" of Latin American markets to forge their own trading empires. Nevertheless, the dynamic of a rural Palestinian market town being thrust so abruptly into a bewildering world of Western-dominated globalization infuses this story with magical properties.

This is not to romanticize Bethlehem's history prior to its emigration explosion. For centuries the town's status as a pilgrimage destination had produced interactions with various kinds of outsiders. A distinctive tradition in souvenir carving that utilized olive wood and mother-of-pearl as its raw materials and catered in particular to European Catholic pilgrims had developed among Bethlehem's artisans. But Bethlehemites themselves remained largely tied to their hometown, acting as subservient local producers in a trade controlled by the resident Franciscan friars and their superiors in western Europe.[7]

The great breakthrough of the 1860s and '70s occurred when a nascent merchant class quite suddenly severed these bonds and took their Holy Land carvings directly to new clients in Europe, and especially the Americas, at the very time that Christmas cards, gifts, and carols about Bethlehem were taking off around the world.[8] With astonishing speed and success, they established their own global networks of trade, quickly progressing to sell a wide range of imported products in the new markets they encountered. Back in Bethlehem, the experience of living through such a sudden shift must have been baffling, to say the least. By the early 1880s, dozens of young men were setting off for the other side of the world every month, bringing back unprecedented wealth and new customs. It is one thing to observe from a distance strange people occasionally visiting your local church. It is quite another when those people are your brother, son, or cousin.

Jubrail Yousef Dabdoub was born in 1860, descended from a proud line of "little bears" (*dabdoubs*). He made his first known trip abroad in 1878 to France, after which he rotated regularly between various locations around the world: primarily Manila, Paris, New York, Chicago, and San Salvador. In

1882 he was married in Bethlehem to Mariam Issa Handal, a woman whose previous marriage at the age of fifteen had ended under mysterious circumstances. Together they had three children, Bishara, Yousef, and Wardeh, at curious intervals of five and ten years. In 1909 Jubrail was presumed to have died from typhoid fever, only to be brought back to life by Sister Marie-Alphonsine. In 1931 he met his final death in Bethlehem, possibly due to pneumonia.

These are some of the few things we can say for certain about Jubrail's existence. The search for more detailed information has led mainly into darkness, punctuated only by the occasional chink of light. Alongside Marie-Alphonsine's account of the miracle, the only surviving written sources consist of fleeting entries in the Bethlehem parish records (birth, baptism, marriage, etc.), colonial immigration records, and the catalogs of international exhibitions, alongside a smattering of business letters Jubrail penned shortly before his final death in 1931. Material traces of his existence have reared their head: the houses he inhabited in Bethlehem and Paris, Holy Land souvenirs bearing his name, a Medal of Honor he received at the Chicago World's Fair. I have been able to supplement these with interviews with some of his descendants (great-grandchildren, great-nieces, and great-nephews), some of whom were able to relate stories of Jubrail as a wise and generous man who put family honor above all else. But these were only vague impressions, related by people who had either never met him or were so young when they had that they could barely summon a direct memory. A more detailed, uninterrupted biography—let alone a window into the man's thoughts, desires, or prejudices—remained off-limits. After more than six years following him around the world, I still know nothing of his physical appearance.

In the end, the silences in Jubrail's story became a creative space to experiment with a more imaginative approach to writing. Perhaps more by accident than by design, the goal shifted from creating a detailed biography to attempting to capture a wider historical "mood"—a recently emerged topic of cultural history.[9] I attempt to do this through a series of flashpoints in Jubrail's life that invite a discussion of Bethlehemites' sudden intrusion into global circuits of capital and culture. This involved letting go of my academic training in historical empiricism—to write only what is directly evidencable—and instead embracing the idea that the act of imagining can produce fruitful historical results.

In trying to conjure these flashpoints through a magical realist style of narrative, I make no claim to literary merit (years of academic training have put an end to that). Rather, I offer an experiment in using some of the standard tropes of a literary genre to narrate a source-based historical project. In practical terms, this involves imitating magical realist authors' tendency to portray encounters with capitalist modernity in the language of wonder, enchantment, and absurdity, while relating interactions with spirits, saints, and the divine using more mundane, quotidian language. I seek to replicate the genre's disruptions of linear time, emphasizing repetition across generations, recurring dreams, and the persistence of ghostly presences. Equally important is the use of Bethlehemite idioms of folklore and storytelling, which anchor the text in the sense of locality that underpins magical realist novels. The author's commentary that introduces the endnotes provides a more detailed discussion of how and where these wider principles are applied, including how certain Arabic terms are preserved as a way to ground these Christian merchants in their Arabo-Islamic socioreligious context.

As I experimented with this magical realist form of prose, I have come to see it as a more honest way of writing such a project. It is self-evident to me that historians are crafters and stealers of stories, conjuring imitations of a past they could never recreate with exact similitude. As Hayden White long ago pointed out, historians already employ the basic plot structures of storytellers, so why not experiment with *how* we tell those stories?[10] Magical realism seems a particularly good fit for the merchants of Bethlehem. The most celebrated authors of the genre, from Gabriel García Marquez to Isabel Allende to Salman Rushdie, openly posit their texts as counter-realities, grounded in worlds recognizable yet simultaneously unrestricted by the laws of physics. These authors deal fundamentally in narrative, meaning the reader feels the writer's presence as a weaver of stories. As the narrator of Rushdie's *Midnight's Children* spells out: "There are so many stories to tell, too many, such an excess of intertwined lives events miracles places rumors, so dense a commingling of the improbable and the mundane!"[11]

Being open about the historical text as an artificial construct is especially important for a book about Bethlehem written by a historian from the UK—a country that relates to Palestine with an uncomfortable combination of physical distance and colonial proximity. All history is appropriation, but this one carries a particular historical baggage that needs to be carefully thought through.

On the one hand, the impact of my entanglement in a colonial set of relations seems to be lessened by the intense mobility of Jubrail and his contemporaries. Jubrail spent much of his life in motion, moving regularly between the Americas, Europe, Asia, and the Ottoman Empire. Many of the book's chapters consequently take place outside Palestine, shifting between the various locations to which he traveled. Simple binaries of Western/Eastern or colonial/native begin to unravel in this context. Would any historian be able to claim belonging in such a cosmopolitan arena?

Nevertheless, it has become increasingly clear to me that those of Jubrail's generation remained deeply rooted in their hometown. Jubrail himself probably left Palestine for the first time at the age of eighteen. When he and his peers were sent out by their fathers and uncles to find new clients abroad, they were encountering distant cultures and industrial technologies for the first time. The generation that followed was born into this lifestyle, hopping between countries and continents as young children. But for Jubrail, Bethlehem remained an immovable anchor—the fixed point of reference through which all encounters were understood. One of the major themes of the book's latter stages is the extent to which Jubrail lamented the unwillingness of his children, nieces, and nephews to remain in Bethlehem.

The book, then, must also be a study of a specific Palestinian locale, rather than a celebration of "faceless globetrotting" that some global microhistory has resorted to.[12] In this more localized context, any claim on my part to authenticity of representation would be ridiculous. No matter how long I spent living and researching in Bethlehem, I would always approach the town as an outsider. No matter how much I immerse myself in Arabic and its local Bethlehemite dialect, I will never know the language as a native speaker. My intense affection for the town and its people will always be shaped by a position of privilege—the mobile Western researcher able to intersperse visits with trips to far-flung locations while Bethlehemites themselves are confined to ever-smaller spaces, thanks in part to the legacies of my own country's colonial policies. The irony of this dynamic in a town once marked by the intense mobility of its residents has weighed heavily on the writing of this book.

I hope readers will treat the resulting text as a deliberately *constructed* narrative whose magical realist form underlines the historian's role as crafter of stories rather than presenter of concrete reality. Many were the times I was tempted to intersperse more analytical passages of writing into the story, but each time I came back to the conclusion that an unbroken narrative was the best way to test out the value of this experiment and make explicit my own role in the process. The solution has been to create an extensive notes section at the end of the book so the story itself can unfold unimpeded by analysis. The reader can follow in more detail in the endnotes the research trail that underpins the construction of the book's main narrative. The emphasis in the endnotes is on explanation: why and how each passage of each chapter has been constructed the way it has, which passages are based on factually verifiable events, and which have been imagined through the use of a wider array of contextual sources. These notes are prefaced by the author's commentary, which serves as a wider meditation on the book's narrative style and the collection of sources that made such an approach possible.

Bethlehem is an outlier within Palestinian history as a majority Christian town that experienced an emigration explosion in the late nineteenth century. But within this exceptional story of global mobility lies a series of wider historical ramifications. First and foremost, the Bethlehemites played a vital role in forging what we might call the first Arab diaspora (or *mahjar* in contemporary Arabic sources). The period from the 1860s to the start of World War I witnessed an outpouring of migrants from the Greater Syria region (today's Syria, Lebanon, Palestine, and Jordan) that saw an estimated six hundred thousand people emigrate to the Americas alone between 1860 and 1914.[13] It is startling how often those migratory histories begin with a tale of young men from Bethlehem selling devotional objects. From Brazil to the United States and from the Philippines to Australia, the descendants of Arabic-speaking migrants tell foundational stories of how their communities were founded through the peddling of Holy Land crosses and rosaries.[14]

Already by the late 1880s it had become a standard trope for young peddlers from Mount Lebanon and Syria to pick up imitation "Holy Land" goods, now cheaply manufactured in Marseille and New York, en route to their eventual destination in the Americas.[15] Setting off with peddle packs slung over their backs, they usually claimed origin in Jerusalem when selling their trinkets. In Haiti, newspapers described how the earliest Syrians to arrive in the 1880s stepped off the boats in Port-au-Prince holding their goods aloft and crying out, "Jerusalem!"[16] Those headed further north to the United States recounted how *Jerusalem* was the first word of English they learned on the steamships.[17] One fourteen-year-old Lebanese boy peddling Holy Land goods in Worcester, Massachusetts, was even nicknamed "Jerusalem" by his customers.[18] But this Holy Land "brand" was unequivocally made in Bethlehem, not Jerusalem. For centuries the town's artisans had been developing a unique style of souvenir, instantly recognizable for its use of mother-of-pearl. In the late nineteenth century, their ability to bring these goods to new markets across Europe and the Americas had forged a path for thousands of others to follow and to imitate.

This is the wider picture in which Jubrail's story unfolds. Following his journeys allows us to glimpse key features of how the earliest routes of this burgeoning Arab diaspora were forged. Most strikingly, this is an acutely masculine story. Historians of the Arab *mahjar* have rightly emphasized the central roles women played in the establishment of new communities in the Americas, working as peddlers and shopkeepers and sustaining families transplanted to the other side of the world.[19] But the case of Bethlehem shows that the very first forays abroad were an almost exclusively male endeavor. The Bethlehem business model was brutally and ruthlessly patriarchal. At the head sat the patriarch himself—represented in this book by Jubrail's father, Yousef—running the family shop in Bethlehem and dispatching his sons to distant corners of the earth. To sustain the model, women were charged with the central task of producing as many sons as possible for the next generation of intrepid explorers, all while maintaining a new type of family home in Bethlehem: a detached villa situated away from the old town, filled with luxury furnishings imported from Paris, New York, or Istanbul. Whereas once men and women in Bethlehem had toiled side by side in the fields, families now relied entirely on income from the souvenir trade.[20]

But it was a system whose very foundations contained the seeds of its transformation. How could a ready supply of sons be produced when the young men were constantly abroad, often for years at a time? Jubrail's story is a case in point: his wife, Mariam, bore only three children, spaced out by gaps of five and ten years due to his unrelenting schedule of overseas trips. To sustain overseas businesses, teenage brides began to be sent from Bethlehem to distant corners of the Americas to marry men they had usually never met.²¹ By the time Jubrail was resurrected by Marie-Alphonsine in 1909, a new generation of his wider family was growing up in France, Bolivia, and El Salvador, immersed in all kinds of "moral depravities," especially concerning the role of women in society. In the eyes of men like Jubrail, Amerka was a terrain where men could make money before returning to family life in Bethlehem. The hypocrisies contained within this mentality are self-evident, not least because stories abound of sexual affairs conducted by Bethlehemite men while abroad. Nevertheless, male resistance to female emigration contained its own internal logic. Everything the merchant families had built was based on securing the family's status and legacy in their hometown. If women began to reside and raise children abroad, the foundations of the system would quickly erode. To recount Jubrail's story is to tap into the anxieties men of his generation felt as they lived through the early stages of this erosion.

A final, equally important ramification of Bethlehem's outward expansion is the way it presents a different picture of Palestine's relationship to nineteenth-century globalization. Historians tend to depict the emergent "modernity" of this period as a set of influences arriving from the *outside* (especially via Zionism), embroiling first the Palestinian elites in cities like Jaffa and Jerusalem where Western influence was most strongly felt and later trickling its way down to a broader segment of the population.²² Changes in dress, technology, architecture, urban planning, education, gender relations, and political ideas are all discussed as a fraught process of adaptation, mimicry, and resistance to external forces. The Ottoman state, too, plays a lead role in this picture through its aggressive modernization of land tenure, taxation, infrastructure, and the military, based largely on a western European set of models.

In the case of Bethlehem, many of these same themes emerge, but through a very different type of historical agency. No longer are Palestinians static recipients of outside forces, waiting patiently for their worlds to be turned upside down. The Ottoman state appears relatively distant from their lives, as do the Zionist settlers making their presence felt in Jaffa and Jerusalem. Instead, we find Bethlehemites as makers of their own modernities, operating as the foot soldiers of globalization not only in Palestine but in the multiple countries to which they traveled. Whether in Honduras, Haiti, Sudan, or the Philippines, the young merchants of Jubrail's generation played a unique role in introducing consumer goods to rural areas thanks to their global networks of suppliers, opening the way for larger European and North American corporations to follow.

Back in Palestine their influence was equally significant, introducing new customs, technologies, architectural forms, and political ideas. Such was the impact of the capital they brought back to Bethlehem that one journalist for the Jaffa-based newspaper *Falastin* was moved to remark in 1913: "Today the visitor is stupefied upon entering [Bethlehem] as the lofty palaces and great buildings come into view, the likes of which are rarely found in our biggest cities like Jerusalem and Jaffa, and it would not be an overstatement to say Beirut either."[23] This was a building spree bankrolled by merchants who spent most of their time abroad, forging their own cultural styles and motifs as they hopped from country to country.

Bethlehem was a trailblazer, but it was soon joined by other towns and villages across Palestine, especially in the country's hilly central spine. Living patterns in Jerusalem, Ramallah, al-Bireh, Birzeit, Nazareth, Beit Jala, Beit Sahour, and Ramleh, not to mention the wider Syrian region, were all significantly affected by these outward migrations. As many as 20 percent of the migrants were Muslim and from Palestinian towns like al-Bireh, where emigration to the United States in the late Ottoman and mandate periods transformed patterns of home ownership and land tenure.[24]

The merchants of Bethlehem are but an extreme example of the profound restlessness of Palestinian society on the eve of its fateful encounter with Zionism. Movement, migration, and exchange were built into Palestinian lives long before the first Zionist settlers set sail for Palestine from the Russian Empire, Galicia, and Romania. They were out in the world, discovering for themselves the bewildering contradictions of the nineteenth century: what it meant to be cosmopolitan and parochial, rational and pious, modern and traditional, all at the same time. In addition to being peasants, notables, and intellectuals, they were arch-capitalists who helped shape the consumerist world we live in (especially when it comes to buying religious knickknacks). In short, they were people. Palestine was a staggeringly diverse, multifarious society that had no idea of the great trauma that awaited under British and Zionist colonization. To retrace Jubrail's steps is to embrace that richness in all its rough-hewn edges.

Following Jubrail through the unpaved streets of his childhood Bethlehem, down to the port of Jaffa, out onto the open seas, and eventually back to a dramatically changed Bethlehem is to follow a ghostly trail that evades as much as it reveals. To capture this in the form of a story, we are obliged to delve into the realm of speculation and conjecture. This is, after all, a story of miracles (economic and saintly), and miracles are rarely verifiable in empirical terms. Today it seems the age of miracles in Bethlehem has long since passed. The city bears the scars of decades of occupation, hemmed in by towering walls of enclosure, military checkpoints, and impoverished refugee camps. But in the years of Jubrail's childhood, a new realm of possibility was only just beginning . . .

Part I

CHAPTER 1

OF A LAND CALLED AMERKA, OR HOW AMMO HANNA WAS SAVED BY AL-KHADR

OF ALL THE EXOTIC CHARACTERS passing through Hosh Dabdoub, it was Ammo Hanna who most fascinated Jubrail. His real name was Hanna Khalil Ibrahim Morcos. He was not an uncle in the strictest sense, but everyone called him "ammo" as a term of affection. Ammo Hanna had traveled to the farthest reaches of the known world and was a walking repository of fantastical stories. Most of all, he was the only person in Bethlehem to have traveled to Amerka and returned to tell the tale.[1]

In those days, Hosh Dabdoub was the first building travelers encountered as they approached Bethlehem along the path that forked off the main road from Jerusalem. Just at the point the road turned the corner at the top of Ras Iftays and offered its first view of Bethlehem on the ridge below, there was the house, hugging the steep hillside, providing a waystation for excitable travelers.[2]

Young Jubrail would creep upstairs from the living quarters and poke his head around the shop door to find a series of arresting scenes unfolding. A pompous Ottoman general, decked out in war medals, tarbush meticulously brushed, might be updating the local mukhtars on how the sultan's troops had crushed the latest rebellion in Crete. Next to them, a barefoot dervish might be debating the merits of Monophysism with the local Syriac priest, his enormous beard showing up all the whiter against the brilliant blue of his brocaded robe. Or perhaps a group of shaven-headed Franciscans would be gathered around one of the European women who visited the shop from time to time, clamoring to offer her lodging in their guesthouse as they admired her voluminous skirts—a most unfortunate design, Jubrail always thought, for the unexpected gusts of wind that swept through town during the khamasin season.[3]

In the midst of these surprising encounters, Ammo Hanna would turn up unannounced, sending ripples of excitement through the house.

"Ahlayn Imm Hanna! What's happening at the top of the hill?" he would greet Jubrail's mother as she opened the door, a mischievous grin on his face. Despite his age, he cut an impressive figure with his wide gait and bushy mustache.

"Khush ya hajj, come in, come in," Rosa would reply, curious to see what strange objects the old man had brought with him this time. Once, he had arrived wearing a bizarre type of headdress, round in shape and surrounded by a curiously stiff brim. He called it his "burnayta," explaining it was popular in some distant corner of Amerka.[4] Another time, he had brought a mysterious device that made a ticking sound as its mechanical parts rotated. He claimed it could measure the hour without needing to be adjusted with the changing of the seasons. This, he explained patiently, was how franji time operated: fixed, mechanical, and measurable to the nearest second. At this point everyone lost interest, agreeing such a contraption held no practical use given the length of the day was constantly changing and they already had the church bells and local muezzin to remind them of prayer times.[5]

Before Ammo Hanna could linger in the hallway, Jubrail's father and elder brothers would usher him out to the rear terrace to drink coffee and puff on arghileh pipes. There the men of the house would talk business as they gazed out over the sea of olive groves that stretched to the east and then gave way to the barren hills of the Wilderness. They discussed exchange rates between unpronounceable foreign currencies, imports of mother-of-pearl shells, and the recent upsurge in Russian pilgrims. All the while, Jubrail sat patiently beside them, waiting for his moment. Eventually the conversation would die down and the old men would start to snooze on the diwan as the hills turned a golden color in the afternoon sun.

This was Jubrail's chance. "Please, Ammo," he would beg, tugging on his abayeh. "Tell us about Amerka!"

A-M-E-R-K-A. Even the word sounded exotic. Some of Jubrail's friends said it was an island in the Red Sea, while others claimed it lay to the east of the Hindi lands. But Jubrail knew it lay somewhere faraway to the west, across a great sea called the Atlasi Ocean. Ammo Hanna had explained to him that to reach Amerka you first had to cross the lands of the faranja—those strange people who stayed at the Franciscan guesthouse and often came to buy mother-of-pearl carvings from the family shop.[6] Jubrail imagined crossing those lands would be a perilous task. The faranja had a reputation for being quarrelsome, always meddling in the affairs of others, even when circumstance demanded a humbler approach. The Bethlehemites had a long history of welcoming them to their town and even finding ways to profit from their presence. But they had also learned to be wary of them. People still told stories about a particularly haughty general named Napoleon whose army had swept across Egypt and Palestine, attracting a few ambitious locals along the way. Among his local recruits had been a man from Bethlehem named Abdallah Hazboun who had found himself in a delicate position when the franji army was defeated at Acre. Facing a choice between the vengeance of the Ottoman armies or a retreat with Napoleon, Abdallah had wisely chosen the latter, traveling with Napoleon all the way back to France. It was said he had found success there, living in a city called Paris with a franji wife and embarking on further military expeditions, where he continued to help the French armies meddle in the affairs of others. But he could never return to Bethlehem.[7]

Jubrail was familiar with these legends of the first people to travel to the lands of the faranja. But only Ammo Hanna had made it all the way to Amerka. The older generation spoke about a man named Andrea Dawid who had set out for those distant lands nearly a hundred years ago. In the year 1796 word had reached Bethlehem of his death, but the event remained shrouded in mystery. The Dawid family lived just down the road from Hosh Dabdoub and still debated poor Andrea's fate. Some of them said he had been consumed by malignant jinn living in the mountain caves of Amerka, while others insisted he had been devoured by sea monsters during the return voyage.[8]

The speculation over Andrea Dawid only served to heighten interest in Ammo Hanna's stories as he turned to young Jubrail on the terrace and launched into one of his tales.

"For thirty days and thiry nights, we journeyed across the great Atlasi Ocean," he would always begin, gazing wistfully across the valley as he stroked his mustache.

"Only Allah knows how we survived the perils of that mighty ocean.

Wallahi, I saw sea monsters with fins taller than our church tower in Bayt Lahm. Waves as high as mountains smashed into the boat, sending passengers and crew rushing below deck!"

Jubrail would listen open-mouthed, straining to imagine this vast, mysterious ocean. There was no river in Bethlehem, let alone an ocean. The only body of water he knew was the Pools of Suleiman to the south of Bethlehem where spring water from the surrounding hills was collected and channeled northward toward Jerusalem. On trips there with his elder brothers he would splash in the pools, battling the sea monsters described by Ammo Hanna.

"Our ship had been battered by storms and the captain lost all sense of direction," Ammo Hanna would continue. "Supplies were running out and the crew had given up all hope of navigating to safety."

Jubrail loved these moments of suspense when Ammo Hanna would pause, shaking his head as he looked down at the floor.

"Then one night, as I looked up to the heavens in desperation, there he was, flying overhead, spear in hand, green robes billowing out from behind him. By the grace of Almighty Allah, it was al-Khadr guiding us to safety! I was not the only one who had seen him either. Several of the crew members saw the same flash of green and knew it was a sign to follow in that direction."[9]

Jubrail knew all about al-Khadr and how he could transport himself from any one place to another in a single instant. "The earth folds beneath them," they would say about that special category of saint known as ahl al-khitmeh.[10] The faranja who came to Bethlehem even had the audacity to claim him as one of their own, calling him Saint George. But everyone in Bethlehem knew he was a local saint who kept special watch over the town's intrepid travelers.

It was only through the intervention of al-Khadr that Ammo Hanna's ship had been guided to the bountiful lands of Amerka. There, on the other side of the Atlasi Ocean, he had found a new world in a frenzy of creation. A land of great cities in the making inhabited by people from every part of the world, all come to make their fortune. Waiving his hands excitedly, he would explain how opportunity there was limitless, especially for a merchant selling Holy Land carvings from Bethlehem.

At this point Jubrail's father would stir from his sleep and begin paying attention.

"The people there profess to be Christians," Ammo Hanna would explain. "They hold anything from al-Quds and Bayt Lahm in great reverence.

I swear to the Virgin, they flocked in great numbers to buy my rosaries and crosses. I only wish I had brought greater quantities from Bethlehem!"

He had arrived in a teeming port city named Rio de Janeiro.[11] Located in a huge bay ringed by densely forested mountains, the city had been his home for several weeks. He had been surprised to discover people speaking the same languages and worshipping the same saints as some of the Franciscan friars he had met in Bethlehem. But once he ventured into the interior, he could no longer understand the people, nor did he recognize their saints. The landscape was like nothing he had seen in Palestine: so verdant and fertile that plants and animals sprouted gleefully from every crevice, no matter how tiny. Strangely, there were no seasons in this evergreen land. Rain fell the whole year, and it was just as hot in winter as in summer. Everyone and everything permanently dripped with water, either from the torrential daily downpours or from the constant sweating brought on by the unrelenting humidity.

Lurking in the forests were all manner of strange beasts ready to devour Ammo Hanna the moment he strayed from the beaten path. As he listened, Jubrail would feel his own skin burning with the poison of a giant tarantula, hear the barking of howler monkeys in the valley below, and see crocodiles slinking across the terrace. He memorized the names of brightly colored birds and poisonous snakes, and he drew maps of the coastline of Amerka as he followed Ammo Hanna's meandering monologue.

Ammo Hanna would explain that the country surrounding Rio de Janeiro was a vast territory known as Brazil. He had concluded it was the ideal base for Bethlehemites to begin trading in Amerka. A powerful emperor named Dom Pedro II was opening the country to international trade in an effort to become one of the world's great powers. Previously, the country had relied on African slaves to work its lucrative sugar and coffee plantations, but now the import of those slaves had been forbidden by the very same faranja who had created the trade in the first place. In response, Dom Pedro was encouraging workers from all corners of the world to travel to Brazil, where they would find bountiful work. New ports and roads were being built to accommodate the immigrants and goods pouring into the country, helping connect the cacao and coffee plantations of the interior to the coast.[12]

Ammo Hanna had seen workmen laying down two parallel lines of iron tracks outside Rio de Janeiro. He had been told this was an invention that would allow a mechanical carriage to travel at great speed along the tracks.

Many years later, he would watch in amazement when the first such carriage rolled into Jerusalem amid a great cloud of steam and excitement. But upon first seeing those tracks in Brazil back in the 1850s, he had laughed at the thought that a carriage could pull itself along those tracks faster than a well-bred horse.[13]

Upon his return to Bethlehem, Ammo Hanna had become something of a local celebrity. The old men would gather in Bab al-Dayr to listen to his tales of Amerka, eager to hear about teeming jungles and strange inventions. Some laughed at his stories and called him a khurafa who had never made it further than the island of Cyprus.[14] Others were more willing to believe he had crossed the Atlasi Ocean but suspected he embellished his tales for dramatic effect. But the young Jubrail hung on his every word, finding himself transported to another world. After hearing about Rio de Janeiro and the Amazon rainforest, he would run down to the terraced slopes beneath Hosh Dabdoub to search for cicadas, lizards, and snails among the apricot and fig trees. He would imagine that the lizards were the crocodiles described by Ammo Hanna and that the olive orchard at the bottom of the valley was a dense rainforest, full of human-eating plants hanging precariously overhead.

On days when he felt more adventurous, he would wander northward instead, up the hill past the last buildings on Ras Iftays. Following the road out of town, he would stop at the fork where it met with the Jerusalem-Hebron Road. Just past this junction in the direction of Jerusalem was Qubbet Rahil, the small domed structure that marked the boundary of the district of Bethlehem and the outer edge of Jubrail's known world. It was said the dome contained the tomb of Rahil, the wife of Yaqub in the Holy Book, who had died when traveling that road. Christian and Muslim women went there to ask favors from Rahil. Occasionally, Jubrail would see strange-looking men dressed in long black coats, rocking back and forth as they uttered prayers in an unintelligible language.[15] Peering in through the window, he would glimpse surprisingly long ringlets of hair descending from black fur caps. Was this how people in Amerka looked, he wondered?

Returning home, he would pull out the maps he had drawn of Amerka based on Ammo Hanna's tales. Following the coastline, he would imagine himself on a great ship and wondered if one day he too would travel the road that stretched beyond Qubbet Rahil toward Jerusalem and the world beyond.

CHAPTER 2

OF THE HALLOWED RIDGE, OR HOW JUBRAIL LEARNED TO PROFIT FROM CHRISTMAS

AT THE TIME OF JUBRAIL'S childhood, everyone in Bethlehem knew each other's business. All four thousand of them lived piled on top of each other, perched on the hallowed ridge that culminated with the fortress-like church at its eastern end.[1] The houses, with their narrow slits for windows, seemed to look out on the surrounding hills with suspicion, happy to remain in the security of their fortified hilltop rather than venture into the valleys below.

Long before living memory, the Bethlehemites had built their houses as separate units: simple cubes of thick stone with vaulted roofs topped by the distinctive shallow domes of the central Palestinian hills. But over time the houses had been extended and welded together as families expanded over the generations, forming a haphazard series of interlocking blocks. From a distance they gave the impression of a single, unified structure—a jumbled mass of gray squares and domes, huddled together on the ridge.[2]

The people of Bethlehem viewed the outside world with a healthy mixture of caution and naked opportunism. Two contrasting domains lay on either side of their town, each offering its own set of dangers and benefits. To the east, the lush hills surrounding Bethlehem quickly gave way to the Wilderness. Only the hardiest of life-forms could exist in those barren folds in the earth's surface that stretched all the way down to the toxic waters of the Dead Sea. There, in the bowels of the earth, Allah had once rained down burning sulfur on the sinful cities of Sodom and Gomorrah, producing a desolate landscape of salt mounds and craggy desert mountains. This was Bedouin country, where the Taʿamreh tribes grazed their sheep and patrolled the mountain passes, extolling hefty tolls on passing travelers in exchange for safe passage. Over time, the Taʿamreh had consolidated their position and even began forming semisettled communities, giving birth to an arc of new villages around the eastern side of Bethlehem: Tuquʿ, Zaʿatara, Khirbet al-Deir, and Beit Taʿmir.[3]

Every Saturday, the Taʿamreh launched a peaceful invasion of Bethlehem. They arrived in droves to sell livestock and buy goods at the town's market. A visitor to Bethlehem on those days would be confronted by a series of arresting juxtapositions. Tattooed Bedouin women bartered with shaven-headed Italian monks over the price of mulukhiyya leaves. Orthodox priests with beards down to their waists eyed the offerings of barefoot children selling maʿmoul sweets. And long-haired men with nervy eyes and long daggers attached to their belts led camels through groups of yellow-haired Russian pilgrims who signed the cross as the camels emptied their bowels beside them. The Taʿamreh were crucial to Bethlehem's survival, providing the town with vital foodstuffs and protection from hostile aggressors. But the Bethlehemites knew how fragile their alliances were. A quarrel between families over grazing rights or the failed repayment of a debt could quickly result in a ruinous raid.[4]

To the west lay a different world. Following the road northward out of Bethlehem, a traveler would arrive six miles later in Jerusalem, that most holy of cities, where the world's great empires and pious seats of learning competed for space. From there, the road led westward, down through the mountains and eventually out onto the coastal plain where Jaffa, Bride of the Sea, lay in wait. Facing the shimmering Mediterranean, Jaffa was the gateway to the world beyond. By the end of the century, it would become the exit point for hundreds of young Bethlehemites setting sail for the gold-paved streets of Amerka. But at the time of Jubrail's childhood it was still more an entry point than a port of departure: the landing station for hordes of pilgrims entering the Holy Land, their eyes fixed on the hills of the interior where Jerusalem and Bethlehem lay in wait.

Over the years, the Bethlehemites had grown used to a steady stream of visitors to their small town and had become adept at profiting from their presence. But they had also learned to keep their distance, aware of how swiftly outsiders could turn against them. Most volatile of all visitors were the faranja from the western lands of Europe: a breed of pilgrim that insisted on imposing their bizarre habits wherever they went. Many of the locals, including Jubrail's own family, had long ago professed their loyalty to a priest in a faraway city called Rome in an effort to gain trade and favors from the faranja.[5] This arrangement worked perfectly well most of the time. The local converts were given jobs by the Franciscan friars who ran the convent of Santa Caterina adjoining the old church. They worked there as translators, tour guides, craftsmen, gardeners, cleaners, or in any other position the friars could find for them. But the friars did not always grasp the economic nature of the relationship, despite being the ones who had established it in the first place. They became infuriated whenever one of their flock married a Rumi or even worshipped the old Rumi saints, threatening immediate excommunication.[6] Such was the fervor of the friars' opposition to the old ways of the Orthodox Church; they could regularly be found brawling with the local Rumi priests while the saints looked on in horror from the icons on the church walls.

To the locals it was all largely the same. Whether Rumi or Catholic, they had always prayed in the old church, and it was only for special events like baptisms or confirmations that the Catholics used the Santa Caterina chapel next door. Even the local Muslims prayed in the old church, worshipping Yasu' and the Virgin in their own particular way. Long before living memory, Muslims from the neighboring village of Faghur had moved into Bethlehem, and they now formed their own district of the town, Harat al-Fawaghreh, just up the hill to the west of the main square, Bab al-Dayr. They had recently built their own mosque on the far side of Bab al-Dayr, complete with its own minaret and muezzin, whose calls to prayer now competed each day with the clanging of the church bells. But this did not stop the Muslims from making their way down to the church on special feast days just as they had always done, lighting candles in thanks to the Virgin and prostrating themselves before the Lord Allah in the main nave.[7]

For some unknown reason, the faranja were implacably hostile to such mixing of traditions, frequently castigating the locals as if they owned the town. Jubrail would always remember a story his mother told about her confirmation in the year 1831 involving a particularly fearsome outburst from a franji spectator. A multitude of locals had crowded into Santa Caterina that day to witness the confirmations. The franji priest had insisted that only those receiving confirmation should be present, but in Bethlehem a confirmation was a public spectacle, attended by Catholics, Rumis, and Muslims alike. Unable to stop the influx of spectators, the priest had become increasingly agitated at the great commotion of conversation and the running commentaries accompanying his sermon. Suddenly, a thunderous voice burst out, sending the entire church into stunned silence.

"USKUT!" yelled the voice from the back of the nave in a bizarre rendition of the Arabic word for "shut up."

A thousand heads turned to see a giant of a man dressed completely in white with a great bushy red beard, eyes popping out of his head in anger. He began to scream in a tongue nobody understood (they later discovered it was called Almani), sending the entire crowd rushing to the door in a frenzied panic. From that day, nobody dared go near the giant, even when he was seen around town in a more peaceful condition.[8]

Each year, the flow of foreign visitors reached a crescendo at Christmas. For the locals, Easter was the most important festival, bringing to a joyous end six weeks of fasting with the Feast of the Resurrection. But it was Christmas when the town attracted the most attention from the world outside. Over the course of two colorful weeks, each of the town's four denominations celebrated the birth of the Messiah at their own time, miraculously transforming Bethlehem into the center of the known universe. On four separate occasions, the town would wait in excited anticipation for a glorious procession to arrive from Jerusalem. Snaking its way down Ras Iftays and into the central plaza of Bab al-Dayr, each procession contained an assortment of illustrious patriarchs, pilgrims, dignitaries, and hangers-on. All came to pay tribute to Bethlehem and the wonderous events that had once occurred there.

The most spectacular processions were those of the two biggest congregations, the Catholics and the Rumis. They were held on the twenty-fourth day of Kanun al-Awwal and the sixth day of Kanun al-Thani, respectively. On these days, the town was full to bursting. Thousands of eager spectators crammed onto the streets, sending the locals onto their rooftops for a better view. Delegations of Bethlehemites would set off on donkeys to meet the patriarch and consuls arriving from Jerusalem.[9] On the occasion of the Catholic Christmas, Jubrail's father and uncles would be among the troop that rode out to greet the French consul, firing their rusty old flintlock muskets into the air as a gesture of welcome. The consul was always preceded by six kavasses—the Ottoman mounted guards employed to maintain a semblance of order. Dressed in their shiny red, blue, and gold uniforms and carrying their mighty silver-headed staffs, the kavasses were an impressive sight to a young boy like Jubrail, and he always made sure he kept a healthy distance. Behind them came the consul himself, surrounded by his official entourage, and finally a motley crowd of followers whose number had grown along the way: pilgrims from faraway lands, musicians playing kawala flutes and riqq tambourines, peddlers selling amulets, and an assortment of beggars and misfits hoping to benefit from the legend that the consul's white mule performed miracles behind his master's back.[10]

Once in Bethlehem, the Catholic procession passed through town with great fanfare, before the dignitaries were forced to dismount from their horses at the entrance to the church in order to pass with stooped heads through the tiny Door of Humility. By ten o'clock in the evening, the crowds had moved into Santa Caterina, where the Latin patriarch sat waiting on his throne, solemnly holding his hooked crozier. Dressed in robes of dazzling gold and white and topped with a mighty jewel-studded miter that seemed poised to topple off his head at any moment, the patriarch sat like a king surveying his subjects. By this time, the crowd had reached such levels of density and excitement that scuffles frequently broke out to determine who would achieve the best view of the ceremony. Ottoman soldiers attempted to restore order by flogging people with their bayonets and shouting all manner of obscenities in their various native languages, but all to no avail. Eventually the chaos was interrupted by the grand entrance of the French consul, accompanied by his six kavasses, who used their staffs to beat a path through the crowd for the consul to follow serenely behind. If all went to plan, the franji hymn "Gloria in Excelsis" would be sung on the stroke of midnight before a wax model of the infant Yasuʿ would be paraded through the thronging crowds. The formalities continued long into the night as various franji prayers and songs were recited, largely inaudible and unintelligible to the mass of bodies packed into the church.[11]

All of this unfolded before the young Jubrail as if in a beguiling dream that made no logical sense. Christmas was the time when his daily existence was put on hold and the rules of everyday life suspended. Bethlehem was no longer the rural village where people eked out a modest living from the land and from selling a few souvenirs to the occasional pilgrim. Instead, it was transformed into a magical spectacle in which foreigners performed the lead parts. Once, Jubrail managed to squeeze his way through the crowds and into Santa Caterina, where he scaled a statue of Saint Jerome to get a better view. He had watched the scene unfold as a curious observer in much the same way he peered at the men in long black cloaks at Qubbet Rahil, the patriarch parading that strangely pale-skinned wax model of the infant Messiah before an assortment of bizarre-looking people wearing colorful costumes from faraway lands.

Many years later, Jubrail would travel to the furthest corners of the earth and find to his amazement people singing songs about Bethlehem and exchanging cards imprinted with images of the town. Gradually, he came to understand that being from Bethlehem carried great economic opportunity, but to exploit that opportunity he must accept a version of his hometown conjured by outsiders. The day he first came across those greeting cards at a stall in Paris, he argued vehemently with the shopkeeper, explaining that the painting on the card looked nothing like the town where he had grown up. But when he noticed a line of customers waiting to buy the cards, he quickly fell silent. In business, he began to realize, it did not matter what the real Bethlehem looked like. To prosper as a merchant, he would have to carry with him two versions of his hometown wherever he went: *his* Bethlehem of narrow-slit windows, feuding families, and chaotic Bedouin markets, and *their* Bethlehem of golden miters, Eastern kings, and curiously white-skinned babies.

Christmas was one of those times in his childhood when he would glimpse the other Bethlehem that lay somewhere out there in the imaginations of the faranja, beyond the domed houses and the olive terraces he knew so well. For those few days each year, ownership of the town temporarily passed into the hands of the faranja while the locals looked on in a state of bemusement, trying to figure out new ways to profit from all that pomp and ceremony.

CHAPTER 3

OF THE TOILS OF YOUSEF AND ROSA, OR HOW THE BETHLEHEMITES ACQUIRED THEIR NAMES

SOME CLAIMED A DISTANT ANCESTOR of the family had walked with a heavy stomp, tilting from left to right as he went—like a little bear (dabdoub). Others said the Dabdoub progenitor had been a poor man who lacked work during the pilgrimage low season. Desperate for food, he would head into the valleys below Bethlehem and stomp on the ground in a bearlike way to separate the mass of weeds from the edible plants.[1]

In later years the family would search through the Franciscan parish records and find the first recorded Dabdoub: a man named Hanna, son of Mikhail, born in 1682. But the story behind the surname remained shrouded in mystery. During Hanna Mikhail Dabdoub's time, many families began acquiring surnames, or alqab, as they called them, for the first time. The general tactic seemed to have been to choose a defining characteristic of the male head of the family, however bizarre or derogatory. Tawil (tall), al-Aʿma (the blind), and al-Atrash (the deaf) had all been chosen in this way. Others had been more imaginative. Faccuse (cucumber), Sarsour (cockroach), Rock (rock), Flefel (falafel), and Babun (baboon) were now honorable names in Bethlehem and the surrounding villages, harking back to some distant family legend. Each family stood ready to defend the sanctity of its name should anybody dare insult it, no matter how comical that name.

The Dabdoubs were proud of their name and would do anything to protect its honor. They belonged to that clan of families known as the Tarajmeh (translators), who were somewhat aloof from the rest of the town due to their connections to the Franciscans. Long ago, the Tarajmeh had embraced the Catholic rites and in return received periodic employment from the friars.[2] For centuries they had worked for them as guides and translators. As the relationship strengthened over time, they had expanded their work at the Franciscan convent, tending the gardens, cleaning the kitchens, carving souvenirs for sale to pilgrims, and occasionally engaging in scandalous sexual affairs with the friars.[3] Many in the town mocked them for their readiness to adopt the European customs, but the Tarajmeh took their role seriously and never tired of telling the other Bethlehemites how they were descended from the blood of European Crusaders. How many times had their neighbors heard the story of the Tarajmeh's noble ancestors—two brothers from the Italian town of Monteforte who had settled in Bethlehem during the Crusades and married into local society? And how many times had those same neighbors laughed at them, retorting that the so-called noblemen had in fact been local mercenaries working as bodyguards for the Venetians?[4]

Whatever the precise ancestry of the Tarajmeh, the benefits they accrued from their close relations with the Franciscans could not be doubted. For centuries they had specialized in the art of souvenir carving, supplying the friars with a steady stream of crosses, rosaries, and all sorts of other trinkets, all carved from the wood of local olive trees and inlaid with shimmering pieces of mother-of-pearl imported from the Red Sea. The friars, for their part, did not shy away from the economic benefits of the arrangement. Despite their founding principles of poverty and mendicancy, they were well aware of the financial necessities of monastic life.[5] Back in the early sixteenth century, they had taken the ingenious step of asking an Italian architect by the name of Bernardino Amico to produce scale drawings of all the Christian shrines in the Holy Land, which they duly used to commission replica models from the Tarajmeh artisans.[6] For months the artisans toiled on those models, producing miniature wooden masterpieces adorned with sparkling stars of mother-of-pearl and tiny columns of camel bone, each one measuring little more than an ayak in length. The friars even demanded that the domes and roofs of the models be detachable to reveal every minute detail of the interior. The artisans were at a loss to explain the friars' obsession with reproducing such precise details. Surely, they argued, an artist should depict the glory of the heavens rather than the limitations of human endeavors.[7] But as long as the friars kept requesting more models, the Tarajmeh artisans were happy to keep carving. Before long, every church, palace, and royal court in Europe had one of those models, or some other form of souvenir, all carved by the dexterous hands of the Tarajmeh.[8]

The Franciscans were running a roaring trade, all backed up by the hard labor of the Tarajmeh. The church models were their showpiece items, but a whole range of smaller items made up their staple sales. Alongside the standard crosses and rosaries, there were brooches, crowns, jewelry boxes, Dead Sea stones, Holy Land soil (dug up from any nearby garden), pressed flowers—anything that might induce the franji pilgrims to part with a few ghurush. The women of the town had become particularly adept at scraping off pieces of the chalky-white walls of the Milk Grotto in Bethlehem where it was said the Virgin had once spilled a drop of her milk when escaping King Herod with her holy infant. After washing the pieces of stone, they would pass them on to the friars, who would mark them with the franji seal of Jerusalem for sale to visiting pilgrims or for distribution around their clients in Europe.[9]

The more adventurous franji traveler, meanwhile, might request from the friars one of the Tarajmeh's famous Holy Land tattoos. Their tried and tested technique consisted of clapping a stencil covered in powdered charcoal onto the pilgrim's arm, and then pricking holes in the skin with two needles bound together, following the pattern left behind by the charcoal. Finally, they would rub dark blue ink over the holes and leave the arm wrapped in linen for twenty-four hours. Upon removal of the linen, the franji would gaze in wonder at the permanent image imprinted on his arm, which, no matter how many times it was rubbed or washed, would remain just as fresh for the rest of his life.[10] Pilgrims could choose from a range of stencil designs, the most common being the franji Cross of Jerusalem or the initials *IHS*, in reference to the Greek initials for Jesus. If they were willing to pay extra, they could even commission the Tarajmeh for a unique design of their own, such as the time a traveler from a faraway country called Iskotlanda requested the crown of his country's king—a man named James. Such work had to be carried out with great discretion if it risked offending the strict Catholic sensibilities of the friars. In the case of the tattoo of King James, the artist in question (a local man named Elias) was severely reprimanded by the friars when they saw the crown imprinted on the pilgrim's arm. They later took pleasure in recounting to the Tarajmeh how the poor traveler had had the tattoo ripped from his flesh when facing the Catholic Inquisition upon arrival in the Spanish port of Malaga.[11]

Living in such proximity and codependence meant the Tarajmeh and the Franciscans often found themselves in conflict. In times of plenty, the wily friars bought in bulk from the artisans, always applying a hefty markup on the sale price. They boxed up thousands of the carvings in their Jerusalem warehouse and distributed them to churches and monasteries all over Europe. But when demand in Europe declined, they turned the artisans away, telling them with typical franji hypocrisy to earn a more honest living cultivating the land.[12] Such was the artisans' desperation to sell their wares that it was not uncommon to see brawls breaking out between the two sides in open daylight. People still remembered the time a young boy drowned in the well of the Franciscan monastery in Jerusalem after the friars had refused to buy carvings from the boy's father. According to the friars, the man had deliberately thrown his son into the well in an act of blackmail. The man denied the accusation, insisting that the friars had performed the dreadful deed in the midst of a scuffle that had broken out between them. When the case was referred to the Ottoman courts, the friars were ordered to pay three thousand Venetian gold coins to the man. It was no surprise to anyone in Bethlehem that they later used their diplomatic leverage with the French consul to have the fine overturned.[13]

It was into this volatile, unforgiving souvenir trade that Jubrail's father, Yousef Hanna Dabdoub, was born in 1816. Yousef grew up carving little wooden crosses and rosaries that his father would take down to Saint Catherine's Convent to sell to the friars. Many were the times the friars turned him away, sending him out onto the streets around the church in search of pilgrims who might be willing to give up a few ghurush. None of this brought much wealth to the family, which continued to live in the old Tarajmeh Quarter, just across Bab al-Dayr from the church. In those days, the Tarajmeh Quarter was largely indistinguishable from the rest of Bethlehem. As much as the Tarajmeh liked to think of themselves as special, they still wore the same clothes, spoke the same Arabic dialect, and prayed in the same church as everyone else. Their houses looked just like all the others, nestled among the dense cluster of buildings that hugged the hallowed ridge.

Yousef grew up in the section of the Tarajmeh Quarter inhabited by various branches of the wider Dabdoub family. The residence was organized around a central courtyard covered by a makeshift arrangement of matting, planks, and vines designed to keep out the winter rains and the summer sun.[14] Yousef lived in one of the rooms surrounding the courtyard, along with his parents and two elder brothers. All domestic activities took place in that single room. By day it was a kitchen and living area where meals were cooked and eaten. In the evening it miraculously turned into a bedroom, thanks to a stash of mattresses and cushions stored in a niche in the wall. Meanwhile, beneath all the human activity, an assortment of chickens, donkeys, and goats slept two feet below them in a room they called qaʿat al-bayt.

By the age of twenty, Yousef had lost both his parents to the vagaries of poverty and disease. It was now down to him and his two brothers to preserve the family's honor and livelihood. This would mean strengthening their ties with the Franciscans in the hope of increasing their income and eventually securing brides from good Tarajmeh families—preferably ones under the age of sixteen who could bear many sons to continue the Dabdoub blood line.

Yousef had always been a capable carver of souvenirs, but now he set about fine-tuning his skills. He toured the houses of the old Tarajmeh carvers and discovered an interesting shift taking place in their work. No longer were they using tiny mother-of-pearl pieces as inlays in their wooden carvings. Instead, they were covering their carvings completely in strips of mother-of-pearl. Making further inquiries, he found out that vast quantities of mother-of-pearl waste fragments were arriving at the Jaffa docks, sent from the factories of Europe and Amerka. It seemed the faranja had developed a craze for making shiny buttons out of mother-of-pearl, producing mountains of waste materials that could be sold cheaply at ports around the Mediterranean. Palestine was awash with the stuff—from Austria, England, the United States, and only Allah knows where else. Bethlehem's carvers were determined to take advantage of this deluge of leftovers, adorning their wooden carvings with a riot of mother-of-pearl panels—all gloss and shine that left the viewer bedazzled.[15]

Yousef's interest was also piqued by a parallel development taking place in the trade. In the old days, the carvers had used mother-of-pearl imported from the Red Sea. It came in the form of small shells brought to the town by the Franciscans in times of plenty who were eager to commission new work from the town's artisans. But now a far larger specimen of shell was appearing in the Jaffa docks alongside all the waste product from Europe. They called them the white-lipped Pinctada maxima, and they hailed from a faraway island called Australia. The Bethlehemites had debated the whereabouts of this island without reaching any conclusion.[16] Some said it was part of the continent of Amerka, while others maintained it lay somewhere to the east of al-Hind. But they all agreed it must be a place of great abundance and beauty, such was the milky thickness of the shells' lining with their glossy, iridescent swirls of whites, greens, and purples. Many years later, Yousef's own sons would travel to that very island, but that was all far in the future, at a time when the brilliance of Bethlehem's artisans would usher in a new age of discovery.

Whatever the provenance of those shells, the impact they exerted on the town's carvers could not be doubted. In the old days, the Franciscans had taught them how to create images of Mar Francis and other Catholic saints by etching sheets of mother-of-pearl in bas-relief, and then coloring in the lines with black, red, and green ink. But such was the plasticity and depth of the lining of the new shells, they could now carve directly into the shell itself. The door was flung open to all sorts of wild and wonderful experiments in high relief carving, pushing the carvers to produce ever-more detailed designs. Whole scenes from the Holy Book were carved straight into the shell, producing the impression of being in perfect harmony with nature itself.[17]

Yousef was quick to grasp the significance of the changes. Bethlehem had always been known for its expertise in souvenirs, but these magnificent specimens had elevated the craft to a new level. A group of highly specialized artists was emerging in the town, each artist pushing the other to produce ever-more exquisite creations unique in style and design to Bethlehem. What might such works fetch on the international market if the buyers knew they had been carved in the sacred town of Bethlehem, birthplace of the holy Messiah? Quickly Yousef invested in a set of tools—files, awls, hammers, and saws—and began to learn the new techniques from the best carvers among the Tarajmeh clan. He made trips to Jaffa to purchase the best shells he could find and spent endless hours experimenting on new designs. Any visitor to the Dabdoub residence at that time would find him sitting cross-legged in the courtyard with a stack of oyster shells piled up behind him, trying out some new pattern he had just devised. By the time he was twenty-four, Yousef had established a solid reputation among the town's mother-of-pearl carvers, making him an attractive marriage prospect among the other Tarajmeh families.

In the year 1841, Yousef's brothers arranged his marriage to Rosa Batarseh, the daughter of one of the highest regarded Tarajmeh elders, Isa Batarseh. Rosa had grown up with a certain haughtiness, instilled in her by her family's firm conviction that they were one notch above the rest of the Bethlehemites. The Batarsehs prided themselves on being the first and most loyal members of the Franciscans' Catholic community. It was true that the Tarajmeh stories told of much older Catholic ancestors in Bethlehem, but the friars' logbooks only went back to 1616—the year they began their "reconversions" following relaxations in the Ottoman rules—and they showed that on the day of the Catholic Christmas that year, a man named Doctor Elias had been the first to receive his confirmation. Elias was the progenitor of the Batarseh family, which from that moment had formed the nucleus of the Tarajmeh community in Bethlehem. That community would grow and grow over the following centuries, forming the majority of the town's population by the time Rosa was born. But the Batarsehs still considered themselves to occupy a special position among the town's Catholic community as the Franciscans' first and most loyal disciples.[18]

Any sense Rosa may have held of elevated status was delivered a rude awakening upon her marriage to Yousef. Like most young brides, she was cast out of the family home at the age of fifteen and sent to live with a man who still shared a room with his brothers and had no parents to support him. She would now be responsible for an endless array of manual labor and household chores, not to mention the pressure of producing children. For years afterward, she bore her marriage to Yousef with an air of disgruntlement, holding him personally responsible for the abrupt end to an agreeable childhood.

In later years, Yousef would never tire of describing to their children the hardships he and Rosa had endured during their youth. In those early days, he would explain, the family still relied for its basic subsistence on the olive, fig, and apricot trees they cultivated down in Wadi al-Jamal, as well as the livestock that slept in the house beneath them. At this point Rosa would interject, reminding old Yousef that the bulk of this work had fallen on her young shoulders. It was she who had set out at sunrise every day to collect firewood from the forests of Wadi Ma'ali or sometimes as far away as Jabal

Abu Ghneim, three miles to the north. When the well in the family house ran dry, it was she who made a detour down the steep slopes of the Anatreh Quarter, on the southern side of the town's ridge, to the fountain known as 'Ayn al-Qanat. The fountain was the town's lifeline, fed by a diversionary outlet of the ancient aqueduct that carried water from the Pools of Suleiman all the way to Jerusalem. Every day in summer, Rosa and the other women of the Dabdoub residence could be seen trekking back up the hill from the fountain, bent over double with the weight of their goatskin water containers on their backs and with great bundles of firewood precariously balanced on their heads. As they entered Bab al-Dayr, the men would sit watching, puffing on their arghileh pipes. Not for Yousef the toil of domestic duty. His role, he had insisted, was to sell souvenirs to pilgrims. His reasoning overlooked the fact that Rosa, like many women at that time, also helped out with the mother-of-pearl carving. But it was the men's job to take the produce down to Bab al-Dayr and barter with pilgrims entering the church. In practice, this meant spending most of the day lounging in the shade of the adjoining Greek monastery, doing nothing but gossiping, smoking, and drinking tea while the women toiled under the hot sun.[19]

Luckily for Rosa, she was not the only woman in the Dabdoub house. Yousef and his brother Isa had decided to carry out a double wedding, marrying their two brides on the same day in the year 1841. Issa was a full forty years old at the time of the wedding, but that did not stop him from taking his thirteen-year-old cousin Hilweh as his bride. In the early years, the two brothers and their teenage brides all lived in the same room within the Dabdoub courtyard, and naturally it fell on Rosa as the eldest of the wives to take over leadership of the household. It was during that period that Rosa grew into the formidable presence that would dominate the Dabdoub family for the next thirty-seven years. She had no time to ease herself gently into the role; at the age of fifteen she had no choice but to learn how to run a family. With Hilweh by her side, she set about tending to the orchards and the livestock, managing the family accounts, and nursing a growing army of infants.[20]

In total, Rosa gave birth eight times over the course of twenty-two years. Thanks to the blessings of the Virgin, five of them were boys, further cementing her reputation as the most venerable of all the Dabdoub matriarchs. In the early years, before the family could afford to employ servants, she could be seen trekking down to Wadi al-Jamal with one child on her back, another tucked under her arm, and two or three more trailing behind her, cursing Yousef as she went. For his part, Yousef would remind her that she was lucky to be given such freedom in their household, free from the prying eyes of a mother-in-law.

"You're the lucky one, ya zalama," she would always reply. "If we had to rely on your mother-of-pearl carving to keep this family afloat, we'd go to ruin in no time."

As much as Yousef hated to admit it, Rosa was right. Every day Yousef went to Bab al-Dayr to spread out his wares on a blanket, just outside the entrance to the church. On a good day he might sell a handful of carvings to pilgrims entering the church, and occasionally the friars would order a larger batch from him. But these sales alone could not support their expanding family. By the time Yousef was forty and Rosa thirty, they already had five hungry children to feed. Yousef could see the potential riches on offer in the souvenir trade, but he could not quite touch them. The pilgrims ignored hawkers like him, keeping their heads down as they hurried into the safety of the church, where they would buy their souvenirs in bulk from the wily friars. The hefty markup the friars applied was plain to see: one only had to set foot in their convent to be dazzled by the glimmering array of gold, silver, and bronze ornaments they had purchased using money from souvenir sales.[21] It was little wonder that some Bethlehemites had been unable to resist the temptation to walk out of the convent with one of those shiny objects tucked under their abayehs, accustomed as they were to more rudimentary standards of living. But nothing passed the attention of the friars. They had implemented a ruthless security regime, enforced by a network of informants and backed up by the power of the French consul in Jerusalem. Many a Bethlehemite had been arrested and imprisoned by the Ottoman police for stealing from his own parish church.[22]

Yousef had tried everything to increase his sales. He had even opened a makeshift shop in the Dabdoub house in an effort to show off his more elaborate carvings. But few pilgrims ever strayed into the warren of backstreets that made up the Tarajmeh Quarter. Besides, everyone knew the real money was in the export market—a trade that seemed completely off-limits to the Bethlehemites. For centuries, the friars had been boxing up souvenirs and sending them all over Europe, where they could charge far higher prices than in Bethlehem. Meanwhile, the artisans toiled away and fought among themselves for the scraps of work the friars offered them.

CHAPTER 4

IN WHICH BETHLEHEM GETS A NEW STREET

YOUSEF SAT OUTSIDE THE CHURCH, watching the day's first group of pilgrims make its descent into Bethlehem. Skirting the hillside, the pilgrims would soon pass under Qoos az-Zarara, the archway marking the entry point into Bethlehem and the site of many heroic defenses of the town. People still spoke of the time an invading army had been pursued through that arch by a swarm of wasps, eventually meeting a grisly death at the top of the hill, which from that time became known as Ras Iftays—"Suffocation Point."[1]

Nowadays, visitors were more likely to be pursued by swarms of a different type. As soon as the pilgrims passed under Qoos az-Zarara, Yousef reflected wearily, they would be accosted by all sorts of hawkers, all selling souvenirs and tours of the church.

The sound of voices caused Yousef to turn around. Some women were making their way into the square from the opposite direction, on their way back from collecting firewood in Wadi Ma'ali. His wife, Rosa, was among them, carrying a great bundle of branches on her head.

"Ya'tik al-'afiyah," she called out sarcastically, praising his hard work.

"Allah ya'fiki," he muttered in response, eyes fixed on the ground.

"By the grace of the Virgin, I don't know why you sit in the square all day like this," Rosa admonished him as she walked past. "By the time those pilgrims reach the square, they'll already be weary of the hawkers. They won't give you a second glance."

"You do your work, and I'll stick to mine," Yousef replied, sensing the smirks on the faces of the other men in the square.

"If you weren't so lazy, ya ibn ʿammi, you might give me a hand fetching water from the well at the top of Ras Iftays. That way you could greet the pilgrims before they arrive in town."

Suddenly Yousef jumped to his feet, spilling his coffee as he did so.

"Malak zalama?" Rosa exclaimed. "Surely you're not coming to help me fetch water?"

"Of course not!" Yousef replied. "I'm coming to see our future."

In an instant he had understood how to grow his business. Rosa was right! Up there on Ras Iftays he could catch the pilgrims long before they arrived in the square and give his carvings the proper attention they deserved. But he would go further. He would build a new house, right at the top of the hill where travelers turned the corner and caught their first glimpse of Bethlehem. Not only that; the house would have its own mother-of-pearl workshop and an adjoining store to attract the attention of the customers.

It was true that people had always feared building beyond Qoos az-Zarara. Who knows what bands of marauding Taʿamreh or rival village gangs might be out there, waiting to enact some age-old vendetta. Not to mention the hyenas and jackals that roamed the countryside, possessed by the spirits of evil jinn who would lure unsuspecting people back to their caves to devour them.[2] For the Bethlehemites, the hills beyond Qoos az-Zarara were farmlands, a place to cultivate olives, apricots, and figs. At best, one might build a small qasr hut to camp out for a few nights during harvest season. But it was no place to live.[3]

Despite the warnings of conventional wisdom, the seed had been planted in Yousef's mind. Why follow convention when it led to the same old place: hawking in Bab al-Dayr and begging from the friars? The time had come to defy the town's conservative instincts and strike out for a new beginning. Besides, the road along Ras Iftays was much safer now that the Ottoman garrison had been stationed up at Qubbet Rahil. It was not that the Ottoman soldiers were looking after the town's best interests. For centuries the Ottoman governors had oppressed the town, sending abusive tax collectors who took more than was owed, backed up by the bayonets of the sultan's guard. For their part, the Bethlehemites had always fought back, launching raids on the tax collectors when they felt they had abused their authority. But something was changing in Jerusalem. The Ottoman garrisons were imposing themselves in the countryside in much greater numbers in an effort to crush the power of the local shaykhs who controlled the routes in and out of the city. People even said that the mighty Mustafa Abu-Ghosh, long the master over the road to Jaffa, had now submitted to Ottoman authority and could no longer extract his extortionate fees from travelers.[4]

The point was, the Ottomans craved stability. Gone were the days of villages and rival tribes going to war every few months, ruining agricultural yields and tax collection. A new kind of order was being imposed on the Jerusalem hills, including on the roads into Bethlehem. Never had there been a better time to build beyond Qoos az-Zarara, up on Ras Iftays. Word had just reached Bethlehem that all land ownership would now have to be registered with the shari'a courts in Jerusalem and taxes paid in accordance with the type of land. As it was outside the boundaries of the old town, Ras Iftays was classified as aradi amiriyya—"miri" lands that the state leased out to landholders prepared to put it to productive use. No one in town had registered their name yet over the miri lands on Ras Iftays, but it was surely only a matter of time before the artisan families would start expanding up the hill in a bid to build bigger, more spacious houses and secure access to the pilgrims ahead of the competition. The Dabdoubs already cultivated small plots of olive and fig orchards up there. It would not take much to establish their occupancy in the courts, but they would have to act swiftly.[5]

The day Yousef led a team of local stonemasons to the top of Ras Iftays, the rest of the town looked on with a mixture of amazement and ridicule.[6] When they realized what he was planning, they quickly dismissed the idea as madness. What man acting in his right mind would subject his family to the dangers of life outside the old town? Yousef and Rosa had five children, and there would doubtless be more to come. What untold perils awaited those poor children if they were cast out onto the hillside? Many in the town put his decision down to the haughty ways of the Tarajmeh, who always believed they were somehow different from the rest of the town. Strange men from Jerusalem had been seen accompanying Yousef to the top of the hill, where they unfurled drawings and pointed across the valley. If these men were not faranja, they certainly looked like them in their ridiculous frock coats and tarbush hats. Had Yousef not learned that you could never trust the ways of the Europeans? Did he not know that working with them only led to scandal, betrayal, and calamity?[7]

In the months that followed, the rest of the town was stunned into silence. In next to no time, a gleaming new mansion was erected at the top of Ras Iftays unlike anything Bethlehem had seen. The house was designed to accommodate only the immediate family: Yousef, Rosa, and their children. Aware that others may seek to follow, Yousef made no mistake in registering the property as the inheritance of his sons, and the design of the house reflected the newfound separateness of their family unit.[8] There was no central courtyard around which different family units could live, no typical fortresslike design with high walls and small windows, and no enclaves for animals to sleep directly below the people. The linear shape of the house followed the line of the road on its eastern side as it descended down the hill. From the road itself, only the roof of the building could be glimpsed, serving to keep at bay nosy passersby, although this did not stop the faranja pilgrims from frequently using the roof as a lookout to catch their first glimpse of the town below.[9]

It was only when viewed from across the valley that the house revealed itself in full, inviting the rest of the town to gaze in wonder at the audacity of Yousef and Rosa's decision. In the ensuing years the house would continue to expand upward and lengthways to accommodate their growing family and to incorporate a new workshop and store at street level. By the time they were finished, a magnificent structure of vaulted arches (the riwaq) had been constructed to the rear, looking out across the valley at the stunned residents of Bethlehem. Despite the warnings of the townsfolk, the house was not raided by bandits or Ottoman soldiers, nor was it ravaged by hyenas and jackals. The Dabdoubs had defied convention and built a house that transgressed the limits of the town's imagination far from the safety of the old town. Bethlehem would never be the same again.[10]

When Yousef erected a gleaming new sign one morning to announce the opening of the family shop, gasps of amazement could be heard in the town below. With its decorative red and blue lettering ordered from the Franciscan printing press in Jerusalem, it was unlike anything the Bethlehemites had seen. "Dabdoub et Fils" read the sign in large franji letters, with the Sacred Heart stationed underneath, embedded in a radiant pearl shell. The town was used to seeing those signs hanging outside foreign hospices or franji churches. But outside the house of a lowly mother-of-pearl carver?

It was almost unthinkable that a Bethlehemite would have the audacity to do such a thing.[11] Before long the sign was drawing in customers in droves, all willing to open their purses when they saw Yousef's shiny carvings of iridescent whites, blues, and pinks.

The new residence was soon known to all as Hosh Dabdoub, standing as a beacon of progress to the town below. Those who had ridiculed Yousef in the beginning now looked on with envy and began contemplating their own move to the top of Ras Iftays. The first to do so were their fellow families from the Tarajmeh clan, who were keen to expand on their trade with Franciscans and gain first contact with visiting pilgrims. The Dawid family, the descendants of Andrea Dawid, who had mysteriously disappeared in Amerka all those years ago at the end of the previous century, built their new residence a short hop down the hill on the opposite side of the road to the Dabdoubs. Long after, the Mikel family constructed a towering mansion just a few paces down the road from Hosh Dabdoub with a three-sided courtyard that opened onto the valley below and featured the same style of vaulted archways. Yousef dismissed the Mikels as imitators, but they were not the only Tarajmeh family to follow the Dabdoubs onto Ras Iftays. Next came the Batarsehs, Rosa's relatives, who opened their own mother-of-pearl workshop on the ground floor of their new residence and quickly began to reap the benefits.

The Tarajmeh families were now in open competition, each competing to build the biggest mansion with the most impressive mother-of-pearl factory. Disputes over land on Ras Iftays became common as families rushed to file their claims with the Ottoman courts in Jerusalem. The Dabdoubs themselves became involved in several quarrels as the expansion of their hosh took up more and more land. Mikhail al-Commandari was one of a few who claimed foul play, insisting the olive groves around the hosh had once been cultivated by his father and therefore constituted his inheritance, as well as that of his brother Francis (who had disappeared somewhere in Amerka) and his mother. As compensation, he demanded to be paid 138 French lira, reasoning that the franji currency would better serve his family's business interests abroad.[12] For his part, Yousef would always refuse such claims, insisting those lands belonged neither to the Ottoman governor, nor to the people of Bethlehem, but to the prophet Musa, who had been given ownership of all the hills around Bethlehem in his covenant with Allah Almighty. As the Dabdoubs were making the most productive use of the land through their thriving workshop, it was they who were the rightful custodians of Musa's land. Keen to maintain good relations with his prophet landlord, Yousef made sure to light a candle of thanks to Musa in their makeshift chapel on the lower floor each time he chopped down an olive tree to make way for the latest round of extensions to the house.[13]

So popular was Ras Iftays becoming with the Tarajmeh families that the area was soon renamed as Harat al-Tarajmeh, or the "Tarajmeh Quarter." For many, the newfound wealth and space afforded by the new quarter allowed them to indulge long-standing fantasies of being European. Anyone entering the houses of these families might have thought they had stumbled into the residence of a franji nobleman. Rather than sitting on the floor during meals and eating with their hands as normal people did, they insisted on gathering around a raised table where each person sat on a wooden chair, eating their own separate portion of food with strange-looking metallic tools, in some cases even allowing the women to eat with the men. After their meals they would retire to upholstered benches they called "chaises longues" or "sofas," where they smoked Egyptian cigarettes with European-sounding names like "Kyriazi Frères" or "M. Melachrino et Co.," instead of puffing on arghileh pipes like ordinary people.[14]

It would not be long before the success of the Tarajmeh businesses and the extravagance of their lifestyles lured families from other clans to Ras Iftays. In a reversal of every word of ridicule and condemnation they had once levied at Yousef Dabdoub, the Jarur, Sabbagh, and Khatir families now scrambled to establish themselves on the street, keen to start their own businesses and gain a share of the profits.[15] As competition grew increasingly fierce, their storefront signs tried to attract the attention of passing pilgrims and tourists with ever-more elaborate motifs and logos. Visitors turning the corner at the top of Ras Iftays to start their descent into Bethlehem were now bombarded with flowery invitations to step inside the shops of Mikel et Fils, Batarseh Brothers, and Sabbagh Souvenirs, all of which claimed to sell the finest souvenirs in town.

By the 1890s, Ras Iftays had been transformed from a dusty track surrounded by open fields into Bethlehem's busiest shopping parade. A continuous row of residences and stores lined the road on either side, producing all kinds of new innovations. At the top of the hill, next to Hosh Dabdoub, an enterprising local baker named Abu Fuad opened a bakery selling fresh bread and pastries to the pilgrims. Meanwhile, the Sabbagh family opened a café where visitors could stop for refreshments and be entertained by an assortment of local musicians, dancing bears, and performing monkeys.[16] When a team of franji archaeologists discovered the remains of a Byzantine church mosaic and an accompanying underground cemetery lying beneath the cisterns at the top of the hill, the street was blessed with its very own tourist attraction, just a stone's throw from Hosh Dabdoub. The Bethlehemites had long referred to the cisterns as Biyar Daoud, believing them to be the wells that had quenched King David's thirst when his armies breached Philistine enemy lines. But the commotion surrounding the discovery of the mosaics elevated the site to a new status among the European visitors. Some of them even speculated with great excitement that this might be the site of King David's burial. Although no evidence existed to support the claim, the local residents were only too happy to support the theory, and before long the site was etched into pilgrimage itineraries the world over.[17]

Amid all the excitement, Hosh Dabdoub stood at the top of the street as the original pioneer and the setter of countless new trends. The house in those days was a hive of activity. Stonemasons heaved enormous blocks of limestone up the stairways, busy completing the latest round of extensions to the house, while pilgrims stopped to browse the souvenirs on display in the storefront. Before long, the house had doubled in size to accommodate the growing family and to expand the size of the shop. An entirely new section was built onto the side of the original structure, creating a mirror image of the original design that accentuated its linear form.

Once again, Hosh Dabdoub was the envy of the whole town. But to maintain such a house was no simple task. With Yousef buried in his business affairs, Rosa was left with the impossible task of looking after the house at the same time as raising eight children. She had given birth three more times since their move, confining her to ever-longer periods indoors. In the old days she would quickly return to her work outdoors after childbirth, thanks to the help of her mother and numerous aunties. But now, with her mother gone and the rest of her family living down in the old town, far from Hosh Dabdoub, she rarely ventured outside the house, so consumed was she with domestic chores.

"If *you* won't lift a finger in the house, then I'll have to pay someone to help me," Rosa declared one afternoon to Yousef as they sat on the terrace looking eastward to the Bedouin villages of the Ta'amreh.

"Pay someone?" Yousef repeated. "Whoever heard of a Bethlehemite paying to have their house cleaned? Next you'll be asking me to wear trousers and funny hats like the Europeans!"

"You wear what you like, ibn ʿammi. I need help, and I know where to get it."

The day the first maid arrived from the village of Tuquʿ, everyone in the family looked at Rosa in shock. Was she really going to allow a Taʿamreh girl into their home? How could they trust her not to steal some valuable ornament when their backs were turned, or at least slip a few figs into the pockets of her tawb? For centuries the Bethlehemites had maintained an uneasy coexistence with the Taʿamreh, tolerating them at their Saturday markets in the knowledge that the arrangement was necessary for the town's survival. But rarely did they invite them into their homes.[18]

In the ensuing months and years Rosa employed a steady stream of them, at first for cleaning, but later for all kinds of roles. They cooked the family's meals, scrubbed their floors, tended their olive trees, and even breastfed their babies. They were the silent workforce that kept the family operation afloat—a small of army of young girls and women working behind the scenes to ensure Hosh Dabdoub maintained its image as the pioneer of Bethlehem's bold new age. Rosa was their commander-in-chief, barking orders, scolding them for mistakes, and spying on them when they thought her back was turned. Long before magazines from Jerusalem and Beirut gave advice to Bethlehem's women on how to treat their maids professionally and humanely as part of the task of "national improvement," Rosa administered regular beatings to the impoverished young girls who came from the Taʿamreh villages. She ruled the house with an iron fist, instilling fear in her subjects and demanding they work long into the night before rising at dawn to prepare the family's breakfast of coffee, zaʿatar, and freshly baked bread.[19]

Freed from the burden of household chores, Rosa turned her attention to the house's interior design, eager to stay one step ahead of the other Tarajmeh families on the street. She ordered strange furniture from Jerusalem—sofas, armchairs, bureaus, cabinets—that nobody had any idea what to do with. The maids served food to guests on silver trays and poured them wine in bronze goblets imported from France and Italy. As the servants cleared away the food and slipped morsels of leftovers into their pockets, the menfolk would retire to the riwaq to talk business, leaving Rosa to tell the women about the latest Damascene silks she had purchased from the Aftimos market in Jerusalem.[20]

All the while, the business kept growing. Yousef's strategy of making contact with pilgrims before they arrived in town had coincided with the biggest growth in visitors anyone could remember.[21] Every day, more and more faranja arrived in Bethlehem, all eager to mark their visit with a precious souvenir. Yousef and his workers struggled to keep up with the demand. They carved Orthodox icons for the hordes of Russian pilgrims who now came to the town, they made splendid scenes of al-Khadr slaying the dragon for the faranja who still believed he was a saint who resided in Europe, and they churned out crosses and rosaries for all pilgrims, no matter their denominational inclinations. Sitting cross-legged and covered in dust, they sang to the rhythm of their sawing and filing, huge piles of shells stacked up all around them.[22] Some would be bent over double making tiny holes in filigree borders, while others rubbed the backs of wooden crosses with a waxy blue material until the words *Jerusalem* or *Bethlehem* magically appeared in Latin characters.[23] All the while, Yousef would be watching over them, barking out orders. Dressed in his red and blue striped qumbaz coat, his head topped with a bright yellow turban, he cut a formidable figure among the workers.

"Leish mlabbedeen hayk? We haven't got all day!"

"Come on, come on, a new order just came in from France!"

"Yallah shabab, my grandmother could work faster than that!"

Alongside the mother-of-pearl staples, Yousef experimented with carving from materials such as the jet-black Hajar Musa stones the Bedouin traders brought from the Dead Sea or the wood of the Mecca fruit tree that could be carved into rosary beads and dyed yellow, red, or black.[24] They even sold cards of pressed flowers collected from the surrounding hills in springtime and dried in the family store.[25] It was a revelation to Yousef that such easily available local materials, used for centuries by the Bethlehemites to decorate their homes and ward off evil spirits, could be sold at inflated prices to the Europeans, all of them eager for anything sprung from the sacred soil of Jabal al-Quds.[26] But it was the mother-of-pearl carvings, the pride of Yousef's workshop, that still brought in the most money. If he got his bartering strategy right, Yousef could sell one of his signature pieces, carved directly into a whole oyster shell, for as much as two hundred ghurush—more than an employee of the Ottoman government would make in a whole month.[27]

At the center of Yousef's strategy were his two prized possessions: his eldest sons, Hanna and Mikhail. He nurtured them in the ways of the business, teaching them the art of mother-of-pearl carving and the more mundane arts of bookkeeping, sourcing materials, and bartering with customers. Any thoughts of marriage were postponed while Yousef groomed the boys as his future associates in the family firm. "Work for the engagement of your daughter, but not the engagement of your son," he would always repeat, making sure he implemented the proverb to the letter.[28] His eldest daughter, Mariam, had already left Hosh Dabdoub by the time she was fifteen, sent to live with her new husband, Yaqub Abu Fheleh, who was nine years older than her. Meanwhile, Hanna and Mikhail were given time to mature, living for many years in the house as unmarried men. Eventually, in 1867 at the age of twenty-four, Hanna was wedded to a sixteen-year-old bride, Nijmeh Jacir, who came to live with him in a newly built wing of the house. Six years later in the year 1873, Mikhail was wedded to the seventeen-year-old Maria Dabdoub (a distant relative), also at the age of twenty-four.

In those days, every marriage was a business transaction, calculated to further the prospects of the family firm. Girls were wedded as young as possible, sometimes as young as the age of twelve, to maximize the number of sons they could bear, while young men were given time to mature as merchants.[29] Alliances were chosen carefully to cement bonds across different branches of the family and to establish new business partnerships. Hanna's marriage to Nijmeh Jacir was a case in point. Nijmeh was the eldest daughter of Yousef Jacir, one of Bethlehem's most respected mukhtars who sat on the town's council of elders. More importantly, he was the Franciscans' bookkeeper, giving him not only valuable knowledge of accounting but also access to the friars' trading networks in Europe, making him the envy of the whole town. Soon his son Suleiman would be embarking on new trading missions in France, eventually rising to become the richest man in all Bethlehem. Hanna's marriage to young Nijmeh secured for the Dabdoub family an early bond with the Jacirs—a bond that would endure for many decades as they set out on dangerous and fantastical journeys to the furthest corners of the world and the highest echelons of Bethlehem society.

CHAPTER 5

OF UNRULY MARKETS AND UNDERWATER SHIPS

ON THE TWENTY-SECOND DAY OF Nisan in the year 1860, Jubrail came into the world to the sound of chisels and saws cutting through oyster shells. It was the beginning of the boom years, a time when every family in Bethlehem had taken to carving souvenirs from any scrap of mother-of-pearl they could get their hands on. From its perch at the top of the hill, Hosh Dabdoub stood at the vanguard, commanding first contact with arriving pilgrims, employing the most skillful carvers, and sourcing the best shells. A constant flow of people moved through the house. Merchants, pilgrims, artisans, builders, servants, and inquisitive townsfolk all came to witness the marvels taking place at the summit of Ras Iftays.

Amid all the commotion, the young Jubrail moved around as he pleased. He was the sixth child of Rosa and Yousef and the first born in Hosh Dabdoub. So preoccupied was the rest of the family with building its commercial empire that it barely paid the young boy any attention. Darting between his brothers' legs as they bartered with customers or clinging to the trails of his mother's tawb as she ordered servants around the house, he explored the colorful world of the hosh as he pleased.

By the time Jubrail was six, he was carrying out expeditions on the terraced slopes behind the hosh, eventually finding his way down to Wadi al-Jamal at the bottom of the valley. There he found an enchanted world of fig and apricot orchards where the sound of cicadas filled the air and lizards darted over stone walls. Far from the commotion of the hosh, he was free to let his imagination run wild, entering a world where fearsome jinn and terrifying ghouls stood guard over glittering treasures hidden in the caves of the stony hillside.

From Wadi al-Jamal, he would head up the other side of the valley until he reached the old town where his parents and elder siblings had once lived. Darting into the old Tarajameh Quarter in front of the church, he would follow the other children through narrow alleyways and up onto the domed rooftops where they played with cone-shaped spinning tops and took aim at goldfinches and sparrows with their homemade slingshots. On windy days in the spring and summer, dozens of colorful kites fluttered in the air as the children maneuvered their paper flying machines across the sky.[1]

Descending back to street level, Jubrail would head to the old Dabdoub residence in search of Elias, his cousin and trusted accomplice. Elias was two years older than Jubrail and attended the same Terra Sancta school where the Franciscan friars taught them how to read and write in Italian and sing unintelligible songs of praise in Latin to the Virgin.[2] These days, however, Elias was rarely seen at the school, as his precocious talent for mother-of-pearl carving had already caught the eye of the owners of the town's new workshops, including Jubrail's father, Yousef, who had begun employing the young boy to carve crosses and rosaries up at the new Hosh Dabdoub. Little did they know it at the time, but this would be the first step on a glittering career that would see sultans, queens, and emperors commissioning his masterpieces, all carved in impossibly intricate detail from mother-of-pearl shells.[3]

The house where Elias lived as a child was the same building where Jubrail's own family had once lived before they had struck out for the heights of Ras Iftays and built the new Hosh Dabdoub. The old Dabdoub residence was arranged around a central courtyard covered by a makeshift arrangement of matting, planks, and vines. Stepping through the exterior door and into the courtyard, Jubrail would check the various rooms for Elias. Usually he would find his mother, Mariam, nursing her baby daughter, Hilweh. Sometimes Elias's grandmother, Sitti Hanneh, would be there too, administering instructions to Mariam on how to care for the baby. There was something fascinating about this old woman with those mysterious tattoos of the Jerusalem Cross and the Virgin Queen etched onto her arms in blue ink. Many were the times she would pluck the swaddled infant from the bright red rocking cradle and place her on Jubrail's lap, muttering "Behold the gift of God" as she did so. Looking down at the delicate creature tightly bound in white and purple linen, Jubrail would observe the relic of Mar Yousef attached to her forehead in its tiny crystal case. "Mar Yousef is always the best saint to keep nearby, should the child fall sick," the old woman would explain.[4]

If Elias was not there, Jubrail would make his excuses and begin the walk back uphill to Hosh Dabdoub, where Elias would most likely be working. To get there, he first had to make his way across al-Manara, the small square given its name by the kerosene lantern that lit up the surrounding streets at night like a lighthouse. On a Friday, Muslim men from the Fawaghreh clan would be filing out of the gleaming new mosque erected on the west side of Bab al-Dayr.[5] The Fawaghreh were greatly outnumbered by the Christian clans in Bethlehem, but they held an important status in the town's affairs, always filling the position of town shaykh—Bethlehem's official representatives to the Ottoman governor in Jerusalem. Despite this lofty honor bestowed by virtue of their religion, they were not among the town's wealthiest families and generally blended in with the rest of the population. Many of them continued to pray in the church, seeing no need to break with tradition, despite the presence of the new mosque. Inside the church, Jubrail often found it difficult to tell Muslim from Christian, as the Muslims knelt in prostration before the Virgin, worshipping her with a fervor that matched that of any Christian.[6]

On a Saturday, al-Manara would be teeming with Bedouins and peasants from the neighboring villages, all come for the weekly market. On these days, the streets would be lined with vendors hawking vegetables, grains, leather goods, and livestock. The tattooed faces of the Ta'amreh women called out in hoarse voices from behind baskets piled high with dates, grapes, and pomegranates, while their husbands led camels through crowds of people haggling over the price of wheat and barley. Many years later, Jubrail would witness the dismantlement of the market by a new imperial power, the British, who seemed obsessed with regulating every aspect of public life. The new market they built between the Farahiyyeh and Najajreh Quarters had its own awnings and specially designated plots that required government permits just to sell a few mulukhiyya leaves. Never again would the market be free to follow its own logic as it did during the days of Jubrail's childhood, fanning out from al-Manara and spreading its long tentacles wherever it pleased. In those earlier times, it could take hours for a young boy to make his way across the market, pushing through dense crowds, frequently distracted by the aroma of roasting almonds and freshly baked maʿmoul sweets.

Jubrail would always remember the day he came back from the market to find his brothers Hanna and Mikhail on the riwaq of Hosh Dabdoub, freshly returned from their first trip abroad. They were holding court with the rest of the family under the arches, telling stories of a faraway city called Paris. The first thing Jubrail noticed was their clothes. Hanna was wearing an absurdly tight-fitting black coat over his abayeh, while Mikhail had donned a pair of dainty black shoes that made his feet look comically small. "Barees," Jubrail repeated when he heard his brothers pronounce the city's name. In what kind of place did people dress in such exotic outfits?⁷

Sitting down next to his sister Miladeh, he caught fragments of tales that were barely believable to a seven-year-old. In a single afternoon, his brothers had circumnavigated the entire globe thanks to the creation of a city within a city where replica streets of every kingdom on earth could be found. At the center of it all stood an enormous domed pavilion where mechanical wonders whirred away, day and night. There were clocks that used water to keep time and lamps that shone instantly brighter than any flame at the mere flick of a switch. Most fantastical of all was a great ship measuring 114 ayak in length that could sail *beneath* the water, propelled by some mysterious force.⁸

So important was this exhibition of wonders that the sultan himself had deemed it necessary to attend. Hanna and Mikhail had seen him with their own eyes when he made his grand entrance through a specially erected archway that replicated the gates of the great Topkapi Palace in Istanbul. With his long retinue in tow, he had glided nonchalantly past the brothers' modest stall in the so-called Turkish Village.⁹ Apparently it was a source of great dismay to the sultan that the Turkish Village had not been deemed sufficiently important to be included in the main exhibition hall and was instead relegated to the adjacent gardens alongside the tribes of Afriqya.¹⁰

Jubrail longed to hear more about the wonders of Paris, but his father insisted on interrogating the brothers on more mundane matters: expenses incurred, exchange rates, and itineraries. When they told him they had spent more than seven hundred ghurush just to reach Paris, he cried out in disbelief and proceeded to reprimand them for not negotiating better deals with the touts, hoteliers, and port officials they had met along the way. Jubrail had heard about the mighty ships that waited beyond the rocky harbor at Jaffa like vast, floating cities. It was said that only the most daring of travelers would board such a boat, as their journeys frequently ended in terrible shipwrecks.[11]

Yousef's anger quickly dissolved when the brothers explained they had more than recuperated the expenses of the journey. Now he asked them endless questions about prices, clients, and supplies. It seemed the family had borrowed money from other merchants in Bethlehem to complete the trip—a situation that caused Yousef great anxiety. Jubrail heard the name Antonio Belloni and remembered the jolly Italian priest with the big beard who gave shelter to orphan children in Bethlehem, training them to carve souvenirs from olive wood and mother-of-pearl. He had often seen his brothers chatting with Father Antonio at the shelter, along with other young merchants like Hanna Mansour and Abdallah Atik. Had the Italian priest somehow been responsible for sending Jubrail's brothers to the distant city of mechanical wonders?[12]

For weeks, the only thing Jubrail wanted was to go down to Wadi al-Jamal with Elias and act out scenes from the exhibition in Paris. One moment they would be bowing down before His Majesty the Sultan, the next they would be inventing new machines that flew through the air or sent them traveling through time. Together they roamed the terraces, looking for fallen branches, rocks, and pieces of discarded old rope to construct their latest contraptions. One day their wanderings took them into Wadi Ma'ali on the other side of the old town, and eventually as far south as the Pools of Suleiman next to the village of Artas—a place their parents forbade them from visiting on their own. For centuries, the pools had collected water from the local springs through a network of pipes and aqueducts that ran slowly downhill all the way to Jerusalem. They were a haven for local families to picnic and bathe in, but they were also a dangerous place where many children were known to have drowned. Arriving at the pools, Jubrail and Elias could not contain their excitement. This was the nearest they had ever been to the rivers and oceans described in the travelers' tales. Tentatively at first, they waded into the largest pool, still in their clothes, and felt the exhilaration of the cool water submerging their trembling bodies.

Before long they had abandoned themselves to the water, splashing merrily alongside the local children of Artas. There they stayed for several hours, traversing oceans and battling sea monsters in the mighty underwater ships of Paris, until at last the setting of the sun sent them scurrying home across the terraced valleys, shivering in their soaked clothes at the prospect of an inevitable scolding from their parents.

CHAPTER 6

OF SUNKEN EYES IN A CASKET, OR HOW BETHLEHEM CAME TO BE COVERED IN DUST

NO ONE WAS TRULY SURE why Allah was angry with the Bethlehemites that year. Some said it was an ancient vendetta for the Virgin's mistreatment at the hands of local farmers who had refused to share their crop of peas with her. Others claimed it was the fault of the young men who had traveled to Paris and been corrupted by the ways of the faranja. The Rumis and Syriacs confirmed this was the natural result of Catholic laxity, pointing out that all the attendees at the Paris exhibition had been Catholics. "They stuff themselves with breakfast and sway along to church at nine o'clock when the sun's already high in the sky," they would say of their Catholic brethren.[1]

Whatever the reasons, the omens were clear. No fewer than three earthquakes shook the town in the year 1868. Not the kind that opened great holes in the ground like those that had forewarned the peasants' uprising of 1834—but nevertheless strong enough to serve notice that a greater calamity was on its way.[2]

There is an old saying that the khamasin always lasts three days. Like most sayings, it is only partially true. The dreaded dust storms that made their way to Palestine from the Sahara took their name from the fifty-day period in spring when they usually arrived. But in the year 1868, the normal order of things was turned on its head. It was not until the end of the month of Aylul, just as the first families were descending into the valleys to harvest their olives, that the khamasin was first sighted on the southern horizon.³ An autumn khamasin was surely another bad omen, the people remarked, and they retired to their homes to wait for the three days to pass. On the fourth day, they reemerged to find the air still thick with a hot haze and the entire town covered in a layer of dust. Returning to their homes, they assured themselves it would surely be gone by the next day, only to be greeted by the same scene when they awoke.

So it continued for twenty-eight days. The great khamasin of 1868 was relentless in its harassment of the town, leaving the streets deserted for an entire month.⁴ Those foolish enough to stray outside were met with a blast of hot air that cut into their faces and a dusty haze so dense they could barely see across the street. Almost immediately, the mucus in their noses dried to a crust and their throats became inflamed and sore. A throbbing headache and fever would quickly set in, as if a vice had been placed over the temples and was being gradually tightened. For the first few days, staying home was the only way to avoid these unpleasant symptoms. But it was not long before the khamasin found a way to penetrate the houses. The first signs of its presence indoors appeared when people's furniture began to inexplicably crack and then suddenly collapse, wilting under the extreme lack of humidity in the air. In Hosh Dabdoub, where they sometimes practiced the franji habit of using tables and chairs, people would sit down to lunch only to fall inexplicably to the ground as the joints of the chairs gave way to the debilitating effect of the khamasin. Gradually and imperceptibly everything indoors became covered in the same thick layer of dust that had already enveloped the town outside. Colors became a distant memory as everything and everyone succumbed to the monotone grayish-brown of the dust. Young Jubrail could no longer perceive the subtle shades of black and gray in his father's mustache or the bright reds and golds of his mother's dress. When he occasionally ventured outside, someone called to him from across the street, but he was clueless as to who it was—all he could make out was a sandy, dust-covered person indistinguishable from every other inhabitant of the town.

The insidious haze of the khamasin was briefly interrupted on the twelfth day when the third and final earthquake of that year struck. Once more the ground shook ferociously, opening cracks in the walls of houses that had been left unrestored for hundreds of years. When people ventured out the next day to survey the damage, they were pleasantly surprised to find the air had become cooler and clearer. Turning their heads to the skies, they saw dark clouds approaching from the west, and a crack of thunder sent everybody running back inside. All that day the people waited for the heavens to open. A few raindrops fell and great claps of thunder continued to ring out. But the threatened storm never erupted, leaving everyone in a state of anguished suspense. Jubrail was at the old Dabdoub house that day, playing with his cousin Elias. From the room across the courtyard, he could hear Sitti Hanneh exclaim, "Allah has not finished with us yet. May the Virgin Mariam, Mar Yusef, and al-Khadr all protect us."

As ever, Sitti Hanneh's predictions proved impeccable. The following day the khamasin resumed its onslaught with renewed fury. It would take another two weeks before it eventually passed, leaving the town a great dusty mess of crumbling furniture and withered faces. When it finally departed, the change was dramatic. The town woke up one morning to find two clouds drifting over from the west, rather than from the south, the usual direction from which the khamasin's wind blows. That evening a heavy shower of rain fell that continued long into the next day, accumulating over an inch of water. When the rain abated, it was as if the weather had switched from the blazing heat of high summer to the chilliest of winters in a single day.[5] Still used to the searing heat of the khamasin, the people of the town were unprepared for such an abrupt change and found themselves shivering from cold as they scrambled to find where they had stashed their winter clothes and blankets.

The unprecedented conditions made everyone nervous. They were pleased the khamasin had passed and the winter rains had come early, but the speed of the change told of further woes ahead. The town waited with trepidation, viewing every mishap, however small, as vindication that something calamitous was coming. The rain continued to fall, forming great pits of mud where the piles of dust had once collected. In Hosh Dabdoub, the family apprehensively returned to their daily lives. The dust was swept from every corner of the house and the latest furniture brought from Jerusalem to replace tables and chairs that had cracked and collapsed during the khamasin. The shop was reopened but with much-reduced stock due to the hundreds of mother-of-pearl carvings that had been ruined by the dust and cracked by the dry, hot air. Yousef fervently set about replenishing supplies, going from door to door encouraging his carvers to return to the workshop. Gradually, the sound of tapping hammers, grinding chisels, and cutting saws began to ring out once more around the hosh.

Just as it seemed things were returning to normal, the disaster foretold by the earthquakes and the khamasin finally unfolded. Jubrail came home one day from one of his forays into the valley to find his brother Murqus in bed, lying in a pool of sweat with a huddle of worried family members around him. Pushing his way through the crowd to take a look, he jumped back in surprise when he saw Murqus's skin had turned blue, his eyes sunk deep into their sockets and his hands and feet wrinkled like an old man. Confused, he turned to his brother Mikhail, who explained that Murqus had contracted the dreaded cholera disease that had reappeared in the region three years ago via Muslim pilgrims returning from Hajj.[6] That year it seemed the disease had finally relented, but in the aftermath of the khamasin it had returned with great vengeance. Rosa did all she could to invoke the assistance of al-Khadr in the struggle against the jinn that had brought the cholera into poor Murqus's body. She placed on his forehead a small mother-of-pearl plate into which an image of al-Khadr on his trusty steed had been engraved, and she cried out to the saint: "Ya Khadr, if my child gets well, I'll buy curtains for your church and a vestment for the priest there."[7]

Despite Rosa's offers of rewards, al-Khadr was unable to defeat the jinn that had taken hold of Murqus's body. By the end of the night, he had passed into the realm of the dead, ushered away by the angel Azrael. When his father told him the news the next morning, Jubrail was left in a state of confusion. How could this have happened? At seventeen years old, Murqus was earmarked for great things in the family business. He had always been studious, listening attentively to his father's instructions as he learned the ways of the souvenir trade. Yousef had even spoken of sending him on the next trip abroad with Hanna and Mikhail. Now, in an instant, he was gone. Why had he not been allowed to fulfill his destiny and discover the riches of Amerka? Why had Allah not taken Jubrail instead? Murqus had worked so hard to take his place in the family business, whereas all Jubrail did was fool around in the fields. And why could Jubrail not rid himself of the terrifying vision of those sunken eyes?[8]

In the hours after Murqus's death, Jubrail watched stupefied as the men of the house laid his body on a bier and scrubbed him with hot water and soap. As Murqus was an unmarried man, they dressed him in a full bridegroom's outfit, complete with qumbaz and turban, to show he was still waiting for a bride in the next life.[9] When the women of the house had finished wailing and beating their breasts on the rooftop of Hosh Dabdoub, a large procession followed the bier all the way down Ras Iftays, across Bab al-Dayr and into the church. A crowd had already gathered at the church, come to catch a last glimpse of young Murqus and to pay their respects to the family. Yousef insisted that Jubrail accompany him to look at the open casket and bid his brother farewell. Jubrail tried to resist and turned to run out of the church. But his father grabbed him by the collar and dragged him up to the body. As he looked down at those milky-white eyes, sunken deep into their sockets, Jubrail was certain they widened for an instant, as if his brother were still alive and struggling to get out of the casket. He screamed and wriggled free of his father's grip. Fleeing through the crowd, he ran out of the church and across the adjoining graveyard in Bab al-Dayr. From there he headed down to his beloved Wadi al-Jamal, trying to rid himself of the vision he had just seen. But as much as he ran, the dreadful image of the sunken eyes remained.

CHAPTER 7

OF MECHANICAL WONDERS ON NEAR AND DISTANT SHORES

FOR MANY YEARS MURQUS HAUNTED Jubrail's dreams. In the months after his death, he would visit Jubrail on a nightly basis, rudely intruding when he least expected it. Usually he would be seated on a white donkey, dressed in flowing green robes. Dismounting the donkey, he would begin digging a canal in the ground before turning to Jubrail with a smile on his face.[1]

It seemed Murqus had come to tell him something, but Jubrail could never make out the words. So transfixed was he by that vacant look in Murqus's eyes that the speech became an incoherent mumble. Jubrail would try to reply, only to find his own mouth was paralyzed. Eventually he would wake up in a pool of sweat, crying his brother's name into the night.

On the streets of Bethlehem, meanwhile, curious events were taking place that made it difficult to tell where the realm of dreams ended. The great khamasin of 1868 had temporarily set back the souvenir industry, decimating pilgrim numbers and ruining much of the merchants' mother-of-pearl stock. But it was not long before visitors were returning in ever-greater numbers, prompting the Tarajmeh families to begin plotting the expansion of their businesses once more.[2]

The key to their success, they reasoned, would be the world's fairs taking place across Europe. Already in 1867 they had seen the potential of these bizarre and wondrous events when young men from the Dabdoub, Giacaman, and Atik families returned from Paris with a trunkful of French francs. Now it seemed every country in Europe was competing to hold a bigger and better exhibition. After Paris came London (1871), Lyon (1872), Vienna (1873), and Rome (1874), followed by an ever-greater proliferation across the globe. A cult of newness seemed to permeate the air at these events, producing a reverence for grandeur and a veneration of mechanical inventions. Exhibitors competed to display the latest gadgets while monumental buildings were erected overnight, only to be taken down again just a few weeks later. It was as if time itself were accelerating and the world's fairs had become the measure of a city's ability to keep pace.

The franji obsession with progress was accompanied by an unquenchable thirst for the traditional, the tribal, and the exotic. According to this formulation, the extent of Europe's advancement could only be grasped when juxtaposed with the timeless habits of folklore, ritual, and superstition. Relentlessly, the faranja scoured the world for artifacts to display at their great exhibitions. They mined their colonies for weavers, potters, and artisans, carting their work onto steamships that plowed their way across the oceans. They cajoled, lured, and ensnared tribal leaders, Pygmies, and snake charmers to appear in some European city, where they would be paraded in human zoos as evidence of how far the faranja had advanced along the path of civilization.[3]

Where the faranja saw backwardness, the Bethlehemites saw possibility; and while the exhibition organizers dreamed of the timeless Orient, the Bethlehemites dreamed of profit. What better way for the faranja to measure their progress than against the land of the Holy Book, that fountain of all Western civilization? And where better to start that story than in the town of the Messiah's birth, the holy Bayt Lahm?[4]

The old mukhtars of the Tarajmeh families quickly realized a world of opportunity awaited them on the exhibition circuit. As the events multiplied in frequency, young men were dispatched on a never-ending tour of the exhibition circuit, hauling great carts of mother-of-pearl carvings from city to city.[5] From Antwerp to Barcelona, stalls could be found all over Europe bearing the name "Holy Land Bazaar" and selling devotional objects carved in Bethlehem. Most of the exhibitions were small affairs: a collection of local traders and industrialists displaying their products in a bid to drum up new custom. At these events the Bethlehemites arrived unannounced, pitched up a stall, and began touting their goods. Many was the time they were evicted by burly guards who insisted they could not sell their wares without an official permit.⁶

All their gritty persistence—days spent trekking along freezing roads, sleeping in windswept railway stations—would pay dividends at the larger exhibitions. It was there, at the great extravaganzas billed as the world's fairs, that a young merchant armed with a suitcase of Holy Land carvings could make his name. At the Vienna World's Fair of 1873, the Bethlehemites participated for the first time as part of the official Ottoman exhibit ordered by the sultan. The Bethlehem bazaar was a great success, helped to no end by the nearby display of a scale model of Jerusalem made by a Hungarian man who had lived in the Holy City and produced an impossibly detailed reproduction of every house, street, mosque, and church.⁷ The enormous model soon became the talk of the entire exhibition. The Bethlehemite merchants spent many hours marveling at the meticulous recreation of the city they knew so well. Only here in the heart of Europe, in the fantastical world of the franji exhibitions, could they view al-Quds in its splendid entirety, as if they had assumed the perspective of Allah Himself. The Ottoman Pavilion, meanwhile, was praised in the franji media for its own replica of the Topkapi Palace, as well as its Turkish bath, café, and bazaar.⁸ Journalists wrote excitedly about its "exotic Oriental charm" and the "juxtaposition of East and West" created by its location next to the franji exhibits.⁹ All this mattered little to the Bethlehemites, who were focused purely on business. One of the merchants among them, Yaqub Giacaman, was so successful in Vienna that he opened his own shop in the city, adding to ones he had already established in Istanbul and Paris.¹⁰

So fast was the pace of change and so insatiable the Tarajmeh's quest for new markets that it would not take long for the merchant families to branch out beyond Europe toward the fabled lands of Amerka. In 1874 two brothers from the Zakhariyya family left town one day, declaring they were following Ammo Hanna's footsteps to Brazil, where they planned to open a Holy Land souvenir store. Few in the town believed they had made it much farther than Jaffa until a year later, when a Franciscan monk turned up declaring he had seen them with his own eyes selling crosses and rosaries on the Rua da Alfandega in the immigrant quarter of Rio de Janeiro.¹¹

News of the Zakhariyya brothers sent ripples of excitement through the town. No longer was international trade the domain of a handful of uppity Tarajmeh families with connections to Catholic churches around Europe.

Now it seemed that anyone capable of raising a few ghurush could traverse the Atlasi Ocean in search of fortune. Children rushed from house to house, telling friends how the streets of Amerka were paved with gold. Young men began packing up their belongings right then and there, declaring they were leaving the next day for Port-au-Prince, Buenos Aires, or New York. Meanwhile, their mothers scolded them for being so impetuous, asking who would harvest the olive orchards while they gone, and their fathers dropped to their knees, beseeching al-Khadr and Mar Yousef to protect them from danger.

Watching it all with interest from their houses on Ras Iftays were the old men of the Tarajmeh clan. Ever since the Paris exhibition of 1867, their business plan had been based on trade in Europe. Now it seemed the process had taken a sudden leap forward, perhaps a little too quickly for their liking. Some were open-minded enough to remember they had voiced the same concerns about the European exhibitions only to find their doubts had been misplaced. Others interjected, saying that trading in France, where they spoke the language and had connections through the friars, was one thing, but traveling across the great Atlasi Ocean into the unknown was quite another. People still remembered the stories of Andrea Dawid's mysterious disappearance in Amerka nearly a century ago. The Dawid family was part of the Tarajmeh clan and was said to have lost a small fortune funding Andrea's fanciful voyage.

Taking his seat among the elders of the Tarajmeh clan was old Yousef Dabdoub. He was sixty-one by the time news reached Bethlehem of the Zakhariyya brothers' success in Brazil and in no fit state to travel abroad himself. Who really knew what lay in wait on the other side anyway? He had heard Ammo Hanna's tales and was sure that for every prosperous city there would be miles of teeming jungle to cross where fearsome beasts and pestilent disease lay in wait. But he also knew the only way for the merchant families to break their reliance on the Franciscans was to take risks by tapping into new markets. He was convinced more than ever that Amerka was the next frontier where the Bethlehemites should expand their businesses. It was a land of devout Christians eager to meet people from the Holy Land they had only heard about in books and to purchase their sacred souvenirs.

The solution, he decided, should be the same one they had employed in Europe. "Let us send our youngest sons on exploratory trips to test the waters," he declared to the Tarajmeh elders. "For years we toiled in poverty to establish our families' businesses. Our boys don't know how lucky they are to be living in these houses we built for them, enjoying all the luxuries money can buy. By the grace of Allah, it is time they gave us something in return."

According to Yousef's reasoning, each family should recruit its most resilient young men, preferably still in their late teens or early twenties with everything to prove, and then pair them up with other families, allowing them to travel in small groups to the distant shores of Amerka. Yousef knew that his eldest surviving sons, Hanna and Mikhail, were no longer suitable for the job. They were grown men with wives and children, no longer desperate to prove their worth to the family firm. But he had two more sons, Jubrail and Ibrahim, who were now approaching adulthood at ages sixteen and thirteen, respectively. The trip to Amerka would serve as a rite of passage for these boys and others like them. If they returned safely with news of business opportunities, they would be accepted as partners in the family business, deserving of the title of khawaja. If they failed and perished on the high seas . . . well, that would prove the old men had been right to be cautious.

Luckily for the young men of the Tarajmeh families, wondrous new inventions were smoothening the long journey to Amerka. Reports of shipwrecks out on the distant seas seemed to be reaching Jaffa with less frequency these days. Enormous steamships, the likes of which had not previously been witnessed, were now laying anchor outside Jaffa's harbor, disgorging hordes of faranja onto little rowboats, all clambering to set eyes on the Holy Land. Some of them came all the way from Amerka and were happy to explain to the Bethlehemites that the journey across the Atlasi Ocean was not as perilous as it once had been. The more scientifically minded among them spoke of iron hulls, compound steam engines, and screw propulsion systems, describing how these new innovations had reduced the Atlantic crossing to a mere ten days. The Bethlehemites listened attentively, struggling to follow the technical details but encouraged to proceed with their plans.

The new steamships also ensured that messages could be relayed back home once the young men set off from Bethlehem. For years now, the Austrians and the French had been operating postal services in Jerusalem, meaning a letter written from Paris or Vienna could reach home in as little as three weeks.[12] This was a lifeline for a young merchant setting out from Bethlehem who might quickly run short of supplies and need to write home to request reinforcements. It was said a similar postal system had been established across the Atlasi Ocean, allowing communication to be maintained if they made it as far as Amerka. There was even talk of an invention that could send messages almost instantly across the ocean via a submarine cable. In the 1870s this seemed too far-fetched for most people to believe and was deemed another one of those frivolous fads of the faranja, just like the underwater ships of Paris. But it would not be long before the Bethlehem family firms were relying on those underwater cables to conduct their businesses, linking together shops established across multiple continents and oceans.

Once the Bethlehemite explorers made landfall, other wondrous inventions would help ease their journeys. In the 1870s, very few people in Bethlehem knew what a train looked like, but the young pioneers soon became acquainted with them. Whether traveling from Marseille to Bordeaux to catch the only steamship to Rio, or from New York to Chicago to attend a great exhibition in the American interior, the railway was the vital artery upon which their journeys depended. Back in Bethlehem, people remained skeptical. For years, there had been talk of a planned railway connecting Jaffa to Jerusalem, but no sign of the project had appeared, causing many to dismiss it as yet another fanciful franji invention that amounted to nothing.[13] The young men who had traveled abroad patiently extolled the virtues of the railway, explaining how a great locomotive wagon was pulled along a pair of iron tracks at great speed by the power of steam. But the old men in Bab al-Dayr just shrugged their shoulders and said such things would have no use in the hill country around Jerusalem. How could steam alone push a wagon up those steep slopes, and why would anyone try such an absurd idea when they already had a newly paved road? Little did they imagine that before long such technological marvels would be forging their unstoppable path deep into the Jerusalem hills.

By 1876, old Yousef was convinced the family could wait no longer to begin their exploration of Amerka. Young men across town were setting off for those distant Western shores, and the Dabdoubs could ill afford to fall behind. He had heard that a city in the northern regions of Amerka named Philadelphia would be hosting a great exhibition to mark one hundred years of independence from franji rule. It was said this exhibition would rival anything the faranja had put on in Europe, and it was already attracting the attention of other Bethlehemite families—the Banayut brothers seemed to be busy preparing their own expedition.[14] Now was the time to strike, Yousef decided. As Jubrail was still too young, he would select his next oldest son, the twenty-five-year-old Mikhail, to carry out the mission along with a cousin, Beshara Dabdoub. The family had spent the past ten years building up the workshop at Hosh Dabdoub for exactly this kind of event. They now had the resources to produce a vast stock of mother-of-pearl carvings and the connections in Europe to transport them safely across the Atlantic. Wasting no time, he wrote to the Ottoman government to secure official approval to open a Bethlehem bazaar next to the Turkish café where they would sell the finest mother-of-pearl carvings ever to come out of Bayt Lahm.[15] Preparations were complete, customs duties paid, and shipping routes confirmed. The Dabdoub discovery of Amerka would soon begin, bringing with it so many new certainties and ambiguities, adventures and calamities.[16]

FIGURE 1. Drawing of pilgrims' approach into Bethlehem in the 1860s. The drawing shows the Qoos az-Zarara archway marking the entrance point into Bethlehem and the lack of buildings beyond this point. Hosh Dabdoub was built around the time of this drawing and is located further back along the pathway, behind the viewer. Source: Andrew Thomson, *In the Holy Land* (Oxford: T. Nelson, 1874), 168.

FIGURE 2. Photograph of Bethlehem, c. 1857, taken from the roof of the Greek Monastery within the Church of the Nativity complex by James Graham, who worked in Palestine as a lay missionary between 1853 and 1857. To the right of the photo, the Ras Iftays road can be seen traversing the hill, forming the main route into Bethlehem. The photo shows that the road remained empty of buildings in the mid-1850s, just before the Dabdoub family and others sparked a building frenzy along Ras Iftays. Hosh Dabdoub was built around three years after the photo was taken just to the left of the cluster of trees in the far right of the photo. Courtesy of the Palestine Exploration Fund: PEF/P/2147-8 (J. Graham, 1853–60).

FIGURE 3. View of Bethlehem, c. 1898, showing Bethlehem's location along the steep ridge, culminating in the fortresslike Church of the Nativity at its eastern end (far left of the photo). The photo shows the extent to which Bethlehem was surrounded by terraced orchards of olive, fig, and almond trees. The Ras Iftays hill where Hosh Dabdoub was built is just out of shot to the right. Source: Library of Congress, Prints & Photographs Division, LC-DIG-matpc-06760.

FIGURE 4. Funeral outside the Church of the Nativity, c. 1900. At that time, the main cemetery in Bethlehem was in the open area in front of the church, immediately to the right as people exited the building. Source: Library of Congress, Prints & Photographs Division, LC-DIG-matpc-05282.

FIGURE 5. Catholic procession entering the Church of the Nativity on Christmas day, c. 1898–1914. The presence of mounted Ottoman police confirms the photo was taken prior to World War I. Source: Library of Congress, Prints & Photographs Division, LC-DIG-matpc-09141.

FIGURE 6. Scene of the street (today's Star Street) from Ras Iftays, Bethlehem, c. 1900. The photograph is taken a short distance down the hill from Hosh Dabdoub when Ras Iftays was already lined with souvenir stores, mother-of-pearl workshops, and the mansions of the Tarajmeh families. The woman in the foreground is wearing the distinctive *shatweh* headdress used by married women in Bethlehem, which contained valuable coins sown into the cone under the white veil. Source: Library of Congress, Prints & Photographs Division, LC-DIG-matpc-04567.

FIGURE 7. Manger Square (Bab al-Dayr) on market day, c. 1900. Vendors from local villages and Bedouin tribes can be seen selling their produce around the square. The Mosque of Omar (built in 1860) is at the far end of the square and the Ottoman police station (the *saraya*) is to the right. Source: Library of Congress, Prints & Photographs Division, LC-DIG-matpc-06765.

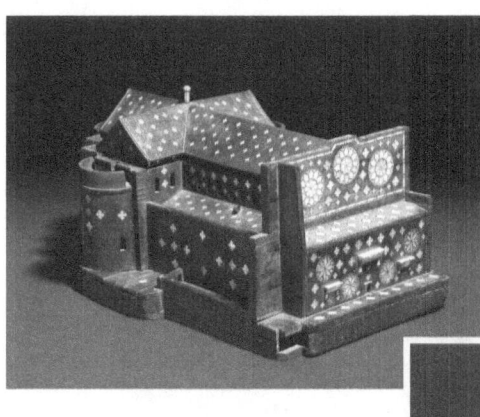

FIGURE 8. Bethlehem mother-of-pearl carvings. Clockwise from top left: Model of the Church of the Nativity, crafted from olive wood and ivory with mother-of-pearl inlay, c. 1600. Source: The British Museum. Nativity scene by Butros Lama, c. 1900. Jordanian coat of arms by Gregory Zoughbi, c. 1960. Model of the Church of the Holy Sepulchre, c. seventeenth century. All reproduced with permission from Enrique Yidi Daccarett, Karen David Daccarett, and Martha Lizcano Angarita, *El arte palestino de tallar el nacar* (Barranquilla: Varios, 2005).

FIGURE 9. Wood engraving of Bethlehem mother-of-pearl workers, c. 1875. Source: Charles William Wilson, ed., *Picturesque Palestine, Sinai, and Egypt*, vol. 1, div. 1 (New York: D. Appleton, 1881–83), 133.

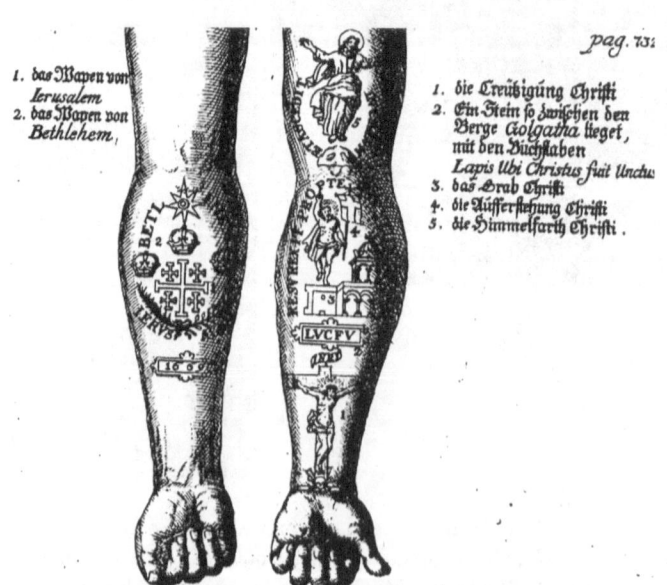

FIGURE 10. Tattoos received by German pilgrim Ratger Stubbe in Bethlehem, 1669. Source: Johann Lund, *Die alten jüdischen Heiligthümer* (Hamburg: Liebernickel, 1738), 732.

FIGURE 11. Jacir Palace, c. 1920. This was one of the most spectacular buildings among the new wave of pink-stone mansions built by the merchants of Bethlehem in the early twentieth century and discussed in chapter 16. Source: Wikimedia Commons.

FIGURE 12. Aerial view of Bethlehem, 1931. Hosh Dabdoub can be clearly seen on the far right in the center with its distinctive double row of arches looking back across the valley. As can be seen, it was the first of the merchant houses lining the Ras Iftays road, which led into Bethlehem. By the time of this photo, a new road (Manger Street) had been built below the Ras Iftays road. Source: Library of Congress, Prints & Photographs Division, LC-DIG-matpc-22176.

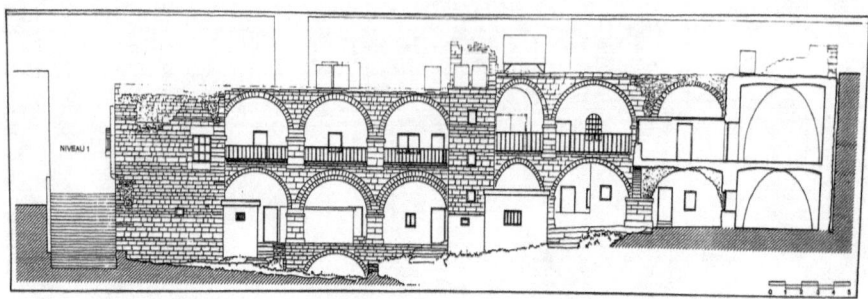

FIGURE 13. Scale drawing of Hosh Dabdoub as seen from the rear, showing the two floors of vaulted corridors (*riwaq*) with their distinctive rounded arches that looked back across the valley toward the old town and the Wilderness further east. Source: Philippe Revault, Serge Santelli, and Catherine Weill-Rochant, eds., *Maisons de Bethléem* (Paris: Maisonneuve et Larose, 1997), 110.

FIGURE 14. Hosh Dabdoub as seen from the rear in the 1990s. The distinctive arches of the house's *riwaq* arcade were extended across the second floor around 1900. Source: Philippe Revault, Serge Santelli, and Catherine Weill-Rochant, eds., *Maisons de Bethléem* (Paris: Maisonneuve et Larose, 1997), 111.

FIGURE 15. The main entrance to Hosh Dabdoub from street level. Photograph by the author.

FIGURE 16. Jubrail Dabdoub's 1923 house as seen from the rear. From the street entrance, only the top floor of the house can be seen, but to the rear, the house's full dimensions are revealed. Photograph by the author.

FIGURE 17. Jubrail Dabdoub's 1923 house as it stands today on Hebron Road, Bethlehem. The front gates bear the inscription "GJD [Gabriel Joseph Dabdoub] 1923." Carved into stone over the front doorway is the Arabic inscription "Jubra'il Yousef Dabdoub." Photograph by the author.

Part II

CHAPTER 8

IN SEARCH OF AMERKA

THEY CAME DOWN FROM THE hill country, headed for the coast on donkeys laden with heavy sacks and trunks. When they got to Jerusalem, they exchanged the donkeys for the daily wagon service that plied the new road to Jaffa, winding its way through the steep hills until it flattened out at the coastal plain. In the port of Jaffa, they struck deals with wily ticket agents who looked nervously around for any sign of Ottoman officials. With their trunks held aloft, boatmen rowed them out to steam ships too large to enter the rocky harbor.[1]

They were the ruwwad of Bethlehem: young pioneers setting out in search of Amerka. Dispatched by fathers and uncles to seek new trade on the other side of the world, they had no choice but to keep looking forward. When they arrived in the great port cities of the Mediterranean, they set about planning the next phase of their journeys, negotiating with shifty looking touts—samasira, as they called them—to secure their passage to Amerka.[2] To their surprise, they discovered that many different Amerkas awaited them. Some traveled east through the Suez Canal, in search of an Amerka that lay somewhere out in the great Hindi Ocean. Others went northward across the Black Sea, toward an Amerka of snow and ice where golden cities of onion-shaped domes lay in wait. Already by 1878 the first Bethlehemite base had been established in Kiev thanks to the enterprising spirit of Elias Kattan—a Catholic Arab selling souvenirs to hordes of pious

Slavs at the largest Orthodox pilgrimage site in the Russian Empire—who set up shop next to the Cave Monastery on the Pechersk Nicolskaia.³

But it was westward that most of them traveled, boarding ships in Barcelona, Cádiz, Marseille, and Le Havre with little idea of where they were headed except that it lay on the other side of the Atlasi Ocean. For weeks they endured the harsh conditions of steerage class, crammed into the dingy bowels of ships, breathing in the pestilential air of a hundred other disheveled emigrants, without a proper bed or toilet, nor the decency of separation between sexes. Many did not survive the journey, succumbing to illness or shipwreck, their names recorded years later in the ledger books of the Bethlehem parish church as simply "morto in America."⁴ Those lucky enough to make it across the great expanse of ocean would stumble bleary-eyed one morning off the deck and onto a land they had only heard about in stories told by the old men of Bethlehem. Fumbling in their abayeh pockets for a crumpled piece of paper where a family member had scribbled the unpronounceable name of a town, they stood blinking into the bright light of Amerka.

The first Bethlehemites to appear in the Caribbean arrived with no plan for how to survive other than to sell the mother-of-pearl crosses and rosaries they carried in their suitcases. In 1879 a group of bedraggled travelers washed up on the shores of Havana. Their boat had sunk as it approached the harbor, forcing them to jump ship and ruining their luggage in the process. Destitute and desperate, they presented themselves to the Spanish colonial authorities, begging to be given free passage back to Cádiz, where they planned to claim compensation from a French shipping company.⁵ Four years later, in 1883, a man from Bethlehem named Giries Kattan appeared at the Havana city hall. He was there to plead with the municipal authorities to waive the license fee required to open a store in the city. Giries wished to establish his shop on the Calle del Obispo, a short distance from the city docks, where he planned to sell Bethlehem-made devotional objects. But he lacked the funds to pay the license fee, and he could not afford a ticket back to his homeland.⁶

It would take years of trial and error, with many aborted projects and ignoble deaths along the way, but gradually the young travelers realized that conditions in the rural interior of the Caribbean islands were ripe for traders of small luxury goods from Europe and the United States. For centuries, European corporations had been shipping vast quantities of sugar and tropical fruits out of the islands, but few products flowed the other way. A merchant with connections to European producers of luxury goods, and with the resilience to brave the rustic conditions of the islands, would find a land of untapped markets and potential new consumers.

Clothing, jewelry, and toiletries were the first products they brought to the villagers of Haiti, Cuba, Jamaica, and Santo Domingo from France and Spain—small goods light enough to carry from village to village in their qashsha wooden trunks.[7] They set off from the port cities with pack animals, targeting rural areas where their goods would still be a novelty. Pushing ever-deeper inland, they made their way along snake-infested paths, drenched in sweat from the unrelenting humidity of the jungle. They looked around nervously every time the call of an unknown beast rang out in the forest. But they kept going, searching for places where European goods had not yet penetrated. When they came across a new village, they went from door to door, showing their array of gleaming luxury items to the curious locals. They set up credit systems with villagers who could not afford to pay outright for their products. Gradually, they began to open stores in the towns where they could guarantee a steady supply of goods.[8]

News of success could not be long contained. By the 1880s, word had reached the Ottoman lands that rich pickings were on offer in Amerka, and especially on those Caribbean islands.[9] News was also spreading of how the Bethlehemites had enjoyed great success selling Holy Land souvenirs at the international exhibitions. Soon thousands of young men and women were heading down from Mount Lebanon to the ports of Tripoli and Beirut, planning to make their fortune by imitating the Bethlehemites' tactics. Already at the world's fair in Philadelphia of 1876, the Dabdoubs had noticed merchants selling fake Holy Land goods.[10] Soon the imitators were making their presence felt all over the great continent of Amerka, selling bucketfuls of cheap crucifixes and rosaries produced in dingy sweatshops in Marseille and New York.[11] The first word these persistent peddlers learned to pronounce on the boats as they made their way across the Atlantic was *Jerusalem*. Once on dry land, their sales routine would always begin with the Holy Land trinkets in the hope of gaining the trust of a pious housewife or catching the interest of a passing pedestrian. Expertly draping the wares along their arm or suspending them at the end of a long stick, they would point enthusiastically to themselves with their free hand, exclaiming their newly learned word: "Jerusalem!"[12]

By the time the Bethlehemites began opening their first shops on the Caribbean islands, a steady stream of Syrians was flowing into the docks of Port-au-Prince, Havana, and Santo Domingo, holding aloft rosaries and stepping off the boat, shouting "Jerusalem!"[13] Before long the locals had come to resent these strange-looking peddlers with their frugal lifestyles and cheap goods that were said to put local traders out of business. In Haiti, the Syrians were blamed for every woe that befell the country, from the poverty of the peasantry to the assassination of presidents, while in Cuba the revolutionaries accused them of being spies in the service of the Spanish colonial government.[14] Sensing conditions were no longer favorable, the Bethlehemites began to eye other opportunities on the American mainland. Their contacts in Havana, Port-au-Prince, and Kingston told them about the small countries that lay just across the sea where governments were welcoming foreign merchants as part of plans for "economic liberalization." Eyes fixed on the horizon ahead, the Bethlehemites set off once more, headed for the new ports of Puerto Barrios, La Ceiba, Puerto Limón, Colón, and Barranquilla. From these Caribbean staging posts, they ventured into the sweet waist of Amerka—a land of teeming jungles, Mayan cities, and bubbling volcanoes where no Syrian imitator had yet ventured.[15]

They found their greatest success in northern Honduras, where a curious accident of history was transforming the region into a vast sea of bananas. Back in 1869, work had begun on the country's first railway, optimistically named the Interoceanic Railroad. The financers of the railway had dreamed of connecting the Pacific and Caribbean coasts of Honduras and in the process making vast fortunes by transporting coffee and minerals out of the country's interior and onto boats bound for Europe and the northern lands of Amerka. But when construction of the railway began at the Caribbean town of Puerto Cortés, the financers quickly realized they would have to export some kind of local product along the railway to fund its ongoing construction. The solution was bananas. Quick and easy to grow in the fertile soil of the northern plains, they could be packed onto empty wagons and shipped out of Puerto Cortés as return cargo on boats headed for the great port city of New Orleans, where the northern Americans were developing a taste for the squishy yellow fruit. Encouraged by the rail contractors, local landowners began planting bananas in the thousands all over the northern regions of Honduras. By 1874, the railway had run out of funds, leaving behind a mere fifty-seven miles of track that led out from the new harbor at Puerto Cortés.[16] The dream of the Interoceanic Railroad had evaporated, but the banana plantations remained.

When the Bethlehemites first arrived in northern Honduras in the 1880s, they followed the line of the aborted railway out of Puerto Cortés and into the Sula Valley, which stretched out to the south between two lines of jungle-clad mountains. Along the way, they stopped at settlements named Baracoa, Rio Blanquito, Cholomo, San Pedro Sula, Chamelecón, Villanueva, and Pimienta—small villages of thatched-roofed adobe houses where people for centuries had lived off the fertile soils of the floodplains. Everywhere they went, they found local landowners busy planting bananas.[17] These plantations seemed to offer rich pickings for a peddler capable of bringing supplies to the workers. The only challenge was how to reach them. Located among the swamps of the Sula Valley, the farms were often flooded during the rainy season, making transportation by road impossible. Leaving the route of the old railway, the Bethlehemites exchanged their horses and carts for makeshift barges and set off down the rivers and canals that led to the farms. Paddling along in the sweltering humidity, they traversed the network of waterways that crisscrossed the plantations, calling out as they went: "Hay algo que le falte?" The workers soon learned to recognize the cries of these traveling salesmen in their strange-sounding accents. They called them "turcos," and they bought from them dried foods, tools, clothes, shoes, and hair combs imported from the Caribbean islands and Europe. As good Catholics, they also purchased rosaries and crucifixes from the Bethlehemites, assured that each one had been blessed by the high priest of the Nativity Church.

From these early beginnings as waterborne salesmen, it was a short step to opening makeshift stores at the entrances to the plantations and in the neighboring villages. Among the first to do so was Salameh Kattan, born in Bethlehem in 1875 as the youngest of eight siblings. His elder brothers Daoud and Jadallah had already established trading bases in Cuba and Haiti when they sent young Salameh to investigate the Sula Valley in the late 1890s. After a few months he had saved enough money to open a store in the plantation town of El Progreso, encouraging his elder brothers to follow him to Honduras.[18] By this stage the banana plantations were already being taken over by giant corporations from the northern lands of Amerka. The biggest of these was El Yunai[19]—a huge enterprise that reached into every corner of Honduran society and consequently gained the nickname "El Pulpo" for its octopus-like tentacles.[20] Rather than relying on local services, El Yunai brought its own infrastructure and workforce: new railways, port facilities, and ships, as well as thousands of laborers from Jamaica. The corporation also insisted on opening its own shops on the plantations, pushing out the Bethlehemites who had previously supplied the workers. But the Bethlehemites were masters of adaptation and would not be deterred so easily. They found new ways to profit from the plantations, selling wholesale to El Yunai's shops rather than directly to the workers. They took advantage of the banana boats that now plied the Caribbean between New Orleans and Puerto Cortés, setting up new lines of import from the United States. And they opened shops selling luxury goods in the fast-expanding towns of northern Honduras.[21]

Sitting in the middle of the Sula Valley was the town of San Pedro Sula. Until the 1880s, San Pedro had been a village of thatched huts. But with the arrival of the banana plantations, it grew at a ferocious pace to become the region's biggest boom town.[22] It was in San Pedro that the Bethlehemites found their greatest success, and it was there that they made their homes. In a town obsessed with novelty and progress, the Bethlehemites of San Pedro prided themselves on being in the vanguard. They supplied the town's residents with all the latest consumer goods required to live a modern lifestyle: perfumes, mirrors, French jewelry, toiletries, and all manner of other products that had no apparent practical use. The houses and shops they built in the 1900s and 1910s were among the first to be made from concrete, their colonnaded exteriors and stylized storefront designs impressing the locals who had not seen such grandiose structures before. They were even assigned the town's first postcodes in the days when the postal service was only just beginning to reach the Sula Valley on a sporadic basis.[23] Later, they opened the first factories in San Pedro, making the switch from importers of consumer goods to local manufacturers of clothing.[24]

As the merchants amassed great wealth, they sent word home for their brothers to join them and to bring brides for them from Bethlehem. Most people in Bethlehem had little idea how to locate Honduras on a map, but they all knew about a town called San Pedro where a life of untold riches was said to await any traveler prepared to brave the journey. For the first time, young girls were sent out to Amerka from Bethlehem, some of them as young as twelve or thirteen, traveling halfway around the world to marry a man they had never met before. Soon they would be raising families in that faraway land of steaming swamps, jungle-clad mountains, and sweltering humidity. Already by 1902, Yusef and Regina Handal were baptizing their newborn baby in the parish church of San Pedro Sula.²⁵ They were followed by a succession of other Bethlehem families, all Hispanicizing their names as they did so. Abu al-ʿArraj became Larrach, Giacaman turned into Yacamán, Murqus became Marcos, and Qanawati became Canahuati. A new Bethlehem colony was born. No longer looking to make a quick fortune before returning home, the Bethlehemites in the Sula Valley were laying down roots in the town that just a few years earlier had only been a village of thatched-roofed adobe huts.²⁶

While some of the Bethlehem pioneers paddled their way into the lush plains of the Sula Valley, others were busy searching out their own Amerka in a land of towering mountains and desert plateaus some 3,500 miles south. For months they had been searching for a place to trade free from the hordes of Syrian imitators crossing the Atlasi Ocean.²⁷ Some had followed the lead of the Zakhariyya brothers and taken boats out of France and Spain headed for the great port city of Rio de Janeiro. Upon arrival, they heard the familiar sound of "Terra Santa!" and "Jerusalem!" ringing out around the streets of the immigrant quarter, sending them back to the docks to reboard ships continuing south to Monte Video and Buenos Aires. But there too they found the marketplaces already crowded with Syrian peddlers selling the familiar Holy Land trinkets and gewgaws.

Consulting with merchants in the docks of Buenos Aires, the Bethlehemites learned of a prosperous land that lay to the west, across a great mountain range where no turco had yet ventured. When they asked how they could get there, the merchants shook their heads and told them it was better to stay in Buenos Aires where the living was good. Only a handful of steamships attempted the journey around the southernmost tip of Amerka in those days. The journey was notoriously dangerous, and tickets were hard to come by, not to mention extortionately expensive.²⁸ That left the overland route, across the Cordillera de los Andes, where no road or railway penetrated. Only the hardiest of local travelers attempted the journey on muleback, taking weeks to traverse the old Camino de los Andes, which offered only the occasional casucha hut as respite from the snowstorms and freezing temperatures.

In those early days, when information made its way back to Bethlehem in confusing fragments, it was said that some of the most daring of the pioneers had attempted to cross the towering peaks of the Cordillera.[29] After weeks of journeying on horseback across the fertile plains of the Pampas, the travelers eventually saw on the horizon a line of snow-clad mountains, dwarfing the hills they knew from back home. When they reached the town of Mendoza, gateway to the Camino de los Andes, they exchanged their horses for mules and hired local Indian men known as baqueanos who knew every twist and turn of the mountain trails. Waiting until the summer weather became sufficiently calm, the young migrants set out on muleback along the stony pathway that led out of Mendoza, through the village of Villavicencio and up into the steep slopes of the Uspallata Pass.

The stories that made their way back to Bethlehem told of how these intrepid young men climbed so high they disappeared into the clouds, some of them never to be seen again. There, on the rooftop of the world, they faced a coldness they did not know existed and snowdrifts deeper than an entire wadi in Bethlehem. The casucha huts, once the pride of the Spanish imperial troops, had long since been left to ruin, providing scant shelter from the ferocious winds, avalanches, and rockfalls. Those who made it to the Punta de Vacas plateau still alive enjoyed some brief respite before ascending once more, this time into the granite gorges around Puente del Inca and Las Cuevas, and then eventually up to the highest point of the pass at over thirteen thousand feet. Here they found themselves surrounded by the tallest mountains in all Amerka, where the air was so thin that breathing itself became the most pressing task. Officially, they were already in Chile by this point, but in reality, they were in no earthly country. They looked around them to see a lunar landscape of soaring granite peaks. It would take weeks for anyone to realize a traveler had disappeared beneath a snowdrift. Praying their mules would keep their footing as they made their way down the steep descent, those fortunate enough to still be alive eventually came to the Chilean border control at Guardia Vieja and, beneath it in the valley below, the welcoming lights of Santa Rosa de Los Andes.[30]

It was impossible to say how many of those young pioneers completed the Camino de los Andes. Tales of miracles made their way back to Bethlehem in which the intervention of saints, French priests, and strong doses of cognac brought travelers back from the dead and carried them down the western slopes of the Andes.³¹ Some of the Bethlehemites opted instead to return to the docks in Buenos Aires and try reaching the other side of the Cordillera by boat, boarding one of the few steamships that attempted the journey around the Cabo de Hornos. Those that survived the bitter cold and vicious storms that battered the boats making their way around the southern tip of Amerka awoke one morning to find they had docked in a beautiful city called Valparaiso. As if in a dream, they blinked at the brightly colored houses that tumbled down the steep hillsides into the sparkling blue waters of the harbor. Stepping off the boat, they noticed the long black dresses worn by the local women and concluded they had stumbled upon a city of nuns who would surely jump at the chance to buy their wares from the Holy Land. "Tierra Santa! Tierra Santa!" they shouted as they rushed toward the women, only to find the women turning around and fleeing in panic. Making inquiries with the local men, they learned the black dresses were simply the local style worn by married women, who were mortified to be seen talking to strange peddlers.³²

Some of the Bethlehemites were so enamored with Valparaiso they decided to stay and find other ways to sell their wares. But most continued their restless search, boarding the train headed across the coastal hills and out into the fertile valley that was bordered to the east by the mighty Cordillera de los Andes.³³ As the train puffed its way down into Chile's Central Valley, the Bethlehemites looked out of their carriage windows and thought about how familiar the landscape seemed, reminding them of the fertile wadis to the south and west of Bethlehem and Beit Jala where their parents still cultivated orchards of apricot and almond trees.³⁴ Their restless search for a trading post devoid of Syrian peddlers had come to an end in the city of Santiago de Chile.

The first to reach Santiago were said to be Elias D'eiq and Yusef Jacir in the year 1881.³⁵ But it was not long before dozens of others began arriving from Bethlehem and Beit Jala. Some of them decided to use the Central Valley as a staging post for explorations further north. Into the high Andes they trekked, following the line of the Cordillera up into the Altiplano region, toward the lands of Bolivia and Peru. Soon news was returning to Santiago of a magical world populated by hardy mountain people dressed in colorful garments who worshipped not one, but many, gods. It was hard for those in Santiago to separate fact from fiction in the tales that filtered back down from the Andes, not least when they heard about the animals those people herded: strange creatures that resembled something between a camel and a sheep and were used by the nomads as both pack animals and providers of wool and meat.[36] From Santiago, these tales traveled in broken fragments across oceans and continents, all the way back to Bethlehem, where they were reassembled in Bab al-Dayr by the town's most gifted storytellers, sending out many more young explorers to see the wonders of Amerka with their own eyes.

Over time, whole communities of Bethlehemites would establish themselves in the mountain cities of Cochabamba, La Paz, Ayacucho, Cuzco, and Arequipa.[37] But it was in Chile's fertile Central Valley that they found their richest rewards. In Santiago itself they colonized the Patronato District on the northern side of the great Mapocho River. There they built churches, established the country's first textile mills, opened banks, and set up football teams. Meanwhile, young peddlers set out into the surrounding hills to find new markets for their goods. Soon they had reached every town and village in the Central Valley, widening the range of products they sold as they went. They tapped into the expanding network of Bethlehem traders that now crisscrossed the coastlines of Amerka, the islands of the Caribbean, and the cities of Europe, allowing them to bring all kinds of novelty goods to the Chilean villagers. Every time they opened their trunks in a village square, an assortment of mirrors, silk scarves, exotic perfumes, hair combs, and shaving soaps would magically appear. For many of the villagers, it was the first time they set eyes on such wondrous objects, and they quickly came to rely on the Bethlehemites to keep them supplied with such fancies, making the peddlers a reassuringly familiar sight up and down the valley. As the proverb would later attest, there were three things that could always be found in a Chilean village: a priest, a policeman, and a Palestinian.[38]

CHAPTER 9

OF TROUBLES ON THE TROCADÉRO

IN THE YEAR 1878, JUBRAIL was pushed into motion at the age of seventeen by his father and elder brothers, precipitating an unrelenting travel itinerary that would not truly subside until his first death in 1909. The occasion was the latest world's fair, held in Paris in 1878.[1]

Jubrail's mother, Rosa, had refused to accept that Jubrail would be traveling to Paris with his elder brothers Hanna and Mikhail. She gave the same curt response every time the trip was brought up in conversation: "Khalas, bikaffi. He's not leaving and that's the end of it."

Old Yousef, on the other hand, argued that it was vital they begin training Jubrail as early as possible. Mikhail's expedition to Amerka two years earlier had been an unprecedented success. Such was the interest generated by their Bethlehem bazaar in Philadelphia that a flurry of imitators had quickly cropped up, hawking various types of bogus Holy Land goods in accents that ranged from the mountains of Lebanon to a distant isle named Ireland.[2] But the competition in Bethlehem was fierce. Every week news filtered back to the town of a young man who had made landfall in some distant corner of Amerka and was now selling rosaries there by the bucketful. The Dabdoubs had to continue to stay ahead of the game at all costs, and the only way to do so was to dispatch their sons on new voyages, old Yousef reasoned. The loss of Murqus to the vagaries of disease had been a devastating blow to the family workforce. Jubrail needed experience as soon as possible, and the exhibition in Paris would give him the perfect opportunity.

When the day of departure finally came, Rosa was taken by surprise. For months she had refused all talk of dates, times, and places. She awoke at dawn one day in the month of Nisan to the sound of donkeys braying and bags being loaded. Pulling on one of her simple house dresses, she rushed out of the hosh with her hair on full display, screaming for Jubrail to come back. But it was too late. The brothers were already making their way past Qubbet Rahil when she caught sight of them, by which time old Yousef was holding her back, beseeching her to return inside.

By nightfall the travelers arrived in Jaffa, where they found accommodation in one of the hospices catering to franji pilgrims. Waking early next morning, they negotiated a deal with the fixers in the docks. Their package included not only a ticket for the ship leaving that day for Beirut but also the cost of the rowboat that would take them out of Jaffa's rocky harbor to the steamer, as well as the bribes required to make it past the Ottoman port officials.[3] Until the 1890s, when the Ottoman government finally understood the benefits of remittances sent home by emigrants, leaving the port was prohibited for Ottoman subjects. The only option was to encourage the officials to turn a blind eye—something they were usually prepared to do if the price was right.[4] Paying them off was just the first of many extra fees and bribes the brothers would pay to ease their passage to Paris. All told, the journey would cost the family over three thousand ghurush—about as much as the shop at Hosh Dabdoub would normally make in a whole year.[5] Old Yousef had staked a great deal on their voyage.

As they rowed out toward the steamship that afternoon, Jubrail was brimming with excitement. He had been to the Jaffa docks before and had marveled at the lumbering giants lying anchored beyond the rocky harbor. But now, as they drew near in their tiny rowboat, he could scarcely believe the size of the ship that awaited them. Amid the shouts of the boatmen and the frightening rocking of the waves, he made out the words *Compagnie des Messageries Maritimes* plastered across the ship's mighty hull in huge franji lettering. Faced with no other option as his brother Mikhail pushed him forward, Jubrail took a leap of faith onto the rope ladder that had been slung down from deck to transport passengers onboard.

Hauling himself on deck, Jubrail was immediately overwhelmed by hordes of people dashing in all directions, clambering to secure their luggage and find their compartments. Only in the church at Christmas had he seen so many faranja gathered in one place. Just as they did in Bethlehem, they pushed and shoved their way about, shouting orders at anybody dressed in the normal Ottoman attire. "You in the fez hat!" one of them barked at Jubrail. "Take my bags to the luggage hold in first class. Run along now, be a good boy." Unable to understand a word the man was saying, Jubrail stared in amazement as he thrust a silver coin into his hand.

"Je suis désolé, monsieur." Hanna's voice intervened from somewhere behind. "This man is my brother. We're passengers."

Returning the coin to the franji man, Hanna pulled Jubrail away by the arm. "Yallah, akhoui, you can't stand around staring at the faranja like that. Stay close to me and Mikhail at all times. We have a long journey ahead of us."

So began a voyage that left Jubrail in a state of permanent dizziness. In his childhood games with Elias, traveling by boat had involved valiant battles against pirates, sea monsters, and tropical storms. Never had he imagined his greatest enemies would be homesickness, squalor, and nausea. Due to the strict budget assigned by old Yousef, the brothers were compelled to travel in steerage class. There, in the dank underbelly of the ship, the constant rocking and putrid smell of unwashed travelers sent Jubrail into a state of acute seasickness from which he would not recover until days after he set foot on land. Hanna and Mikhail passed the hours playing tawilah and tarnib with unsavory travelers who flashed furtive glances as they lay their bets and occasionally erupted into accusations of cheating. All the while, Jubrail lay on his back in a state of torment, his head spinning and stomach churning. On several occasions he was sent rushing onto deck to throw up what little food he had dared eat from the helpings of mush served up in the ship's canteen. How he wished during those long days and nights to be back in the comfort and familiarity of Hosh Dabdoub!

When he finally looked out to sea one morning and saw the glistening port of Marseille coming into view, he had the premonition that his life would never be the same from this moment forward. Stepping tentatively off the boat, he stuck close to his brothers as they made their way through the noisy immigrant quarter, the voices of touts and hawkers ringing in his ears. How thankful he was that Hanna and Mikhail knew how to rebuff their sinister advances, batting them away like flies along the narrow streets of Le Panier.

Unfathomably to Jubrail, his brothers knew their way to the railway station, and that same evening, Jubrail was bundled onto a train for the first time in his life. Amid a great cloud of steam and the piercing whistle of the engine, the train puffed and hissed its way out of the station while a dazed Jubrail looked out the window in bewilderment, wondering how he had come so far from the terraces of Wadi al-Jamal. Before long, the unrelenting speed of that formidable contraption and the steady clickety-clack of its wheels passing over the rails beneath sent him into a slumber from which he would not awake until they pulled into Paris the next morning.

For years Jubrail had heard the word Paris pronounced in tones of hushed reverence. His brothers had returned from their voyage of 1867 telling of a fantastical city of sumptuous palaces, majestic fountains, and magical gardens where exotic plants were gathered from all corners of the earth. But now, as he stepped off the train at the Gare de Lyon, all he could make out was a sea of people. They scurried about in all directions, dressed in the most bizarre clothing he had ever seen. Some of the men looked like the faranja who visited Bethlehem with their silly, tall hats and their austere, tight-fitting jackets. But here they wore their jackets open, revealing further layers of waistcoats, shirts with stiff collars turned over into little wings, and mysterious devices hanging from their pockets that made a ticking sound as their mechanical parts rotated. Strangest of all were the women whose robes had been gathered at the back in large bunches. With their tiny hats perched on their heads and their dresses jutting out at right angles to the rear, Jubrail had the distinct impression he was watching a parade of ostriches prancing around the station concourse.[6]

Following his brothers out of the station, he was greeted by a scene even more chaotic and beguiling. Long streets of towering buildings led off in all directions, each one identical to the next in its perfect symmetry. People darted in and out of shops, trying to avoid the fearsome contraptions that rattled up and down the streets. Suddenly, Jubrail was pulled by Mikhail onto a horse-drawn tram that went hurtling down the road at a ferocious speed. Noticing his brothers had taken off their tarbush hats, Jubrail did the same and looked out the window. An endless array of shiny cafés and brightly lit stores rushed by, the tram passing too quickly for him to make out the franji lettering. "Try not to look so naive," Hanna whispered to him. "There are many here who make a living out of picking the pockets of innocent boys like you."

Jubrail was unsure at what point they had entered the exhibition grounds. Everything around him was already so eccentric that he had not noticed when the regular streets ended and the attractions of the exhibition began. It was only when he found himself strolling through a busy marketplace with the sounds of the Arabic tongue ringing out that he realized something had changed. All around him people were arranging displays of carpets, jewelry, and fabrics. Out of nowhere, a camel lolloped its way across the street in front of him, led by a Bedouin man wearing the hatta and iqal. Had he somehow been transported back to the Jerusalem Wilderness without realizing?

"Yallah Jubrail, we have to sign in at the registration desk." Hanna's stern voice brought him back to the reality of the situation, sending him scurrying up a series of steps to catch up with his elder brothers.

At the top of the steps Jubrail looked up to see a mighty palace looming before them. There was something about its imposing size and strange mixture of styles that filled him with fear. The base level consisted of an enormous circular structure of columns and rounded arches. It was topped by an octagonal edifice completely out of keeping with the rest of the building that would almost have reminded Jubrail of the Dome of the Rock in al-Quds were it not for the winged angel standing on its roof. Completing the bizarre arrangement were two giant towers on either side of the building, rising high into the sky and adorned with fluttering flags of red, white, and blue. As he entered the palace through a great archway at the base of the building, Jubrail let out a gasp. He was standing in a huge open hall with a mighty domed ceiling. At the rear of the building, he could make out an imposing wooden structure with a series of great metal pipes running vertically up the center, surrounded by elaborate wooden carvings of angels, saints, and fearsome jinn.[7] Unable to deduce the purpose of such a structure, Jubrail turned to Mikhail and whispered, "Where is our stall, akhoui?"

Mikhail let out a burst of laughter that echoed across the hall. "Ya hmar! They don't allow the Eastern peoples in here. We'll be outside in the gardens."

Having waited for an eternity to sign the registration book, the brothers made their way back outside and onto the steps. Facing the other way this time, Jubail could make out the entirety of the exhibition. He realized a mighty river passed right through the middle of the grounds, plied by an assortment of steamers, schooners, and rowing boats. Across a bridge on the other side was an enormous rectangular structure of glass and metal, not as tall as the palace behind them, but far larger in its surface area. Through the glass Jubrail could make out hundreds of tiny people making their way around the exhibits. Looking beyond the great glass building, the curiously metallic rooftops of Paris stretched into the distance as far as the eye could see.

As the brothers took in the view from the top of the stairway, Hanna let out a sigh. "Keef helwa Paris. How beautiful this city is!" But all Jubrail could feel was the seasickness returning as his legs gave way beneath him.

"Jubrail, shu bitsawwi!" Mikhail yelled as he grabbed Jubrail just in time to stop him falling down the steps. "What are you doing?"

"I'm ok," Jubrail replied sheepishly. "I just need to sit down for a moment."

A few minutes later, they were back down in the gardens at the foot of the palace, making their way along a street that Jubrail later learned had been constructed specially for the exhibition and consisted of pavilions built in the style of various countries around the world.[8] As they walked down the street, Jubrail made out the names of places he had read about in books at the Franciscan school. Here was "La Belgique," there was "L'Italie," and there, in a small rectangular building with a red sloping roof, was "Les Etats-Unis d'Amérique"—a place whose very name had inspired so much excitement in Jubrail as a young boy but now seemed strangely underwhelming, contained here in its orderly little pavilion.

By the time they reached the far end of the street, the atmosphere had changed completely. Once again Jubrail could hear Arabic ringing out, accompanied by the shrieks and howls of strange-looking birds and monkeys locked up in cages. They were back where they had started, where he had first seen the camel. All around them, people were busy erecting market stalls offering various kinds of clothing, jewelry, food, and drink. Familiar smells made their way into Jubrail's nostrils—roasting coffee infused with cardamom and the fruity fumes of arghileh pipes—producing in him a sudden pang of homesickness. The familiarity of the scene was a facade, a mere display in a franji shop window. As soon as he looked upward, the sight of that monstrous palace could not be avoided, with its red, white, and blue flags fluttering in the wind, reminding him how far he was from home.[9]

Jubrail was soon to discover there was no Ottoman Pavilion on the Rue des Nations. Instead, old Yousef had written to the owner of the Tunisian Pavilion, a franji of course, and persuaded him to rent out one of their stall spaces. It was not ideal to be selling Holy Land devotional objects in a pavilion designated for a country thousands of miles from Palestine. But once the exhibition opened, the franji visitors did not seem to care. They let out squeals of delight when they came across the "Objets de piété de la Terre Sainte" sign the brothers had erected and eagerly browsed the rows of carefully arranged mother-of-pearl crucifixes and rosaries the brothers had prepared. Jubrail watched as his brothers worked their audience, recounting tales from back home but changing the locations to make them resemble scenes from the Psalms of the Bible or the birth of the Messiah. He noticed how they always related their stories back to the carvings on display in the stall. This rosary had been carved from olive trees in the very fields where Ruth had met Boaz, or that crucifix had been blessed by priests in the very grotto where the Virgin had nurtured the holy infant. He also noticed how they had put their abayeh robes back on, as well as the tarbush hats they had taken off earlier on the tram.[10]

"Rassemblez-vous, mes amis. Gather 'round!" Hanna would declare in the French he had learned from the friars of Bethlehem. "We present to you sacred objects from the Holy City of Bethlehem," he would continue, gesturing to onlookers with a magnanimous sweep of the hand and adding for good measure: "Don't believe the imitators! Only here will you find the original and authentic rosaries and crosses from the Holy Land, sculpted by hand and blessed by the priest of Bethlehem."

The effect was magical. The faranja queued up to purchase their products or discuss how they might go into business together. Before long, the stall was also attracting the attention of envious merchants and peddlers who had traveled to Paris from the Ottoman lands without a designated stall space. Jubrail watched the way they mimicked his brothers' sales techniques as they wandered around the exhibition grounds hawking all sorts of goods, none of which appeared to have been made in Bethlehem.

An idea came to Jubrail one afternoon as he sat puffing on an arghileh pipe in the Tunisian café next door to their booth, watching a pair of young men trying to sell some old wooden boxes in a distinctly Damascene accent.

"Terre Sainte! Terre Sainte!" they exclaimed to the customers in the café, between bouts of conversation with each other in Arabic.

Jubrail put down his waterpipe and approached the two young men. "Ya shabab, surely you'd be better off selling these boxes in your own booth bearing a large sign with the words *Terre Sainte* in franji lettering?"

"Ya reet, habibi. If only we could do such a thing," one of them replied ruefully. "We've begged the stewards, but they refuse to give us our own stall."

As Jubrail made his way over to the Dabdoub booth to explain his plan to his brothers, he congratulated himself on the ingenuity of his thinking. Ever since they had left Jaffa, he had felt like a liability to the operation, his brothers constantly reproaching him for his naivety. This scheme was the very thing he needed to show them his worth and cement his reputation back in Bethlehem.

As with anything Jubrail suggested, Hanna and Mikhail were skeptical, not least because they were already doing so well selling their own goods in the stall. But when they finally agreed the next day to test the scheme for a couple of hours, they were surprised at how easy it was to implement. Soon they were subletting the stall on a daily basis to a rotating cast of Beirutis, Homsis, Zahlawis, and any number of other Ottoman merchants, all prepared to pay high prices for a few hours of selling their goods in the Dabdoub family booth.[11]

What riches awaited the brothers now! Making a profit on the markup they charged for the rental of the booth, they were now free to wander around the exhibition grounds and drum up new business on foot. Jubrail also took the opportunity to browse the many wonders of the exhibition. Strolling through the gardens, he came across an enormous sculpture of a woman's head ten times the height of a fully grown person, wearing a spiked crown, with the words *La Liberté* inscribed on the plaque at the front.[12] Most amazingly, he was able to enter inside the head for a small fee and ascend a winding staircase to the base of the skull, where he looked out on the brightly colored world beneath through two vacant eyeballs.[13] Years later, Jubrail would come across that exact same head once more, this time sitting atop a mighty statue with her torch thrust high in the air, greeting his steamship as it made its way into the Bay of Manhattan.[14]

Jubrail's wanderings also took him across the bridge and into the mighty Gallerie des Machines on the other side of the river. This was his favorite part of the exhibition to explore. Everywhere he looked, he saw the most wonderful and unfathomable inventions, useless to any normal person but nevertheless enchanting to behold. There were candles designed by a Russian gentleman named Yablochkov, lit by a mysterious flame he called the "electric current," which illuminated the room at night as if with daylight.

There were megaphones and phonographs, dynamos and combustion engines. Most bizarre of all was a device designed by a man named Bell, who claimed his invention could carry the sound of a person's voice across hundreds of miles, simply by speaking into a microphone connected to a jumble of wires and cables.[15] Never for a moment did Jubrail imagine such a device would one day connect him to his brothers and cousins across continents and oceans.

One afternoon, as he strolled back across the bridge, he that saw a crowd of people had gathered around the Dabdoub stall, many of them gesticulating excitedly. Assuming at first that demand had further risen to sublet their stall, he realized as he drew nearer that the commotion was far from friendly. A circle of exhibition stewards had surrounded the booth, and they were shouting at Hanna and Mikhail, their batons held threateningly in the air.

"Sortez d'ici!" he heard them shouting as he approached. "Take your stuff and never come back!"

By the time Jubrail got to the stall, his brothers had been thrown onto the street and were desperately trying to gather as many of their belongings as they could. Hanna gave him an icy stare. "All thanks to your wonderful idea," he scowled." "I knew we shouldn't have listened to you."

Over the coming days and nights, as the brothers made their way back to Bethlehem with sunken spirits, Hanna and Mikhail explained how the franji owner of the Tunisian Pavilion had found out about the scheme and reacted with furious indignation. Immediately, he had marched to the exhibition commissioner's office to demand the ejection of the Dabdoub brothers from the exhibition grounds. Despite protesting that they were innocent, Hanna and Mikhail could only look on helplessly as the stewards set about smashing their treasured mother-of-pearl wares and throwing their belongings onto the Rue des Nations.[16]

It was at that point that Jubrail had arrived on the scene, just as the brothers were being threatened with arrest and imprisonment if they ever dared to reenter the exhibition grounds. Left with no choice, they had gathered what little was left of their stock and made their way to the Gare de Lyon, boarding the first train headed for Marseille. In a flurry of threats and insults, Jubrail's first trip overseas had come to an inglorious end under the cloud of his own ingenious scheme.

CHAPTER 10

OF THE DECLINE OF HOSH DABDOUB, OR HOW JUBRAIL'S SCHOOLING CAME IN USEFUL

JUBRAIL AND HIS BROTHERS RODE back into Bethlehem one windy afternoon on the twenty-ninth day of Tishrin al-Awwal, bracing themselves for their father's reaction. Instead, they found old Yousef in such a state of agitation that he paid no interest to the outcome of their trip. Shortly after their departure, Rosa had been struck with tuberculosis. For weeks she had been on the verge of passing into the next life but had somehow defied everybody's expectations and was still alive.

"I'm not dying until my sons return alive and well," she had stubbornly declared on a daily basis to anyone prepared to listen. "I've already had one of them die before me. I want to make sure I haven't suffered the same indignity twice."

The day Jubrail, Hanna, and Mikhail returned, she finally relieved herself from her struggle. As the brothers entered the bedroom, their heads hung low, she caressed each of their faces to confirm they were still alive, then promptly closed her eyes and left them forever.[1]

Immediately, the whole family went into a crisis from which they would take years to recover. For as long as anyone could remember, Rosa had been the bedrock of the Dabdoub family. She was the foundation upon which the whole enterprise of Hosh Dabdoub was based. Not only had she raised eight children and overseen all domestic duties, she was also vital to the management of the family business. She always kept a watchful eye on the accounts and was the voice of reason when important decisions had to be taken, acting as a counterbalance to Yousef's capriciousness.²

With Rosa departed, Yousef became a ghost-like figure—a shadow who stalked the house but was somehow no longer there. He stopped eating with the rest of the family at mealtimes, choosing instead to sit out on the riwaq for hours on end, surveying the Wilderness with his empty eyes. He lost interest in the family firm and paid no attention when his sons presented him with various plans to recuperate the losses they had suffered in Paris.

Hosh Dabdoub entered a period of neglect and sadness. Lacking direction or leadership, the family firm stagnated. Yousef dispatched occasional shipments of souvenirs to Europe, sending some of his poorer nephews on low-level trips to France and Belgium.³ But he had lost the capacity for innovation at a time when the other Tarajmeh families were sending their sons on daring new missions to unknown corners of Amerka. Even families outside the Tarajmeh clan were moving ahead of the Dabdoubs, especially those from the Farahiyyeh and Najajreh clans. Word reached Bethlehem that young men from the Jacir, Kattan, and Jaʻar families had made it across the Atlasi Ocean and were trading on islands off the coast of Amerka.⁴ Meanwhile, the Handal, Hazboun, Giacaman, and Murqus families were all strengthening their bases in Paris, where they plotted their next trips to Amerka.⁵

Yousef and his sons moped around Hosh Dabdoub, unable to muster the enthusiasm or the funds for new ventures abroad. In Rosa's absence, the house fell into a state of disrepair. Dust gathered on the Parisian furniture, and the family no longer bothered to eat with the knives and forks they had once proudly used as a sign of their sophistication. No longer receiving any payment, the servants trickled away to find work with other families on Ras Iftays. So too did the mother-of-pearl carvers gradually leave the workshop, despite Hanna's assurances that they would be paid as soon as the next trip abroad was organized. Even young Elias abandoned them, declaring he was going to set up his own business down in the old Tarajmeh Quarter. So depleted had their stocks become that the family rarely bothered to open the shop anymore.⁶

Jubrail watched the decay taking hold and became racked with guilt. The incident in Paris was never spoken of, nor did old Yousef ever ask about it. But Jubrail was certain the botched scheme on the Trocadéro was to blame for the malaise that had taken hold in Hosh Dabdoub. So desperate had he been to prove his worth that the thought that his own actions had brought calamity upon the family left him overwhelmed with shame. He became increasingly withdrawn, no longer able to look his brothers in the eye.[7]

He took to taking long walks in the hills, sometimes staying out for days on end. Such walks were known as sarhat—a kind of retreat where a person could escape the toils of daily life and lose themselves in nature.[8] Jubrail's favorite destination for a sarha was Wadi al-Makhrour, the valley to the west of Bethlehem, where the family still owned a small apricot grove. There he would camp out in the little qasr built for the harvest season, alone with his thoughts. Sitting on the roof of the qasr, he would look out over the mighty hills, watching them change color in the evening light, from dusty brown to brilliant reds and pinks. Here the landscape was more verdant than the stony terraces around Bethlehem. In the springtime, wildflowers poked their way out of every crevice, and the sound of running water was never far away. In front of him, to the west, the steep hills gradually subsided as they made their way toward the coastal plain and, eventually, the sparkling waters of the Mediterranean. Behind him stood his hometown and, further to the east, the barren hills of the Wilderness, which dropped down toward the toxic waters of the Dead Sea.

Caught between these two worlds, Jubrail pondered his future. He was still only eighteen, on the cusp of manhood but unsure how to grasp it. His childhood world had been one of certainty. Certainty that he would always follow his father and elder brothers. Certainty that one day he too would travel the world and make his fortune in Amerka. The trip to Paris was supposed to be a first test of his mettle before his father sent him on longer ventures to Amerka. Now everything seemed precarious and undefined. He thought of his brother Murqus with those sunken eyes staring back at him from the casket. He still haunted his dreams, reaching out to tell him something that Jubrail could never make out. Had Murqus still been alive, it would have been him, not Jubrail, on that trip to Paris. Why had Allah not taken him instead of Murqus all those years ago?

Out there in the solitude of Wadi al-Makhrour, Jubrail came to realize that the world had changed beyond recognition. Every week a traveler was returning from some previously unknown corner of Amerka with new tales of riches to be made. The world itself was shrinking, and there was no telling where the next trading post might be established. The Jacirs were in Haiti, the Kattans in Cuba, the Handals in Honduras, and the Dʿeiqs in Chile. Even old Ammo Hanna had packed up and gone to Mexico.⁹ The young men returning to Bethlehem had not reached those distant shores by following the footsteps of others. Their families had sent them out into the unknown, leaving them to fight for themselves in the bustling ports of the Mediterranean and then out on the great Atlasi Ocean.

Returning to the hosh, Jubrail began to involve himself more closely in the management of the family business. Under normal circumstances, it would have been impossible for someone so young to take a lead role, but the apathy of his elder brothers and father afforded him new opportunities. He began to study the account books and retrace the unfulfilled orders of clients in Europe. He visited Elias down in the old town and persuaded him to sell some of his work at Hosh Dabdoub. Unnoticed by his brothers, he took trips to Jaffa to source mother-of-pearl, learning about the various types of oyster shells sold by the merchants in the docks.

Back in Bethlehem, he opened the shop more regularly and worked on his bartering techniques. Drawing on his experience in Paris, he refined his French vocabulary to appeal to the sensibilities of the franji customers.

"Ils ont été fabriqués ici à la main," he would declare with a sweeping gesture of the hand, remembering how Hanna had captivated his audiences in Paris. "Every one of the rosaries has been blessed by the priest here in Bethlehem."

One day, while on one of his trips to Jaffa, he found himself in one of the merchant houses browsing crates of oyster shells. Noticing a particularly impressive box of Pinctada maxima shells, he approached the merchant to ask where they had come from.

"Al-Filibeen," came the merchant's response.¹⁰

The Philippines . . . Jubrail's thoughts rushed back to his days at the Franciscan school. He remembered a weather-beaten old Spanish friar who was said to have traveled the seven seas in his quest to spread the word of Allah. Jubrail and his friends used to accost him after class, begging him to tell them tales of Amerka. The old friar would usually shoo them away as he hurried up the steps to Saint Catherine's Church, rushing to make it to vespers on time. But one time they had found him in a more relaxed mood after finishing catechism early. They stopped at the school gates, and he began to tell them about his travels to a part of Amerka he called "Mehico." He told them about the blasphemy of the Christians, how they used to paint icons of the Virgin with a brown face and dress her in colorful fabrics of red, gold, and green.

From this Mehico, the friar had journeyed further west onto a vast ocean called the Pacifico that extended to the other side of Amerka. The boys became transfixed. In their minds, Amerka represented the furthest extremity of the world, the final destination for any traveler heading westward. The thought that an ocean lay on the other side had not occurred to them. They listened with wide eyes as the friar described an archipelago of jungle-clad islands where the people were ruled by the Spanish king but were even more blasphemous than in Mehico. Nevertheless, he beamed, the firm hand of Spanish rule was steadily civilizing those islands and opening them up to foreign trade. At this point, he leaned closer to the boys and whispered in a conspiratorial tone: "They even say a great channel of water is being dug through the Egyptian desert that will connect the Mediterranean to the Indian Ocean, allowing travelers to reach those islands from the other direction." At that point the boys burst out laughing, reminding the old friar that he had just told them the islands were west of Amerka, not on the eastern seas. The friar just tutted and made off to vespers, muttering "niños majaderos" as he went.

"Al-Filibeen . . ." Jubrail repeated to the merchant, now realizing the old friar had been right all along.

For the past few years, merchants in Jerusalem and Jaffa had been talking about the canal at Suez and how it had opened up new trade on the Hindi Ocean.[11] But the news had attracted little attention among the Bethlehemites, whose sights were firmly fixed on the westward routes to Amerka. Jubrail had once heard Armenian merchants in Jaffa talking about the lucrative trade on the Philippine islands and how the people there were all Catholics. But he had assumed a merchant would first have to establish a base in Amerka to reach the islands. For the first time, it dawned on him that the route to Amerka might also lie eastward. Surely the Catholics on those islands would be interested in buying mother-of-pearl carvings made in the Holy Land. He might even be able to establish direct import routes for the oyster shells harvested there.

Everybody in Hosh Dabdoub thought he was crazy when he told them about the idea.

"Don't think I haven't forgotten about the last time I listened to one of your crazy schemes," Hanna told him.

When he told old Yousef he would need around two thousand ghurush to cover his expenses, the old man just laughed and told him they could barely afford to pay the few carvers they had left in the workshop.

Despite their objections, nobody had the energy to oppose Jubrail's scheme, leaving him free to make his own plans. He commissioned new supplies of crucifixes, boxes, rosaries, and medallions from the carvers in the workshop. He studied the old maps Ammo Hanna had left them, and he made further inquiries with merchants in Jaffa. Back in Bethlehem, he knocked on the doors of the Tarajmeh families, telling them of the great opportunities on offer if they were prepared to provide credit for the trip. Most turned him down, but Jubrail persisted, visiting families from the Farahiyyeh and Najajreh clans as well. After weeks of soliciting, he had persuaded a handful of families—the Jacirs, the Sa'di, and the Abu Hamameh—to contribute small shares, eventually reaching a sum of one thousand ghurush.[12] The rest he would take from his own family coffers with Hanna and Mikhail's agreement, but in strict secrecy from old Yousef.

The final task was to find a traveling companion. Jubrail knew he could not undertake such a long and dangerous journey alone, but his elder brothers resolutely refused to go. Trying to convince others in the town to accompany him was no easier. All the young men in those days were traveling west, following their brothers and cousins to the promised lands of Amerka. Most people had never heard of the Philippines and certainly did not how to locate the islands on a map. But a family with nothing to lose has everything to gain from taking a risk. So it was that the Sa'di family, just starting out in the souvenir business, entered into talks with Jubrail and his brothers. The head of the family, Anton Sa'di, had already agreed to supply a few ghurush on credit to Jubrail's venture. Now he saw an opportunity to secure a bigger share of any profits Jubrail might make on those distant islands. His youngest son, Issa, was the perfect choice: just twenty years old, and with everything to prove.[13]

CHAPTER 11

OF A STREET NAMED ROSARIO

BY THE TIME HE STEPPED off the boat in Manila, Jubrail was no longer capable of feeling surprised. For over a month, he and his companion Issa had circumnavigated the globe in a state of bewilderment, witnessing scenes more beguiling than anything his childhood imagination had pictured.

On the first evening, their boat from Jaffa had pulled into the gleaming harbor at Port Said, joining a long queue of steamships waiting like well-mannered giants for their turn to enter the Suez Canal. Exchanging their ship for a Spanish vessel named *Francisco Reyes*, the two travelers stood on deck in open-mouthed amazement as they sailed for a hundred miles through the Egyptian desert.[1] They drifted past camel caravans, sand dunes, and the occasional Bedouin encampment, the width of the canal too narrow for them to see the water below. They seemed to glide across the desert itself, in full defiance of the laws of nature.[2]

A day later, they reached the town of Suez, the point where the canal opened out into the Red Sea. For three days and three nights they sailed along the eastern coast of Africa, passing through the very waters where most of the mother-of-pearl shells that ended up in Bethlehem's workshops were fished. Docking eventually at the port of Aden, the *Reyes* was soon on its way again, sailing out into the open waters of the Indian Ocean.[3] It was at this point that the journey began in earnest. Never had Jubrail imagined that such an immense body of water could exist. So vast was the ocean that he lost all sense of time. Was it a week, a month, or perhaps even a year that they spent crossing that endless expanse? He quickly gave up recording the days once the seasickness set in again. From that point, the journey became a blur of endless dark blue, punctuated by the occasional silhouette of mysterious creatures passing ominously alongside the ship. In his dreams, his brother Murqus appeared once more, his eyes transformed into swirling whirlpools that led down to the ocean depths.

Twice they docked in strange cities, Jubrail still swaying from side to side as he stumbled off deck. He wandered around palm-fringed streets in a sweat-drenched state of confusion, unsure if he was hallucinating from the effects of the seasickness as he stared at magical temples covered in intricate carvings, whitewashed churches, bell-shaped domes, and grandiose palaces. Galle, Singapore—the names meant little to him as he struggled to comprehend the alternate reality in which he now found himself.[4] A strange and bewildering array of people had converged on these cities. Faces, costumes, mannerisms he did not know existed. They rushed around the docks in every direction, all seemingly performing tasks for a handful of franji officials. Straining to make sense of it all, Jubrail thought he recognized the sounds of the English language he had occasionally heard spoken among pilgrims in Bethlehem. "Chinese? Arab? Malay? Hindu?" These were the words the officials barked at each migrant stepping off the boats, directing them in lines toward sentry posts dotted around the harbor. How had such a small number of faranja managed to impose their curious form of order over these people, Jubrail wondered, so far from the franji heartlands in Europe?[5]

Long before he could find answers to such beguiling questions, they were back on the *Reyes*, passing this time through the Strait of Malacca and out into the warm waters of the South China Sea. Jubrail's seasickness quickly returned, leaving him in a stupor from which he feared he would never return. To the outsider, he looked like a man possessed by jinn, frantically thumbing his rosary beads for hours on end, his eyes staring vacantly into the ocean. But in his head, Jubrail was praying fervently to Mar Yusef, al-Khadr, and the Virgin, beseeching them to release him from his torment. Somehow, he felt sure they were there with him, guiding him through his moment of crisis all those thousands of miles from home. On more than one occasion he saw the Virgin's silhouette on the ocean horizon, guiding him like a beacon toward those distant islands he had heard about all those years ago from the Spanish friar.[6]

One morning, as he lay festering in the semi-darkness of the steerage cabin, he heard cries of excitement coming from the passengers above. As he staggered on deck, blinking into the sunlight, he found they had passed into a vast bay lined by dense mangrove forests. Ahead of them stood the harbor of Manila, shimmering in the distance. It was the seventeenth of Tishrin al-Awwal in the year 1881.[7]

Jubrail was dismayed to find that his arrival in the port of Manila did not bring him onto firm ground. Stepping off the *Reyes*, he was greeted by a floating city where the streets were just as likely to be canals and rivers as they were roads of solid earth. Ahead of him was the main docking area, teeming with waterborne activity. Steamships competed for space alongside flat-bottomed barges with strangely squared ends and heavy tarpaulin covers that protected their cargo. These were the casco boats of Manila: long enough to carry large loads but narrow enough to continue sailing up the Pasig River, which made its way through the heart of the city, delivering their goods down myriad estuaries that branched off on either side. Jubrail looked across the docks at the city, the smell of putrid water in his nostrils. Directly opposite he could see the red roofs and bell towers of the walled city of Intramuros, where franji conquerors had long ago built their luxurious villas and churches. Beyond it, the river continued its murky course, surrounded by a dense network of warehouses, canals, and residential streets.[8]

It was a good time for a foreign merchant to arrive in Manila. For centuries the city had been a magnet for Chinese, Malay, Indian, European, and Japanese merchants. But the opening of the Suez Canal had brought new traders flocking to its docks from all over Europe. Sensing an opportunity to increase their revenue, the Spanish colonial masters had relaxed their restrictions on immigration, lifted the ban on foreign property ownership, and removed the islands' protective trade tariffs.[9] The year before Jubrail and Issa's arrival, the city had been struck by a dreadful earthquake, but already its industrious residents were rebuilding their neighborhoods to accommodate more traffic of commercial goods. Once again, the faranja were arriving in droves, along with new waves of Asian and American traders.

Dazed by the journey and unsure of their first move, Jubrail and Issa stood gazing at the multitudes of people and cascos making their way across the harbor. Quickly they realized that very few Ottomans were trading in the city, and certainly no Arabic speakers from the Syrian lands, save for the occasional Jew or Armenian. They would have to rely on the French they had learned from the Franciscans, as well as the smattering of Spanish they had picked up from some of the friars. There were no networks of Syrian traders to fall back on, no cafés where they could retreat into the familiarity of an arghileh pipe or a cup of cardamom-infused coffee. Here they would have to forge their own path.

In the absence of any other starting points, Jubrail and Issa boarded a casco and followed the crowds of new arrivals into the district of Binondo. Located across the Pasig River from the walled colonial city, Binondo was a natural first port of call for a newly arrived merchant.[10] The neighborhood had been established back in the sixteenth century to house Chinese merchants who had converted to Christianity. By the 1880s it had developed into a bustling business district: the commercial hub of the city and a magnet for foreign traders. As Jubrail walked down the main thoroughfare, the Escolta, which ran parallel to the Pasig River, he looked around him. Chinese stores jostled for space alongside European warehouses. Street vendors hawked their goods in Hokkien Chinese while Spanish governors dressed in frock coats and top hats passed hurriedly by in horse-drawn carts.

The confusing jumble of people made Binondo an easy place to blend in. Sikhs, Portuguese, Japanese, Mexicans, and British had all flocked to the district to rub shoulders with the older Chinese and Spanish communities. The elegant three- and four-story buildings lining the Escolta were occupied by the wealthier merchants who imported goods from all over the world, while the street itself was the domain of the hawker. New buildings were springing up all over the street, and some of the latest inventions from Europe were being installed. A steam-powered tram shuttled its way up and down the Escolta, forcing people and animals out of its way. Workers were fitting a new waterworks system that brought water directly into people's homes, and before long the magic of electricity would be lighting up the houses and shops. When the sun went down, the city transformed itself into a riot of entertainment: theaters, circuses, opera houses, and drinking dens all stayed open into the early hours of the morning. Jubrail and Issa had stumbled into one of the world's great melting pots, where all of the confusion and paradoxes of the modern age could be found condensed into one city.

Wandering up and down the Escolta, Jubrail and Issa made inquiries with the shopkeepers and chatted with the hawkers in broken Spanish. Lacking any leads, they began hawking their rosaries and crucifixes on the street. Opening their cases to shop owners and passersby, they exclaimed, "Terra Santa!" and "Jerusalén!" hoping for an instant reaction. Most people just ignored them, but a few stopped to take a closer look, thumbing the shiny beads of the mother-of-pearl rosaries with great interest.

"De donde viene este nácar?" they asked, offering to sell them the raw material more cheaply.

Making inquiries at the docks, they asked how they could send shipments of the best shells directly to Palestine. To their disappointment, they discovered that the famous shells of the Sulu islands were all sent to Singapore, where the British had already monopolized the trade, bypassing Manila altogether.[11] Returning to the Escolta with sunken spirits, they went back to selling their goods on the street, making the occasional sale but mostly failing to stand out from the throngs of hawkers lining the road.

One day, they befriended a Jewish merchant by the name of Simon Semora who owned a jewelry shop on the Escolta. Simon claimed to be from Jerusalem but spoke only in French and Spanish, leading Jubrail to conclude that he must be like the Syrians he had met in Paris who claimed affiliation with the Holy Land purely for commercial purposes.[12] But whatever his origins, Simon was kind to the young Bethlehemites, explaining how things worked for foreign merchants in the city.

"First you have to register with the Spanish authorities to get your residency permit," he told them, describing the various forms they would have to complete. "Then you can buy some premises that will give your goods the proper display they deserve."

"Ya khawaja," Jubail retorted, "We barely have enough money to pay for our lodgings, let alone buy our own shop!"

"No te preocupes," Simon winked back at him. "We'll find you something cheap to rent to get you started. In the meantime, we'll put a few of your rosaries in my shop window to see how they sell, okay?"

Simon's advice was all they had to go on. Leaving him with a selection of their stock, they made their way to the Intramuros colonial district to make their applications. Following the Jew's instructions, they declared to the stern-faced Spanish official in the immigration office that they wished to apply for residency permits. To their surprise, he handed them a stack of forms to complete, just as Simon had predicted. How Jubrail was grateful in that moment for the Franciscan school, where he had learned to read and write in the franji alphabet! Without it, they would have drowned in that sea of papers, unable to decipher the information they were supposed to provide. How grateful they were, too, for Simon's arrangement of a guarantor for them—a respectable man by the name of Mariano Rodriguez who worked as a port official in the city docks.

Leaving their papers with the official, the two young Bethlehemites returned to the Escolta, where they found Simon beaming at them across the counter of his shop.

"I've already sold three of your crosses!" he exclaimed. "Because I like you and you're from Belén, I'll give you 20 percent of the sale price, vale?"

Lacking any other source of income, the Bethlehemites begrudgingly accepted Simon's offer and set about looking for their own shop to rent.

Over the coming weeks and months, they gradually learned to get by in that chaotic and beguiling city of commerce. Simon taught them that being the only merchants from the Holy Land would be a great advantage once they understood how to harness it. He showed them how he carefully arranged their goods in his storefront window with a sign saying "Hecho en Jerusalem" hanging overhead, and he took them to the Basilica of Saint Lorenzo Ruiz, or Binondo Church, as it was more commonly known, where they discovered that people were much more inclined to buy their products as they filed out after Mass.

Before long, they had earned enough money to rent a small shop space on the Calle del Rosario in the Binondo District.[13] Their choice of location was as pragmatic as it was poetic. Named after the patroness of Binondo, Our Lady of the Rosary, the street was the perfect match for a shop specializing in the sale of rosary beads. But it was also the ideal place to sell Holy Land wares. Not as upmarket as the Escolta, Calle del Rosario was lined with cheaper shops, mostly owned by Chinese merchants but increasingly joined by Indians, Persians, Europeans, and Americans. One end of the street looked out onto the Pasig River, where a nearby bridge, the Puente de España, connected Binondo to Intramuros. Conveniently located at the other end of the street was the Binondo Church, where the two Bethlehemites now went to give thanks to the Virgin and al-Khadr for protecting them on their perilous adventure in the Philippines, as well as to sell their goods to the exiting worshippers.

Soon word was circulating around the neighborhood about the Holy Land goods on offer at the small shop on Calle del Rosario. The Manileños had never seen such a store before. Schooled by Jesuit priests in the importance of revering the land of Jesus and the early saints of the Catholic Church, they were drawn to these strange-looking merchants and their shop selling the iridescent, shiny white carvings of biblical scenes.

On the thirteenth day of Kanun al-Awwal in the year 1881, Jubrail and Issa received their residency permits from the immigration office. Now they were certified residents of the city, able to own property and legally run their own business.[14] In the space of two months, they had gone from clueless immigrants to proud owners of a Holy Land business with the official approval of the Spanish governor.

For the next two months, the shop on Calle del Rosario prospered. Jubrail and Issa spent their first Christmas away from home praying in the Binondo Church and selling record quantities of rosaries and crucifixes. But they knew they could not remain much longer in Manila. Their stock had almost been depleted, and they had no supply line to furnish them with further goods from Bethlehem. The purpose of their mission had been purely exploratory: to test the waters so that others might follow. Having proven the feasibility of trading in the city and having established a new base of clients and partners, it was time to brave the long journey home and pass on the word for others to follow. Four months after arriving in the city, they set sail once again across the South China Sea toward the mighty Indian Ocean. Looking out across the vast expanse of ocean, contemplating his return as his stomach churned from the rocking of the boat, Jubrail realized the world had changed beyond all recognition.

CHAPTER 12

BY THE TRUTH OF AL-KHADR, I WENT AND CAME BACK!

WHEN JUBRAIL WALKED THROUGH THE door of Hosh Dabdoub one morning in the spring of 1882, old Yousef spat out his breakfast in surprise. "Masha' Allah! You're back!" the old man cried. "Wayn ha al-ghaybah? I thought you were dead."

Everyone in the hosh had feared the worst. They had heard nothing since he left town eight months ago. Now here he was, like an apparition from another world, weary and disheveled but very much alive.

"I made it to the Philippines, Yaba." Jubrail stood tall, fixing his gaze on his father. "By the truth of al-Khadr, I went and came back."[1]

Jubrail's return breathed new life into Hosh Dabdoub. For the first time since the death of Rosa, people flowed in and out of the house, great banquets were held, and the sound of singing could be heard from the mother-of-pearl workshop. Old Yousef had been convinced he would never see his son again and had resigned himself to living out his last days in a state of steady decline. But Jubrail's return sent the old man into a frenzy of excitement as he listened to his son's descriptions of the riches on offer on those distant islands.

Yousef was back at the helm of the family firm, directing affairs from his office once more. He checked the account books, placed new orders for oyster shells, and went looking for new carvers to employ in the workshop. He held meetings with his two eldest sons and decided they should carry out their own voyage to the Philippines. "Now is the time to capitalize!" he exclaimed. "We have found our Amerka on the eastern seas!"

Meanwhile, Jubrail basked in the glory of his return. He and Issa were the only ones in the town to have traveled across the Hindi Ocean, making them the object of great curiosity. In church, unmarried girls whispered excitedly when Jubrail took his seat between his brothers, and the priest gave a special prayer of thanks for his return. As the crowds left Mass and made their way out into Bab al-Dayr, the old men of the Tarajmeh families rested their arms on Jubrail's shoulder and offered their congratulations.

Soon crowds were gathering in the Sabbagh café on Ras Iftays to hear Jubrail's tales of adventure on the eastern seas. His stories had an air of the khurafiyya about them, opening with the young hero leaving his village in a quest to find a great treasure on a mysterious, faraway island. To get there, he had to outsmart various kinds of ghouls, jinn, and wicked rulers.[2] Captivating his listeners with tales that stretched even the most fantastical of imaginations, he spoke of floating cities that glided through deserts, giant monsters of the deep, and enchanted islands of magical temples.

When he was not holding court in the Sabbagh café, Jubrail took great pleasure visiting each one of the merchants who had provided credit for his trip, as well as those who had not. They all remarked how he had changed beyond recognition since they had last seen him. He was a man now, they told him, entering his prime years. Referring to him as "Al-Khawaja Jubrail," they welcomed him into their homes and introduced him to their families.

"Tafaddal, stay and drink coffee with us. Our maid makes the best ma'moul in Bethlehem."

"Tell us about your next business trip, ya khawaja. Perhaps we can form a new partnership."

"Uq'ud, ya zalama. Please sit on our new diwan. We just had it shipped from Paris. They say the raised style is in fashion there. They call it *sofa*.[3]"

"Did I mention my daughter will soon be ready for marriage? She is already twelve."

"Beitna beitak, ya khawaja. Our home is your home."

On the tenth day of Huzayran in the year 1882, just three months after his return from the Philippines, Jubrail was married to Mariam Issa Handal in the Catholic chapel of Santa Caterina, next to the main church. The two families had rushed through the marriage ceremonies so that Jubrail could depart in time for his next business assignment: the latest franji exhibition, which would be held in a northern city called Amsterdam. They had hastily arranged the khutbah to allow bride and groom to exchange rings in front of their extended families and the town elders. That night, hundreds of guests had packed into Hosh Dabdoub to feast on the stewed mutton cooked with yogurt and rice, all commenting on what a favorable match Jubrail and Mariam were.[4] The final stage of the preparations was the two-day celebration that culminated in the signing of the ʿaqd marriage contract in the church. As the final act of union approached, Mariam's family held the henna night for the bride and received guests from the heads of each clan, who gave gifts of gold coins or whatever else their means allowed. Meanwhile, Jubrail and his brothers danced through the streets until they reached Dar Handal, where they serenaded the bride in their best hadda voices.[5] The next morning Mariam was dressed in her wedding robes, with their elaborate couched embroideries of gold, orange, red, and purple thread, and the cone-shaped shatweh was placed on her head for the first time. After being paraded through the town in the bridal procession, she was finally presented to Jubrail, who stood waiting nervously in the church in his plain tawb and hatta.[6]

The Handal family was one of the most prosperous families in all Bethlehem. Giries Suleiman Handal had attended the ill-fated Paris exhibition back in 1878, alongside Jubrail and his brothers. Now he was busy expanding his business into Amerka, sending his sons and nephews on various missions to the Caribbean.[7] One of those sons, Suleiman, would later go on to build a mighty empire in the great city of New York, where he would forge close ties with Jubrail, marrying his daughter Afifeh to Jubrail's second-born son, Yousef.

Over the years the Dabdoubs and the Handals would form lucrative business partnerships that stretched across Amerka from Honduras to New York and as far east as the Philippines. But it was back in 1882 that the alliance was first formed, when a cousin of Giries Suleiman Handal by the name of Issa Anton Handal approached old Yousef with a marriage proposition. At twenty-one, Issa's daughter Mariam was just a year younger than Jubrail: relatively old for a bride in those days. She had already been married to Ibrahim Giacaman, a man from another one of the town's leading Catholic families, when she was fifteen. But just a year later Ibrahim had died, and now the Handals were searching for a suitable replacement. Jubrail's return to Bethlehem from the Philippines had caught Issa's eye as he searched for a new husband for his daughter. Old Yousef Dabdoub considered the proposal long and hard. He considered Mariam's age to be an impediment, as she had already missed several years of potential childbearing. On the plus side, the Handals' recent exploits in Amerka made it an attractive proposition for the Dabdoubs. Now that Yousef had decided to focus the family's efforts on the Philippines, it could prove invaluable to maintain alliances with families trading in the other direction. Jubrail's triumph in the East had also opened a door to the West.

The marriage between Jubrail and Marriam restored the Dabdoub family to its rightful place among the elite merchant families of Bethlehem. The ceremony was a public announcement of the family's return to the forefront of the town's great overseas expansion. Within a few months, Jubrail's eldest brother had departed for the Philippines. He was followed shortly after by Mikhail, who stayed on the islands for ten months in 1884 and returned home with a profit of eighty French francs.[8] He had discovered it was more profitable to sell goods imported from Europe than it was to transport their own mother-of-pearl wares halfway across the world. With each subsequent trip, the brothers solidified their base, slowly building up a trusted network of importers and distributors. They opened shops and warehouses across Manila, trading jewelry, lenses, fabrics, and incense.

As money poured into the Dabdoub family coffers, other families took notice. Suleiman Jacir had been busy making his fortune importing goods from France to Haiti. But now the Dabdoubs' forays across the Indian Ocean caught his attention. For years the Dabdoubs had been cultivating an alliance with the Jacir family. Hanna was already married to Suleiman Jacir's sister Nijmeh, and now he took the alliance to the next level. In 1884 he created a partnership with Suleiman that would see the two of them living in the Philippines for a year and a half, eventually returning home with the enormous sum of 250 French francs.[9]

By the end of the 1880s, the Dabdoubs and the Jacirs were being joined in the Philippines by a long list of Bethlehem families: the Abu Hamamehs, Haddads, Ayoubs, Banayuts, Sabats, Mikels, Musallams, al-Aʿmas, Tarags, Salmans, Asilis, Sabbaghs, Aludans, and Salems. They had all made their way to Filibina Bilad al-Hind, as they called those distant islands, a reference to the vast Hindi Ocean that first had to be crossed to arrive there.[10]

By that time, the Bethlehem merchants were not the only ones from the Ottoman lands rushing to do business on the islands. As with the migrations across the Atlasi Ocean, young men and women from all over Mount

Lebanon and the Syrian lands had caught wind of the Bethlehemites' success. A system developed in which the Bethlehem merchants in Manila became wholesale suppliers for young peddlers arriving from Syria who would set off into the more remote areas of the Philippines: to the verdant hills of northern Luzon, where villagers working on rice terraces were eager to see the new goods they brought in their trunks, or as far south as the jungle-clad beaches of Mindanao, where the young peddlers were surprised to find fishermen praying to the same Muslim god they knew so well from back home.[11]

Of all the Bethlehem families that established themselves in the Philippines, the most successful was the Abu Hamameh family. The three brothers—Elias, Basil, and Khalil—arrived on the islands in 1889 having heard about the success the Dabdoubs had enjoyed there. Quickly they went about establishing a formidable range of import routes that ran through a series of European ports, through the Suez Canal, and into the Philippines, allowing them to sell a dazzling array of goods in their shops.[12] Soon they were acting as guarantors for dozens of newly arriving Syrian immigrants, building a reputation with the Spanish authorities as "persons of reputable character."[13] The centerpiece of their operation was the store they named "El Belen" out of fidelity to their hometown. Located at number 6 Calle del Rosario, the store stood on the very same street where Jubrail and Issa had first set up shop all those years ago. Renowned all over the Philippines for its fine range of European and "Turkish" goods, El Belen was estimated by the Spanish authorities to be worth a staggering ten thousand Philippine pesos—a major fortune back in the 1890s, standing as an emblem of the Bethlehemites' success on the islands.[14]

By the end of the century, there were over two thousand Syrians living in the Philippines.[15] The Dabdoubs had long since moved on, but many of the Bethlehemites had made the islands their home. Their children now grew up speaking Tagalog with their Philippine nannies and sneaking out to watch the sabong cockfights when their parents' backs were turned.[16] Defying their mothers' orders to stay away from those "barbaric" cockpits, they would push their way through the crowds to place bets with the kristo and catch a glimpse of the owners of the cocks attaching knives to the birds' legs.[17] Before long, the cocks would be launching brutal attacks on each other in the sandy arena, spurred on by the shouts of a thousand excited spectators.

CHAPTER 13

OF WHITE CITIES AND BRONZE MEDALS

"*IT IS TRULY BEAUTIFUL, MASHALLAH.*"

"*Feel how heavy it is. Such an object must be worth a fortune!*"

A small crowd had gathered in Bab al-Dayr to touch the solid bronze medal. Amazed by its heavy weight, people took turns caressing the lifelike carving of Columbus.

"*Tell us, khawajat, how did you come across such a wonderous thing?*"

Jubrail and Mikhail looked at each other. They both remembered the day a man in a white coat had visited their stall in Chicago.

"You've been awarded a Medal of Honor for the excellence of your carvings," he had informed them. "Your display denotes improvement in the condition of the art that it represents."

Jubrail had no clue what that meant, but he could see that some other exhibitors in the Turkish Village had been given the same medal, including the Imperial Fez factory and the Syrian cigarette producer, Yusuf Wakid. Even the Ottoman Naval Ministry had been given one for transporting boats and equipment to the exhibition. He later found out that thousands of exhibitors in Chicago had been given the award.[1]

"*Isn't it obvious, shabab? They won first prize at that exhibition!*"

"*It must be true! No other family has brought back such a medal from the franji exhibitions.*"

"*Perhaps it was the sultan of Amerka that presented it to them.*"[2]

Jubrail and Mikhail looked at each other again, not sure what to say.

They had not won any competition, nor had the medal been presented by any dignitary. But they were proud of their achievements in Chicago. They alone among the Bethlehemites had been given the medal, and they alone had been mentioned by name in the official Ottoman newsletter. They had even been visited by an American journalist named Kunz. Jubrail still kept the cutting from his article:

> The utilization of mother-of-pearl carving was also well illustrated in the exhibit of the Dabdoub Brothers and by that in the Turkish Village. Here the polished mother-of-pearl shells are engraved with allegorical and ornamental designs and are known as Jerusalem shells, serving for trays, light screens, and similar objects.[3]

Hanna insisted that they must advertise their success as widely as possible. He had already designed a new letterhead proudly bearing the words "Médaille d'Honneur à l'Exposition Universelle d'Amérique 1893." Now Jubrail and Mikhail were planning to use the same design for their next venture in Paris.

The key, Hanna explained, was to stay one step ahead of the competition. In the old days it had been easy: their father just had to build his shop at the top of the hill to gain an advantage over his rivals. But now the marketplace was crowded. Everywhere they traveled they found Bethlehemites already doing business, not to mention the hordes of peddlers from Mount Lebanon, holding their fraudulent Holy Land curios aloft as they stepped off the boats.

Hanna had warned Jubrail and Mikhail that the Bethlehemites would flock to Chicago in greater numbers than ever before. The Americans were determined to celebrate the four-hundredth anniversary of their continent's conquest with a spectacle more extravagant than any previous exhibition. Every merchant in Bethlehem knew this was a golden opportunity to expand his business into the lucrative markets of Amerka.

Had Hanna not been right in his efforts to prevent other Bethlehem firms from attending the Chicago exhibition? Their success in Philadelphia all those years ago had encouraged a spate of other Bethlehem families to set off in search of the latest American exhibition. The Dabdoubs had had to act to prevent the competition from overwhelming them. Hanna's plan had been ingenious: he traveled to Istanbul to negotiate with the contractors of the Ottoman Pavilion. There he had struck a deal with a Jewish man by the name of Elia Souhami—the person appointed to oversee the allocation of stall spaces within the Ottoman sections of the Chicago exhibition.[4] Before the other Bethlehem families even knew how to apply, Hanna had secured exclusive rights to the sale of Holy Land goods at the biggest exhibition the world had ever known.[5]

The only thing he had not considered was the tenacity of their rivals. When news had reached Bethlehem about the monopoly agreement, a storm of protest had broken out. Petitions complaining of foul play had flooded into the Ministry of Public Works and Trade. Tensions had simmered in Bethlehem. Everywhere they went, the brothers had been met with glares and stony silences. To counteract the hostility, they had sought out allies, explaining that the plan had always been to sublet stall space to their most trusted partners. They had struck a deal with Suleiman Jacir, brother of Hanna's wife, Nijmeh, and longtime associate of the Dabdoubs in the Philippines. On the other side of the divide, an incensed group of merchants had sent their own delegation to Istanbul to insist on their right to participate.

In the end, it was the sheer indifference of the Ministry of Public Works and Trade that had defeated Hanna's plans. Officials at the Sublime Porte cared little for the parochial squabbles of a faraway village they would never visit. In the face of a barrage of protests, canceling the agreement was the easiest option for a bureaucrat in Istanbul. In the name of the sultan's eternal magnanimity and impartiality, new regulations were put in place that allocated four plots for the sale of Holy Land goods in Chicago. These goods would be supplied by a consortium of twenty different Bethlehem merchants. In accordance with official regulations, they were required to pay half the rental price in advance, with the rest of the money to be paid once the specific stalls had been allocated at the exhibition.[6]

Hanna had been livid when he read the notification posted in Bab al-Dayr. "They're all backstabbing liars!" he had declared upon returning to Hosh Dabdoub. "Those hamir will see who has the last laugh. We'll get one of those plots if it kills us. And we'll be the first to reach Chicago. We'll set off next week with the Jacir brothers."

Jubrail had looked at Mikhail and rolled his eyes. He had only just returned from his latest trip to Paris. He was tired of life on the road and longed to spend more time with his wife and young boy Bishara.

But had Hanna not been right all along? Chicago had been a resounding success. The brothers had returned as conquerors of the American continent—the only family in Bethlehem to be awarded the Medal of Honor. Why disappoint the old men in Bab al-Dayr with the finer details of how it had been awarded?

The crowd in Bab al-Dayr had grown as news of the medal made its way around town. Young boys pushed their way to the front, eager to hear about the famous exhibition in Chicago.

"*Is it true the exhibition was held in a city of white palaces?*"

"*How can it be reached from here, ya khawaja?*"

A camel made its way through the crowd, led by a Bedouin woman carrying a bundle of mulukhiyya leaves. Jubrail perched himself on the steps that led up to the first floor of the Ottoman saraya and cleared his throat.[7] He began to recite lines of poetry:

> Were I mighty to conquer and
> subdue the seas
> As Columbus overpowered the
> waves—his adversary;
> From her fathomless depths a
> pearl would I have seized
> To crown His sepulchre—a
> Gem to memory![8]

"*See how Amerka has turned him crazy!*"

"The White City is even more strange than they say," Jubrail now proclaimed.

A hushed silence descended.

"To reach it, you first have to cross the great Atlasi Ocean and make landfall in the city of New York."

As the people below jostled for a better view of the speaker, an Ottoman soldier poked his head out of the saraya window, curious to see what was causing the commotion.

"Young Jadallah Jacir and I were the first to leave Bethlehem," Jubrail continued. "We journeyed from France on a mighty ship named *La Touraine*, braving storms in the discomfort of our second-class cabins for ten days before finally reaching New York on the twenty-first day of Adhar.[9]

"I still remember my surprise as we sailed into the bay that day. There in front of me stood a statue that was strangely familiar. Looking out from the deck of the *Touraine* I thought I must be hallucinating, and I rubbed my eyes. But by the glory of Allah, it was true! I had once climbed inside that very same head at an exhibition in France. That unmistakable spiked crown, and those very same eyes through which I had once looked out over the city of Paris now greeted me as I arrived on the shores of Amerka for the first time."

"*Ad-dinya zgheer. The world is small!*" someone in the crowd shouted.

"Small but wondrous! Young Jadallah was still only nineteen when we made landfall on the island of Manhattan. As we disembarked from the ferry, he stared in wonder at the spires and towers being erected all over the city. Naturally, it fell on my more experienced shoulders to take the lead and arrange our onward journey. I was determined we would be the first to reach the White City.

"To our surprise, we discovered a little corner of Syria has been transported across the ocean and implanted in the heart of New York City. Thousands of Syrians, all living and working on a street named Washington, just a short distance from where our ferry docked. Wallahi, you can drink proper coffee, smoke arghileh, and have a game of tawilah on that street, all the while speaking in the Arabic tongue, as if you were back here in Bayt Lahm.

"They say that the city is the richest in the world and that many Syrians are making a fortune there. They trade all kinds of goods—clothing, jewelry, devotional objects. One of them has even opened a bank. One day we will surely open our own businesses in that city, ya shabab. But Jadallah and I could not delay our quest to find the White City! I made inquiries on Washington Street and was directed to a vast railway station, where we boarded a train headed west."

"*Those trains are the work of al-Shaytan. I will never trust them!*" an old man's voice rung out across the crowd.

Just the previous year, some of the town's residents had made their way to Jerusalem to witness the arrival of the first train from Jaffa. For years they had heard that a great chariot of iron and steel would be making its way up the steep slopes of the Jerusalem hills. They had even heard the stonemasons in Bethlehem talking about the work they were doing cutting a path through the rocky hillsides around the village of Battir so that three iron rails could be laid along the route.¹⁰ But nothing could have prepared them for the scene that awaited them that day in Jerusalem. Thousands of people had gathered at the gleaming new station building. Ottoman officials waving flags in honor of the sultan, imams smearing sheep's blood on the tracks as they recited verses of the Quran, and all manner of clingers-on come to witness the historic event—priests, shopkeepers, nuns, notables, beggars, franji consuls, prostitutes, pilgrims, lepers, and marching bands. It seemed the entirety of Jerusalem, in all its rough-hewn diversity, had turned out that morning to witness the arrival of the train.¹¹

At first all they heard was a piercing whistle in the distance, followed by a curious panting sound. The onlookers strained their necks apprehensively to catch a glimpse of the approaching train. No railway had ever been built in the Arabic-speaking lands of the Ottoman Empire, and most of the people assembled had never heard such strange sounds. As the panting came nearer, many people threw up their arms and began to plead to Allah, Yahweh, or whatever God they worshipped for protection. Others simply bolted, ignoring the calls of the Ottoman officials for dignified calm. Amid all the commotion, the most bizarre and frightening contraption suddenly came into view, puffing out great clouds of smoke as it went. Like a chain of enormous chariots, pulled by horses of iron and fire, it pulled into the station in a whir of sparks and steam, sending many of the onlookers into a blind panic.¹² When the dust settled, and the fearsome creature finally ceased its angry panting, those who still remained in the crowd watched in astonishment as hordes of people calmly disembarked from the carriages carrying flowers they had picked along the way from Jaffa.¹³

"You may curse those trains, but they are shrinking the world before our very eyes," Jubrail called out in reply to the old man. "Can you not travel from Jerusalem to Jaffa in just three hours where once it took you a whole day? And will the railway not allow us to supply our workshops with far greater quantities of mother-of-pearl shells?"¹⁴

It was true—the opening of the railway was already providing a great boost to the merchants of Bethlehem, bringing down the costs of raw materials and connecting them more easily to Jaffa and the world beyond. Some enterprising merchants were even building their own warehouses in Jerusalem where they planned to open new businesses as specialist wholesalers of mother-of-pearl shells.¹⁵ But not everyone saw the benefits of the railway. Franji pilgrims complained of the deafening roar, local camel caravans and horse-drawn carriage services found themselves out of business, and many of the old people in Bethlehem remained convinced that such a fearsome contraption could only bring disaster and calamity.[16]

"In the space of just two days we traveled eight hundred miles on the Nickel Plate Road across the mountains, plains, and forests of Amerka," Jubrail continued, oblivious to objections from the crowd. "We arrived at our destination on the twenty-fourth day of Adhar. The great city of Chicago now stood before us!"

"*But you said you went to the White City!*" someone called out.

"*Ah, he's a khurafa!*"

"If patience is bitter, its results will be sweet![17] The story has not yet reached its climax, my friends. When we stepped off the train at the Chicago Union Depot, we found a city in a whirl of excitement. Streams of people getting off their trains, carrying suitcases overflowing with merchandise, strange costumes, and mechanical devices. All headed for the White City!

"We noticed many of them speaking strange versions of the Arabic tongue. An Arabian invasion of the city of Chicago! Hundreds of them gathering on the concourse, plotting their route to the exhibition. They were quite a sight, dressed in their colorful turbans, baggy trousers, embroidered Bedouin dresses, raqs sharqi costumes, and brightly painted jewelry. There were carpet weavers, fortune-tellers, and sword swallowers. Many of them carried fearsome looking daggers on their belts, making us afraid to go near them.[18] Jadallah and I stood open-mouthed as four of the finest Arabian stallions cantered past us, led by four men in a curious kind of Bedouin clothing. We later found out these were in fact Syrian men working for the Ottoman Ministry of Agriculture who had dressed up for the occasion.[19]

"Following the crowds, we made our way out of the station and jumped onto one of those magical machines they call streetcars. Unlike trains, these wagons are pulled along by the track itself, which makes its way around the city in a giant loop, constantly turning as it goes. You should have seen the terror on Jadallah's face as we hung out the side of the crowded wagon, clinging to the handrail! Naturally I had experience with such vehicles and so managed to keep an eye on our route through city.

"At first we passed through a district of towering steel buildings, taller than anything we had seen in New York, stretching so high they disappeared out of sight as we craned our necks through the streetcar window.

The locals even call them skyscrapers! By the grace of Allah, I swear some of them reach as high as fifteen or even twenty stories.[20]

"Soon we reached the edge of a lake so massive I could make out no sign of the other side. The streetcar made a wrenching turn, and we proceeded to skirt along the shore for what seemed like an eternity with nothing but an endless expanse of water to look upon. Eventually I poked my head out the other side of the wagon and saw a skyline of shimmering domes and towers coming into view."

"Akhiran he gets to the point."

"About time!"

"There it was, my friends. The White City, standing before us in all its beguiling beauty."

The crowd quietened down, hanging on Jubrail's every word now.

"Words cannot describe the strangeness of that place. The dome of the Palace of Fine Arts. The enormous golden arch of the Transportation Building. The never-ending hallway of the Forestry Building.[21] Countless other palaces, all covered in ornate facades, columns, minarets, and sculptures. Everything painted a brilliant white that shimmered in the lagoons and canals where Venetian gondolas transported people from palace to palace."[22]

The crowd went silent, everyone trying their best to picture the scene.

"What's a gondola, ya khawaja?"

"And what's a forestry building?"

Jubrail carried on, undeterred. "At night the White City was lit by thousands of lights, much like the ones I saw demonstrated in Paris where the mere flick of a switch magically lights a candle. To be in the White City at nighttime was to be plunged into a state of bewitchment, never sure what was real and what was imaginary, what was solid and what was reflection, as if floating through a dream of flickering palaces casting their lights across an endless lake.

"But let me tell you the strangest thing about that place." Once again, the crowd went quiet. "Everything in that white city—the domes, the towers, the palaces, the ornate facades, even the gondolas—everything was erected purely for the exhibition. The buildings were not made of stone but of cement and jute fiber that seemed like they might crumble when touched. Now that the show has finished, they're already tearing the whole place down. It was all just an illusion, a trick of the eye!"

The listeners let out a collective gasp.

"*Why would they do such a thing, ya khawaja?*"

"That is the way of the Amerkan, my friends. They are not like us. They do not measure time by the turning of the seasons and the passing of the years. Time is measured in money. If something no longer makes profit, they tear it down and start on the next project. Everything is new in the land of Amerka. A land constantly being reborn."

A few of the old men shook their heads and took their leave, murmuring to each other as they went.

"*What about the wheel, khawaja?*"

"*Yes, tell us about the wheel!*"

"Ah yes, I nearly forgot. To behold that bizarre construction was to feel you had entered a realm of giants where an ordinary object had become a hundred times larger. Some said it reached as high as three hundred ayak—taller than any church tower or minaret you've seen in Jerusalem. It was made from the most enormous metal spokes, radiating out from a giant axle planted in the middle of the fairground. At the outer edge of the spokes, thirty-six cabins rotated day and night around the axle."[23]

"*But why build such a ridiculous structure?*"

"*The Amerkan are truly possessed by jinn!*"

"I already told you, everything in Amerka is measured in money. You must realize that each of those cabins could hold sixty people. That means more than two thousand paying customers could be crammed onto that wheel at any one time. People queued for hours to pay their fifty cents and ride for the twenty minutes it took to make two revolutions. The man who designed it was a genius! He has made a vast fortune from that wheel."[24]

"*Did you ride the wheel yourself, ya khawaja?*"

"Tabʿan, of course I did! But to get to the wheel, you first had to traverse the Midway Plaisance—a mile-long walkway where all the exhibition's entertainment took place. Never have I seen such a cacophony of shops, cafés, peep shows, drinking dens, sword swallowers, jugglers, dancers, theaters, and animal rides—all crammed into one long street. It won't surprise you to hear that this was where all the Arabic speakers we had seen at the railway station had ended up. They dominated the Midway Plaisance in their dazzling costumes and bizarre props, selling every kind of trinket and entertainment you could imagine. Our booth was located among all that madness, on the so-called Street of Constantinople in the heart of what they called the Turkish Village.[25] Next to us was the Tunisian Village, then the Algerian Theater, and even a masjid they called the Moorish Mosque of Tangiers that had been erected just for the pleasure of the exhibition visitors."

"So the Amerkan are Muslims?"

Jubrail tutted and rocked his head back. "You're still not understanding! The exhibitions are just a show to satisfy their insatiable curiosity. They desire to see the inside of a mosque for no other reason than to see what it looks like. They don't go there to pray. They go to enact a fantasy they have about a land they will never visit. They call it 'the Orient'—a place they imagine is full of seminaked women, snake charmers, and fortune-tellers, all smoking arghileh inside the mosques."

"*Astaghfirullah.*" A couple of the Muslim men clucked their tongues as they looked up at the minaret of the Bethlehem mosque standing a few paces across the square.

"But it is the Syrians, the Egyptians, and the Moroccans who feed these fantasies! Everywhere in the White City there were hawkers enticing customers into their booths, stores, theaters, and mosques, offering them 'a taste of the Orient.'"[26]

"*Were you and your brothers not doing the same thing, ya khawaja?*"

"Of course not! Our business is different. We are artists who depict the glory of Allah and his saints in the town where the Messiah Himself was born. That's why they gave us the medal. Our booth was not some cheap form of entertainment. We were recognized for the beauty of our workmanship."

"*But you, too, exploit their fascination with us for financial gain. Is it not the same?*"

"Haram 'alayk! We allow the Amerkan and the faranja to glimpse the true Holy Land, not some depraved fantasy. We spread the good name of Bayt Lahm. Everywhere in Amerka now they take interest in our sacred town. They have taken to singing songs in the month of Kanun al-Awwal that mention Bethlehem by name. They have developed a craze for sending greetings cards with images of our town to friends and relatives living on the other side of the country. Even the great wheel in the White City was made by an enterprise named the Bethlehem Iron Company. None of these things bear any resemblance to our town. What we are doing is educating the Amerkan about the real Bayt Lahm.[27]

"How can you compare that to the depravities we witnessed on the Midway Plaisance? A place where the most popular attraction was 'Cairo Street'—a full-scale imitation of a road in al-Qahira, full of trinket shops, cafés, and scandalous shows.[28] Baʿid ʿan is-samiʿin![29] For a fee of just ten cents, visitors could enter its souqs, cafés, the mosque of Sultan Selim (complete with a real muezzin), bridal processions, two obelisks, and a theater where a strange version of raqs sharqi was performed by women in shameful costumes exposing their midriffs. The Amerkan called them 'belly dancers.'"[30]

"*May Allah protect our women!*"

The bells of the church began to ring out, calling the town to prayer.

"Amerka is no place for a woman," Jubrail muttered as he descended the steps. "We should never expose our wives and daughters to such habits."

CHAPTER 14

OF FERTILITY POTIONS AND
THE DIZZYING HEIGHTS OF SUCCESS

THE ELEVATOR HAD RISEN SO high, cranking its way up those enormous iron beams, that Jubrail had lost all sense of proportion. Clinging to the railing, he looked out from the summit of the tower to find the world had shrunk. The whole of Paris stood stretched out beneath him, merging into a carpet of green fields at the outer edges. A cloud drifted by, increasing his feeling of light-headedness. It all seemed strangely distant and unreachable from up there, like a painting in one of those franji galleries where visitors could look but not touch.

Trying to regain his bearings, he followed the line of the river eastward from the base of the tower. There it was! The tiny church of Saint-Julien-le-Pauvre—still his first port of call every time he arrived in Paris—standing just across the water from Notre Dame. Following the streets north, he eventually came to the open space of Place de la Republique with its statue of Marianne in the center, just a dot on the urban landscape from here. Somewhere to the south, tucked away in the narrow streets of the Temple District, was the Dabdoub shop.

From his perch at the top of the tower it all seemed so inconsequential: the church, the shop, the exhibitions. They all blended into an expanse of uniform streets, each one identical to the next.

Paris was celebrating the arrival of the new century and with it the dawn of progress. But to Jubrail it seemed as if time had moved in a circle, bringing him back to where it had all started. It was here, immediately below him, that he had first marveled at the strange buildings and fantastical inventions of the Paris exhibition. Just there across the river, he had sat in the Tunisian café and concocted his ill-fated scheme. That was twenty-two years ago. Now here he was, returned for the latest Exposition Universelle, looking out from this frightening tower of iron beams and steel rivets erected on the very spot where the Gallerie des Machines had once stood. Soon they would tear this tower down, just as they had torn down the Gallerie des Machines before it.

From his vantage point in the clouds, Jubrail thought about everything he had done since that first trip to Paris. He felt dizzy recalling the litany of cities he had visited: Manila, Amsterdam, Antwerp, Liverpool, Barcelona, Copenhagen, Chicago, New York. He and his brothers had earned vast sums of money, unthinkable just a generation before.[1] Together they had seen the world change beyond recognition, right before their very eyes.

Among all the places he had visited, Paris was still the city where every Bethlehemite aspired to open a shop. The "bride of the world's cities," as they called it, drew in the rustic young merchants like moths to a flame.[2] They were transfixed by its glittering arcades, dazzling department stores, and alluring nocturnal entertainment. Soon they too were adopting the Parisian customs, exchanging their abayehs and turbans for frock coats and top hats, eating with knives and forks, even frequenting the scandalous shows on the Montmartre.

Jubrail had sampled the pleasures of Paris too. But he never forgot the purpose of his visits. Ever since the failure of that first trip in 1878, he had devoted his life to the prosperity of the family firm. It was as if every time he set out from Bethlehem, he had to prove his worth to his brothers all over again. While others reveled in the Belle Epoque, Jubrail kept his eyes on the account books and learned how to get ahead in a city enchanted by consumption. Everything was a fantastical illusion: a trompe l'oeil designed to induce the swelling middle classes to part with their money. Shopping had been turned into a leisure activity in which browsing the department stores and strolling the arcades became an end in itself. Each week, new fashions were born on the city's streets, exhibited in lavish window displays, and exported to countless cities around the world. For a merchant capable of keeping his head and staying focused on his work, the commercial possibilities were boundless.

To maintain his equilibrium among all the confusion surrounding him, Jubrail had never forgotten his father's advice from that first day he had set out from Bethlehem as a seventeen-year-old boy. "Always remember where you come from," old Yousef had told him, before adding for good measure: "He of little prayer sees his business affairs go to ruin."[3] Wherever he had found himself in the world, Jubrail had always found a place to kneel in prostration, thanking the Virgin, al-Khadr, and Mar Yousef for their protection as he thumbed his trusty prayer beads.

Soon the saints were repaying him. Having toured the streets of Paris for weeks searching for an affordable shop space, he finally found a small, ground-floor warehouse for rent at number 6 Rue Saulnier. The building was located in the heart of the Temple District, where so many Syrians were congregating at that time. They had even established their own church in the ancient chapel of Saint-Julien-le-Pauvre back in 1889, complete with a priest dispatched from Beirut to give sermons in Arabic. The Bethlehemites were an integral part of this Syrian community and had led the campaign to consecrate the Arabic church.[4] Many of the Bethlehemite businesses were located around the Boulevard de Strasbourg in the Temple District.[5] With the opening of their new shop on the nearby Rue Saulnier, the Dabdoubs had taken their place among them, making Paris the headquarters of their global operations.

From their base in the Temple District, Jubrail and his brothers had taken turns traveling to New York, where they plotted the next phase of their expansion. Their success at the Chicago exhibition had encouraged them to target the United States as the next frontier. Before long, they had opened a new shop at 35 Broadway, in the heart of the Syrian colony of Lower Manhattan, selling the usual assortment of religious wares, jewelry, and fabrics imported from all over Europe.[6] From there, they had followed the Syrians out of the crowded streets of Manhattan and into the more spacious surroundings of Brooklyn.[7] Soon they were renting their own apartment in an elegant building on Wyckoff Street just off Atlantic Avenue, where the next wave of the Syrian colonization of the city was taking place, all the while maintaining their shop across the water on Broadway.[8]

"At what cost, all this success?" Jubrail murmured as he turned his gaze toward the newly built Gare d'Orsay and the tangle of railway lines leading out from the station. He could not deny it: a life of constant travel had distanced him from his family. He had grieved the death of his father thousands of miles from home in the company of strangers.

"Allah yarhamu," Jubrail muttered under his breath as he remembered the letter he received in Antwerp one morning in 1885, informing him of old Yousef's death.

He barely saw his brothers these days. At any given time, any one of them would be stationed in some distant corner of the world on his latest business assignment. Even his younger brother Ibrahim was traveling the world now, shuttling between Bethlehem and Honduras, where he had recently opened a new shop. Once the brothers had always traveled together as a team. Now, the scope of their operations demanded each maintain his own sphere of the empire.

Back in Bethlehem, Jubrail could only watch from afar as his youngest sister, Sara, was plunged into a crisis that would divide the family for decades. He had barely noticed Sara growing up until one day he came back to Bethlehem to find she had left Hosh Dabdoub to marry a cousin of theirs, Yaqoub Yuhanna Dabdoub. A year later, Jubrail returned to find her back in the hosh again. Yaqoub had contracted tuberculosis on a business trip to Australia, leaving Sara a widow with two young children.[9]

Jubrail and his brothers had seen to it that Sara find another husband, but many tribulations lay in wait. Her two boys, Yousef and Daoud, were taken into the custody of their father's brother, Ibrahim Yuhanna Dabdoub, who now insisted he was their sole guardian, as was the custom in those days. For a while, Sara and her new husband tried living with the boys in their uncle's house, but the tension became so unbearable that Sara was cast out of the house and once more separated from her children. From that time onwards, a bitter feud enveloped the family, pitting Sara and her allies against her former brother-in-law, Ibrahim.

"Ya haram!" Jubrail exclaimed from the top of the tower. The man standing next to him moved sheepishly away.

Stranded thousands of miles from Hosh Dabdoub, Jubrail had been helpless in preventing the feud, which caused untold damage to the family's reputation in Bethlehem, not to mention their business interests abroad. Had he been so focused on the accumulation of the family's wealth that he had neglected the wellbeing of his own siblings?

Worst of all, his long absences meant he had been unable to raise a family of his own. For years, whispers had circulated that Mariam was infertile. But no woman could conceive if her husband was never there. After more than six years of childless marriage, she and Jubrail had turned to the Virgin for help. Everyone in Bethlehem knew that the chalky walls of the Milk

Grotto could cure even the most barren of women, not to mention bring abundant milk to mothers struggling to lactate. But could they compensate for an absent husband?[10]

It was in those caves that the Virgin herself had stopped to nurture her baby as she fled from King Hayruds, turning the walls white as she spilled a drop of her holy milk. By the time Jubrail and Mariam visited the caves, the Franciscan friars had erected their gleaming white chapel, giving the place an air of franji formality.[11] But Jubrail could still remember accompanying his mother there as a young child when it was still a network of musty caverns. Anyone in those days could just walk in and slice off their own piece of the cave wall. Now the friars had imposed their orderly system of handing out prewrapped parcels of powder stamped with the franji Cross of Jerusalem to those who proffered a Catholic prayer.[12]

Once back in Hosh Dabdoub, Mariam and Jubrail had eagerly unwrapped the package and emptied the contents into a cup of water. As they took turns drinking the potion, they had thumbed their rosary beads and dutifully prayed the third of the Joyful Mysteries, recalling the birth of Yasu', followed by a quick Our Father and ten Hail Marys.[13] Having dispensed with the formalities, they had proceeded to make their own appeals to the Virgin, offering her various rewards if she brought them a child.[14]

Repeating the same ritual every day for three months, Mariam had awoken one morning in the winter of 1888 to a violent sickness and realized she had not bled that month. So great was Jubrail's joy when he heard the news that he sank to his knees and heaped lavish praise on Allah and the Virgin.

Just a few weeks later, he was on the road again, journeying back to Paris to attend the great exhibition of 1889. That was the year the great tower had first been constructed. He had thought he could attend the exhibition and still make it home in time for the birth of his first child. But he had been delayed on the way back, and by the time he reached Bethlehem, Mariam had already named the boy Bishara—bearer of good news.

It was not until five years later that a second child was conceived. This time, Jubrail had made it home from Chicago in time for the birth and insisted they call him Yousef in honor of the baby's grandfather. But before long he was traveling again, now to Paris to complete the purchase of the shop on the Rue Saulnier.

"Al-ghurba murra," Jubrail muttered as he got back in the elevator, the bitterness of his exile mixing with the acute vertigo he was now experiencing.

The problem with the business model he and his brothers had created was that it could never stand still. The rivalry between the family firms was so fierce that a constant supply of new markets had to be found just to keep pace with the rest of the town. Staying in Bethlehem to concentrate on local sales would never satisfy the rapacious demands of the trade. They would be forced out of business in no time by more powerful souvenir firms making their money abroad. He had created a life that required him to live in constant motion.

As the elevator car descended to earth at breakneck speed, Jubrail struggled to recall the last time he had spent the Easter feast in Bethlehem.

Stepping out of the lift, his legs felt wobbly as he took his first steps back on solid ground. For months now he had been yearning to return to Bethlehem, not just for another fleeting visit, but to live in tranquility with his children in his beloved Hosh Dabdoub, where he would once more sit under the arches of the riwaq and look eastward across the terraced hills, down as far as the barren hills of the Wilderness. He was forty years old, ready to take his place in Bethlehem as a respected khawaja who had traveled the world to secure the honor of his family. His eldest son Bishara was ten, little Yousef already five. He had barely seen them these past few years, so busy had he been with the shops in New York and Paris.

Some of the merchants in Bethlehem were starting to take their families with them on trips to Amerka, exposing their women and children to all kinds of scandalous influences. Jubrail had seen with his own eyes how the American men and women frolicked at the seaside in bathing costumes that left little to the imagination. He had seen how unmarried couples held hands in public, openly flirting with each other.[15] As long as it had been just the men of Bethlehem who were exposed to such shameful customs it was possible to keep them at a safe distance. But now the younger generation seemed intent on moving permanently abroad, bringing their wives and children with them.

"I will never allow it," Jubrail muttered to himself as he hurried along the Champ de Mars to return to his exhibition stall.

The world had changed beyond recognition, but he would not permit the bonds that connected his family to Bethlehem to be broken. What had been the point of all this travel and absence if not to secure the legacy of the Dabdoub name in their sacred hometown?

FIGURE 18. A Bethlehemite family on its way to Jerusalem, c. 1900. Three of the women in the foreground can be seen wearing the cone-shaped *shatweh* headdress worn by married women in Bethlehem. Source: palestineremembered.com

FIGURE 19. The first Jaffa–Jerusalem train arriving in Jerusalem on September 26, 1892. Source: Wikimedia Commons.

FIGURE 20. Rosario Street and Binondo Church, Manila, 1899. This is the street where Jubrail established his store in 1881 selling Holy Land devotional objects. Source: Library of Congress, Prints & Photographs Division, LC-DIG-stereo-1s35453.

FIGURE 21. The Bethlehem stall at the Philadelphia Centennial International Exhibition of 1876. This may have been the stall run by Jubrail's brother Mikhail, or that of the Banayut brothers (as described in chapter 7). Courtesy of the Free Library of Philadelphia, Print and Picture Collection.

FIGURE 22. The Medal of Honor awarded at the World's Columbian Exposition of 1893. Jubrail and his brother Mikhail received one of these medals, as described in chapter 13. Source: The Metropolitan Museum of Art.

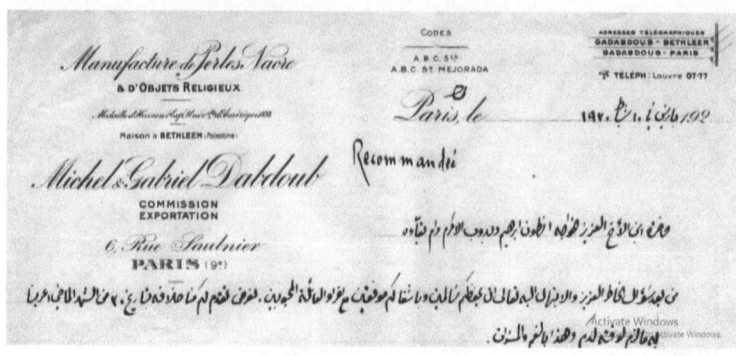

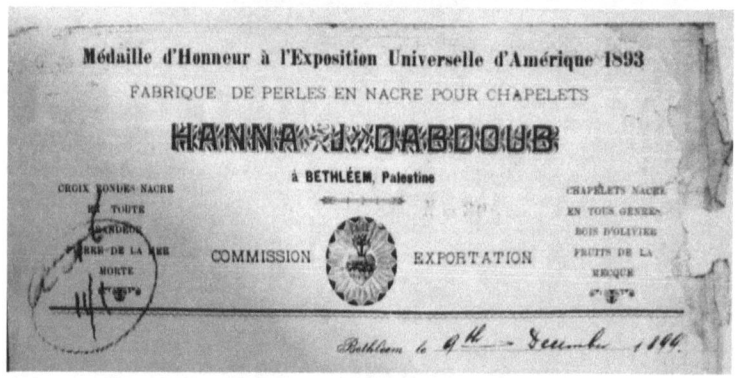

FIGURE 23. Dabdoub family logos and letterheads. Top to bottom: Letterhead used by Jubrail ("Gabriel") and his brother Mikhail ("Michel") from 1930, a year before Jubrail's death, advertising their Medal of Honor from Chicago. Source: Private collection of Peter Dabdoub. Business card used by Jubrail's younger brother Ibrahim, c. 1920. Source: Private collection of George Michel al-Aʿma. Letterhead used by Jubrail's elder brother Hanna in 1899, again making reference to the Medal of Honor in Chicago. Source: Private collection of George Michel al-Aʿma.

FIGURE 24. Yaqoub Yuhanna Dabdoub (1857–1890), brother of Ibrahim Yuhanna Dabdoub, whose unpublished memoir has been used extensively in this book. Yaqoub was the first husband of Jubrail's sister Sara. He took trips to Europe, the Philippines, and Australia in the 1870s and '80s that sometimes overlapped with Jubrail's own trips. Yaqoub's clothing and posture in the painting appear designed to portray him as an important *khawaja*—a title bestowed on merchants in Bethlehem who had achieved success overseas. The painting is signed in the bottom right by Zachariah Aboufhele (b. 1885), a Bethlehem artist who photographed and painted several of the merchant families in the late nineteenth and early twentieth centuries. As Aboufhele was only five years old when Yaqoub Dabdoub died, the painting must have been adapted from an earlier drawing or photograph after Yaqoub's death. Source: Private collection of Antonio Dabdoub Escobar.

FIGURE 25. Painting of Jubrail's brother Mikhail Dabdoub, along with Mikhail's wife, Maria, and their two sons, Abdallah and Khalil, in 1900. The identity of the young girl is unclear: Mikhail and Maria had a daughter, Jamileh, but she was twenty years old by the time of the painting. The painting is signed by Zachariah Aboufhele (b. 1885). This painting is thought to have been painted over a photograph taken in the Khalil Raʿad studio in Jerusalem. Source: Private collection of Abdallah Michel Dabdoub.

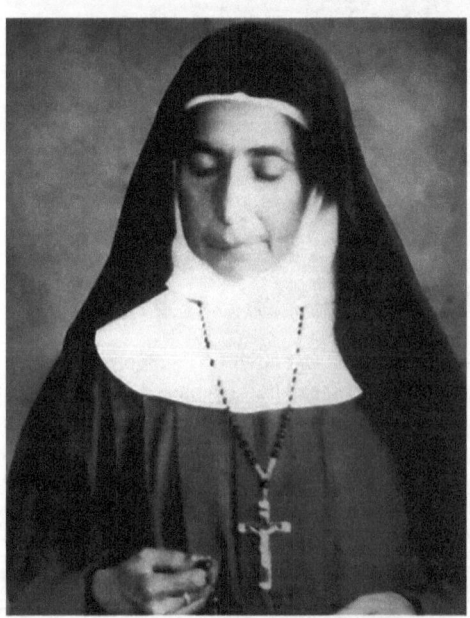

FIGURE 26. Photograph of Marie-Alphonsine Danil Ghattas, c. 1895. Courtesy of Rosary Sisters Congregation, Beit Hanina.

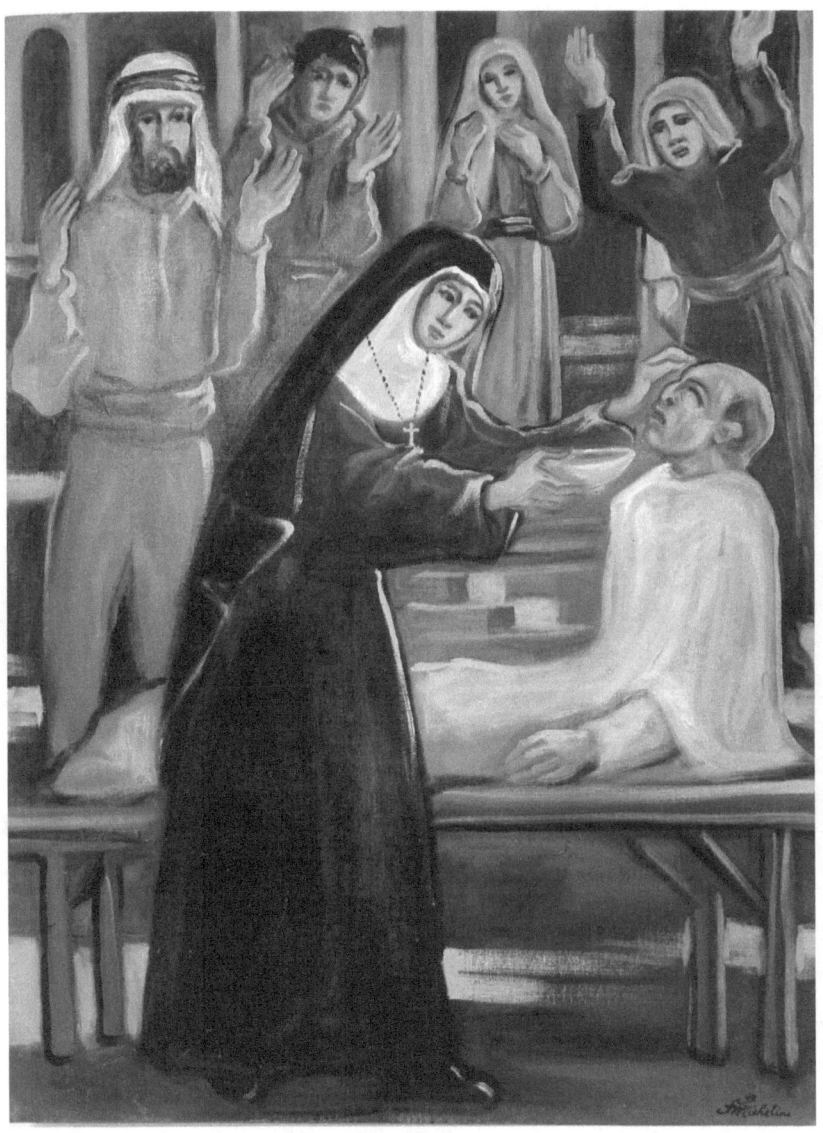

FIGURE 27. Artist's impression of the resurrection of Jubrail Dabdoub in 1909, signed "Michelini." The painting is one in a series commissioned by the Rosary Sisters in the 1980s. Photograph by Carol Khoury. Courtesy of Rosary Sisters Congregation, Beit Hanina.

FIGURE 28. Wedding of Daoud Dabdoub and Jamileh Freij, Bethlehem, May 2, 1920. Daoud was the son of Jubrail's sister Sara, and his marriage to Jamileh is described in the epilogue. There is a good chance that Jubrail is present in this photo. He was sixty years old at the time. Source: Private collection of Antonio Dabdoub Escobar.

Part III

CHAPTER 15

OF WEEPING ICONS, GHOSTLY ARMIES, AND VISIONS OF THE VIRGIN

"A GIRL IS BORN IN the home of the carpenter!" whispered the women who had crowded into High Mass in the Church of San Salvatore in Jerusalem. It was the fourth day of Tishrin al-Awwal in the year 1843. The women's faces bore a mixture of excitement and trepidation. "May she at least make it to her baptism," one of them murmured.

Her name at birth was Sultaneh Danil Ghattas, but in later years she would be known as Marie-Alphonsine. At baptism, her parents added the name Mariam in thanks to the Virgin, who had kept her safe during those perilous early weeks of life.[1]

They were right to be thankful. Sultaneh's mother, Cattoun, gave birth nineteen times, but only eight survived infancy. Little Sultaneh was the first of the eight to survive, forever imbuing her with a special aura in the eyes of her parents. The precise reason she had been spared during the early weeks by Azrael, the angel of death, was unknown. Perhaps it was because Cattoun had secretly asked a neighbor for salt to rub into the newborn baby. It was well known that obtaining the salt from somebody's else's home, especially an east-facing house, could help distract Azrael's attention away from the baby's own home. As an extra precaution, Cattoun had also insisted on dressing the infant in clothes begged from the neighbors.[2]

Or perhaps it was because Sultaneh was born on the feast day of Mar Francis, that most heavenly of Catholic saints. The Ghattas family had a special connection to Mar Francis and his friars. Sultaneh's father, Danil, worked for the Franciscans as a carpenter and lived with his family in the house opposite the friars' monastery in Jerusalem. At that time, the western part of Jerusalem was being transformed into an imposing Catholic fortress thanks to the sultan's readiness to grant favors to the faranja rulers. Entering the city at Bab al-Khalil, visitors walking northward would pass a series of walled compounds containing Catholic hospices, schools, and churches, as well as the gleaming new headquarters of the Latin patriarch himself, whose presence in al-Quds was restored in 1847 after five hundred years of absence. The Catholic stronghold extended up to the northwestern corner of the old city, where the sultan even ordered that a new gate be built into the city walls in 1889 to allow direct access into the Christian neighborhoods. Veering eastward from the new gate along the street of Saint Francis, the Ghattas family home was nestled among the buildings opposite the Franciscan monastery of San Salvatore. Continuing in this direction, a visitor would arrive at that most sacred of Christian shrines, the Church of the Resurrection, before passing into the more colorful streets of Souq Khan al-Zeit and al-Wad—Jerusalem's two commercial thoroughfares.

It was in that newly Catholicized corner of Jerusalem that little Sultaneh spent her early years, learning the catechism at the recently opened girls' school run by the Sisters of Saint Joseph and dreaming that one day she too would enter the religious life. The Ghattases were known to be one of the most pious families in al-Quds. Originally from Bethlehem, they had been among the Franciscans' early converts back in the seventeenth century, later moving to Jerusalem to work in the service of the friars. In those days it paid to be Catholic, and the Ghattas family made a good living working for the friars. Sultaneh's father, Danil, was always kept employed as the Franciscans continued to expand their monastery complex at San Salvatore.

Danil was known to everyone for his fierce devotion to the Virgin. Every evening he would invite friends and neighbors to his house to pray the Rosary and give thanks to the Virgin for his family's protection and prosperity. Kneeling before his diverse collection of statuettes and icons, and enveloped in clouds of incense, he would loudly beseech the Virgin to deliver lost souls from purgatory, thumbing his treasured prayer beads as he did so.[3] There was no doubt among those who knew him that Danil was rewarded for his unswerving devotion. Tales abounded of wondrous events occurring in the Ghattas family home. There were apparitions of saints, an icon that expelled drops of mysterious oil to heal one of his sickly daughters, and even a whole squadron of the lost souls of purgatory escorting Danil through the treacherous hill country as he made his way back to al-Quds one evening.[4]

Danil's devotion to his icons was matched only by his fierce opposition to Sultaneh entering the religious life. He was intent that his eldest daughter should marry into a good Catholic family to cement the Ghattas's high standing among the Christians of al-Quds.

"By the Grace of Allah, no daughter of mine will become a lowly nun!" he retorted when Sultaneh informed him of her plans one day. "They might even send you to Europe for your training. Ya rab, the scandal it would cause!"

Poor Sultaneh was overcome with grief. From a young age she had displayed unusual piety and had become fixated on the idea of joining one of Jerusalem's Catholic convents. But she would not be easily discouraged by her father's opposition and continued to pray incessantly to the Virgin. She was eventually rewarded in an unexpected manner when Danil suffered a terrible accident, caused by an exploding bottle of methylated spirits. Confined to a long and painful period of recuperation from his burns, Danil was forced to reflect on the meaning of the episode as his daughter lovingly cared for him. How else could he interpret the accident other than as a sign of heavenly displeasure at his refusal to grant his daughter's wishes?

Upon his recovery, Danil summoned Sultaneh to his room and explained that he would no longer stand in the way of her destiny. Overcome with elation, Sultaneh embraced her father and profusely thanked the Virgin for her intercession.

"But there is one condition," added Danil solemnly. "You will never leave this country."[5]

Sultaneh would never find the words to describe the beauty of her first vision.[6] She was thirty years old and had already been a member of the Sisters of Saint Joseph for thirteen years. When she had first taken the habit and changed her name to Marie-Alphonsine, she had been the only local girl in the order, surrounded by haughty franji nuns with their disdain for Arab customs. No matter how hard she tried, she would never look or sound like them. Her upbringing in al-Quds had rooted her in the local culture, and she could not prevent her Arabic tones from creeping into the French she was forced to speak with the sisters. Over time, she had become withdrawn, dedicating herself to her prayers with ever-greater fervor.[7]

It was the sixth day of Kanun al-Thani in the year 1874, the day of the Epiphany. Her prayers that day seemed like any other in her life of devotion and piety. Reciting the Mysteries of the Rosary in the Bethlehem parish school of the Sisters of Saint Joseph, she had just entered one of her deep states of meditation as she contemplated her love for the Virgin Mariam. As she reached the tenth mystery, a radiant light suddenly appeared above her, unlike anything she had seen before. Once her eyes adjusted to the brilliance of the light, Marie-Alphonsine realized the unmistakable figure of the Virgin was standing before her. There she was, as clear as day, hovering among glittering clouds, her hand outstretched toward the dumbstruck nun. Marie-Alphonsine saw a rosary fixed to a cross on the Virgin's breast, forming a luminous circle in which each bead was a glowing star. Looking more closely, she saw that each star contained a scene from the corresponding Mysteries of the Rosary, so that fifteen scenes simultaneously played out in miniature around the Virgin's breast. Immediately Marie-Alphonsine burst into a flood of tears, so intoxicated was she by the power of the Virgin's love.[8]

Such was the strength of that first vision that it sent Marie-Alphonsine into a trance from which she did not emerge for several hours. When she finally returned to consciousness, she was left pondering a series of questions. Why had the Virgin chosen to visit a lowly servant like her?[9] What did she want from her? Could it be mere coincidence that she had made her appearance on Eid al-Ghattas, the feast of the Epiphany, from which Marie-Alphonsine's family took their name? As the days passed, another more disturbing question crept into her mind. Was this the work of some evil jinn, trying to trick her into a state of hubris?

Over the course of the next five years, the Virgin visited Marie-Alphonsine no less than ten times, leaving the nun in no doubt over the nature of the visits. Every time they met, Marie-Alphonsine was further reassured that this was no devilish trap. So strong was the love that washed over her each time she set eyes on the Virgin that she knew this must be the work of a divine force. A sense of ecstasy, the likes of which she had never experienced, surged through her body during those encounters, leaving her in a state of pure bliss for hours after.[10] Each visitation left her desperate for more, but she quickly discovered that she could not conjure the visits at will. The Virgin would visit her in her own time and only when she deemed the moment to be right.

The Virgin was surely a busy woman in those days, spreading her work across the whole of Palestine. Every town and village, Muslim and Christian, contained shrines to her munificence. Many Muslim villages still paraded effigies of her mounted on a wooden cross as a way to persuade the annual rains to come.[11] In Jerusalem, pilgrims came from far and wide each year to take part in Eid Intiqal al-ʿAdhra on the fifteenth day of Ab—the great celebration of the Virgin's assumption to heaven. Hundreds of tents were erected around the shrine where the Virgin's empty tomb lay at the foot of the Mount of Olives. In the daytime, Muslim and Christian pilgrims circumambulated the shrine together, as if it were the Kaʿaba of Mecca. In the evening, the chapel was illuminated by dozens of gold and silver lamps, lit as votive offerings to the Virgin. The worshippers brought with them sick, young babies and anyone else in need of the Virgin's attention, and they shuffled in chaotic procession around the tomb, the Christians praying the Rosary and the Muslims thumbing their own prayer beads and amulets.[12]

Amid all the demands on her time, the Virgin still maintained a special relationship with Bethlehem, scene of her most heavenly act. Every street, well, and shrine in the town and the surrounding hills had some legend or other associated with her. Usually, she played the role of the town's protector, like when she unleashed a vast swarm of wasps onto an invading army that had attempted to breach the Church of the Nativity. Or when she had halted an earthquake by grasping the columns of that same church, leaving holes in the columns that were still visible hundreds of years later.[13]

It was natural, then, that every time Marie-Alphonsine was visited by the Virgin it should be in Bethlehem. The town at that time was in a whirlwind of activity as young men set off to seek their fortunes in a distant land called Amerka while their parents built elegant new mansions at the top of Ras Iftays. All the while, the merchants prayed to the Virgin to protect their sons on the other side of the world and to bless their businesses with success. As ever, the Virgin was happy to give them her special blessing, but only on the condition they remain steadfast in their prayer and devotion. It was well known the Virgin could quickly turn against them if they betrayed her trust. People still spoke about the time she asked a group of local peasants if they could spare her some peas from their field. When they tried to trick her by claiming there were only stones in the field, the Virgin simply replied, "Then let it be so," and the peas were instantly transformed into stones.[14]

Amid the clamor of requests by the Bethlehemites for the Virgin's protection, she somehow found time to visit the young nun. Upon each visitation, the Virgin drew nearer to Marie-Alphonsine and even began talking to her directly. She showed her visions of the future, allowing Marie-Alphonsine to foresee the horrors of the First World War some forty years in advance. She introduced her to Jesus and various saints, and she conjured scenes from the Holy Bible before her very eyes.[15]

As the visions multiplied, Marie-Alphonsine took on a new aura. To those who looked closely, she seemed perpetually bathed in a heavenly light, and everywhere she went, the Virgin accompanied her in the form of a beautiful star.[16] She walked around in a state of constant bliss, taking particular delight in earthly suffering, which she actively sought out by indulging in self-mortification.[17] In a dream that would later prove prophetic, she flew hand in hand with the Virgin across the hills of the Wilderness, over the River Jordan, and into the land of Moab. There she remained in the dream for many years, living among the local Bedouin tribes, serving Allah in the blissful hardship of poverty.

Gradually, Marie-Alphonsine learned from the Virgin that she had a special calling. She was to establish a new religious order formed exclusively of local Arab girls. In her visions, the Virgin appeared encircled by two rows of young girls dressed in religious habits with the words "Virgins of the Rosary" written in letters of fire above them. With every visitation, the message became louder and clearer: she must form the new congregation and lead them in their devotion to Marian prayer. Their mission, explained the Virgin, was to help the poorest women and girls in the most remote parts of Palestine and teach them the true path of Allah, using the Rosary as their guide.

At first, Marie-Alphonsine was confused. "Why, oh heavenly mother, would you be concerned with such despised and forgotten people? Surely there are more pressing matters to attend to in the lands of the faranja?"

"Remember, my daughter, that out of the thorns grow roses," came the Virgin's reply. "It was in this country that I was filled with joy, sorrow, and glory, and so it is from you and in you that I reveal the power of my hand."[18]

CHAPTER 16

OF THE ENCHANTED PALACES OF BETHLEHEM

IT WAS THE SPRING OF 1909, and the money was pouring in from overseas, producing a beguiling effect on the streets of Bethlehem. Fantastical inventions were being paraded through the streets, leaving people in a state of permanent bewilderment. The merchant families competed to bring the most outrageous contraptions from Europe, causing ripples of excitement each time something new arrived. There was the Primus stove that could cook things without the need for charcoal but left everyone cursing its deafening noise. There were Edison phonographs that mysteriously emitted the sounds of singing and musical instruments, and there were cameras that could conjure the exact image of a person if they were patient enough to stand still for several hours. Most frightening of all was Hanna Mansour's famous Berliet motorcar imported from France—a white streak of wheels and hissing pistons that sent people running for cover the day it came hurtling into town.[1]

No longer were the fabulous tales of the khawajas a distant source of curiosity that occurred in faraway lands. Bethlehem itself was now thrust into a period of such rapid transformation that no one was sure what they might see from one day to the next. Just a few months earlier, people had come from as far as Jerusalem to marvel at the gas lantern hung from the church and the joyously bright light it emitted. But such was the pace of change that the gas lamp quickly become outdated when the wealthiest merchant families began erecting electrical lanterns outside their houses and in their hallways. People came from all over town to test out the remarkable invention, endlessly pressing the magic button that instantly illuminated a whole house and then plunged it back into darkness. Everybody quickly agreed that these lights were a greater wonder than the church's gas lamp, and they thanked Allah for allowing them to witness such wondrous things in their own town.[2]

All these fantastical developments occurred against the backdrop of constant construction, leaving the impression of an entirely new town being raised from the rubble of the old. The clink-clink of chisels on limestone and the scraping of gravel and mortar could be heard on every street while women shouted orders at workers and kept a watchful eye on the stonemasons.[3]

"Taharrak, ya zelama. Get a move on man, I've seen donkeys work faster than that."

"Watch what you're doing with those mizzi ahmar stones. They're the expensive kind! My husband will string you up if he finds any marks on them when he gets back from Amerka."[4]

"Imshu bi-sur'a. We haven't got all day!"

One by one, they popped up in quick succession around the edges of the town: lavish pink-stone palaces, the likes of which had never before been seen in Palestine. Each one pushed the level of architectural experimentation to new heights of flamboyance. Pointed Islamic archways competed for attention alongside turreted towers resembling the old franji castles. Regal external staircases rubbed shoulders with Roman columns, Renaissance balustrade balconies, and Damascene courtyards. The merchant families had embarked on an orgy of spending, and nothing could restrain their enthusiasm. The combined effect was to leave the passerby in a state of dazzlement and confusion, unsure if they were looking at an Umayyad palace, a Roman villa, or a Crusader fort.

The lavish exteriors were only the tip of the iceberg. The interiors of these palaces contained so many rooms that the residents would occasionally come across new ones they had not known existed after years of living there. Unlike the merchant houses on Ras Iftays, the new mansions made no provision for workshops or stores, leaving behind the hustle and bustle of commerce for a new type of residence modeled on the villas glimpsed during travels across Europe. Husband, wife, and children now lived in spacious comfort, perched on hilltops surrounding Bethlehem, looking down on the old town with a sense of detached satisfaction.[5]

Impossible as it sounded, the humble village of the Messiah's birth had become the richest town in all Palestine. In just a few years, the Bethlehem merchants had acquired such vast sums of wealth that their new palaces outstripped anything seen in Jerusalem, Jaffa, or even Beirut.[6] Now young men and women were setting off from villages up and down the Palestinian hill country in an attempt to emulate the success of the Bethlehemites and find their fortune in Amerka. But the Bethlehemites were already far ahead of them, sending back vast sums of money to expectant wives ready to direct the next prestige building project.[7]

The miraculous transformation taking place on the streets of Bethlehem was a sure sign the saints were smiling on the town. As if to prove it, miracles of other kinds were taking place on an ever-more frequent basis. Old women were being cured of blindness, icons of the Virgin were weeping tears of joy, and young children were being pulled alive from the depths of wells after having long since been pronounced dead.

Some even proclaimed a political miracle had taken place. Young men educated in the new public schools of Jerusalem and Istanbul were returning to Bethlehem and declaring that the Ottoman Empire had been transformed in the space of a single day into a bastion of liberty, equality, and fraternity. Some of the merchants had seen those same words imprinted on public buildings in Paris, but never did they believe they would hear them on people's lips in Bethlehem. Yet here they were, these young men fresh from their studies, describing excitedly how the word *huriyya* (freedom) was ringing out on the streets of Jerusalem and that Christians would now be placed on an equal footing with Muslims for the first time.[8]

Most of the old people laughed off these reports as one of those fantastical khurafiyya tales, designed more to entertain than inform. Others took them more seriously but questioned the usefulness of equality if it meant their sons would be conscripted into the Ottoman army like the Muslims, instead of being sent abroad to serve the family business. But the enthusiasm of the young intellectuals was infectious. As censorship laws relaxed, bundles of newspapers printed in Jerusalem and Jaffa began arriving in Bethlehem each week. Never before had people been exposed to such a flood of information. Until that time, the only publications that reached the town had been the newsletters of the Franciscan and Rumi printing presses that stuck scrupulously to the affairs of the church. Now the residents of Bethlehem could find out about all kinds of events occurring in distant corners of the world just days after they happened. Strange new ideas began to circulate, proclaiming the birth of an Arabic-speaking nation and, most shockingly, the end of the church's authority over earthly matters.[9]

Naturally, the Franciscan friars were alarmed by these developments and began to issue apocalyptic pronouncements about the dangers of reading such newspapers.[10]

"Son figlioli del diavolo!" the friars exclaimed to worshippers in the monastery of Santa Caterina. "Those who heed the words of these godless creatures will surely burn in hell!"

The Rumi priests and friars were equally worried, not least because a new campaign was being launched in Jerusalem to rid the clergy of its Greek-speaking leadership and install local Arabs instead. The rebels even had the audacity to boycott the Christmas procession to Bethlehem in protest, sending the Rumi patriarch into a vitriolic rage when he delivered his sermon on the day of the Orthodox Christmas.[11] Those who attended listened patiently but remained largely immune to the alarmism of the priests. Such was their confidence that their town had entered a new era of miracles that they were not prepared to rule out the possibility that new prophets were among them. Had the Franciscan friars and the Greek priests not fought among themselves like children all these years, oblivious to the needs of the town's residents? Had they not looked down on the town's residents with scorn all these years? The only reason they had ever worked for the friars and studied in their schools was in the hope of being thrown a few scraps to improve their meager existence. Now that the money was pouring in from Amerka, they were free to go their own way. Perhaps the young men preaching the new gospel of equality and liberty were right. The town was awash with mystics and sorcerers, conjuring all kinds of miracles. Anything seemed possible in those heady days.

Such was the feverish excitement that gripped Bethlehem when Jubrail returned from his latest venture to Amerka in the spring of 1909. This time he had come with the intention of settling for a longer period. His baby girl, Wardeh, was four, and his sons were already growing up. He would assess the conditions and reestablish his status in his hometown.

He first noticed the palaces after attending Mass one morning in the old church. Taking a stroll down the steep streets of the Anatreh Quarter where he had played with his cousin Elias as a child, he turned onto one of the narrow pathways he knew so well and stopped dead in his tracks. Towering before him was a dazzling pink mansion, standing with its back to the church as it looked out across Wadi Ma'ali below. Its vast walls rose three stories above the surrounding buildings, completely at odds with the rest of the neighborhood. For a moment he thought he had been transported back to the suburbs of Paris as he gazed up at the European-style shutters and the ornate balustraded balconies. The area behind the house had been cleared of the old ruins that had once stood there and a team of workers was busy building a garden fountain. Jubrail rubbed his eyes. How could such a thing exist in Bethlehem? Who had had the audacity to build it?[12]

Asking around, he discovered the house belonged to Morcos Nassar, a young man who had been sent to Europe to train as an architect. Now Morcos had returned and was putting his training to use. His mansion in the Anatreh Quarter had laid down a new marker for the rest of the town. Modeled on the villas Morcos had seen in the affluent suburbs of Paris, the house was designed so the Nassar family could live in the comfort of their own detached house, no longer having to share a central courtyard with a network of extended clan members.

As he called on family members and business associates around town, Jubrail quickly discovered that Dar Nassar had already inspired a string of imitators. Some of the merchant families had been so impressed by young Morcos's design that they had immediately commissioned him to build them a pink palace of their own. By the summer of 1908, he had completed the new residence of Saleh Giries Giacaman, a short distance up the hill from the Bab al-Zqaq crossroads that divided the boundaries of Bethlehem and Beit Jala. This time Morcos was even bolder in his design, incorporating a sumptuous external staircase leading up to the front door, where the visitor's gaze was drawn upward toward a poem engraved in the finest Arabic calligraphy over the entrance.

Walking uphill past the Giacaman mansion, Jubrail quickly came to another one, this time belonging to one of his business associates in New York, Suleiman Giries Handal.[13] Jubrail stared in amazement at the house's stately Corinthian columns, the elegant archways, and the grandiose staircase. How had Bethlehem been transformed so dramatically since his last visit? He was used to thinking of himself as one of the town's trendsetters, but these palaces left him feeling like a relic from a bygone era. Where once the distinctive riwaq arches of Hosh Dabdoub had been a landmark on the

Bethlehem skyline, they now faded into the background as the shiny pink palaces competed for attention.

Jubrail did not know it then, but those palaces he encountered in the spring of 1909 were just the first of a trend that would leave Bethlehem unrecognizable from just a few years earlier. By 1910, the Hirmas brothers would complete their masterpiece on the northern slopes behind Ras Iftays. Saleh and Giries Hirmas had been among the first merchants to arrive in Chile, rising from humble beginnings hawking rosaries on the streets of Santiago to earning a vast fortune in the textile trade. Soon they had sent word for their wives and children to be sent across the ocean to start a new life in Chile, leaving their brother Mitri to maintain the family business in Bethlehem.[14] Building a palace in Bethlehem was the brothers' way of ensuring their legacy in their town of birth. The result was the largest building Bethlehem had ever seen, bigger even than the old church. Once again it was Morcos Nassar who supplied the designs, this time letting his imagination run wild with a double-sided facade that incorporated elegant symmetrical staircases and columned archways in the Damascene style. The house was a vast mirror image of itself, leaving poor Mitri in a state of confusion every time he returned to the house, unsure which entrance to take to reach his living quarters, which were tucked away at the end of a corridor in some distant corner of the palace.

Just when it seemed the Hirmas brothers had reached the uppermost limits of extravagance, the richest of all Bethlehem's merchants set a new standard of opulence. Suleiman Jacir had watched the building spree with great interest, increasingly convinced that he must build his own palace that would outstrip all others in its magnificence. By 1909 he had applied to the Ottoman governor in Jerusalem for a license to build on a five-dunum plot of olive groves near Qubbet Rahil, the exact point where travelers approaching Bethlehem first veered off Hebron Road to begin their descent into town.[15] Suleiman had just completed his second stint as the town's mayor and could now combine unrivaled political influence with his indubitable economic muscle. For the next four years, an array of builders, stonemasons, and franji architects buzzed around the site, leaving the whole town in a state of anticipation. Bethlehem's finest sculptor, Issa Mikhail Hazboun, was hired to oversee construction and provide the flourishes on the palace facade. The renowned calligrapher Najeeb Al-Hawawini was brought from Istanbul to adorn the towers with Arabic script, and an Italian painter named Marco showed up to decorate the interior hallways with sumptuous frescoes.[16]

Finally, the day arrived in 1914 when Suleiman Jacir threw a lavish party to mark the completion of the palace. It seemed the whole of Bethlehem was there that day, eagerly awaiting the first official viewing. When they laid eyes on the building, a collective gasp of amazement rang out. The palace was a riot of turrets, columns, and arches, combining the finest franji, Ottoman, and Syrian styles. Its scale was breathtaking: three floors made up a total of almost eight thousand square feet, with elegant landscaped gardens stretching to the rear. Passing through wrought-iron gates bearing the initials "S. J.," guests were greeted by a stately Islamic doorway that led into the interior courtyard, complete with an Italianate fountain surrounded by Romanesque columns. Strolling the corridors and stairways that framed the quadrant, visitors encountered portraits of the patriarchs of the Jacir family and frescoes of scenes from the Bethlehem hills.

Rumors were soon circulating about the cost Suleiman had incurred building this enchanted palace. The matter was finally settled when a journalist arrived one day from Jaffa to write an article about the town's mansions. When the article was read out loud in Bab al-Dayr one morning, a crowd of eager listeners gathered to hear which families had been mentioned by the journalist.[17] It did not matter that the journalist had written the article as a rebuke to the Bethlehemites, urging them to invest their money instead in land acquisitions to ward off the threat of Zionism. All the listeners really wanted to know was how much each of the khawajas had spent on his palace. As expected, Suleiman Jacir came first with a sum of fourteen thousand lira, followed by Said al-Quwwas, Anton al-Jaʻar, Yaqub Babun, and Saleh Giacaman, all in the range of ten thousand lira.[18]

When Jubrail came back that spring of 1909, Bethlehem was only on the cusp of those wondrous transformations. Upon his return, he could already sense that a remarkable change was in the air, producing an atmosphere of feverish excitement among the town's residents. Anything seemed possible in those heady days. Diseases were being miraculously cured, children pulled from the depths of wells, and saints regularly sighted strolling through the town in broad daylight.

Amid all the excitement, one person in particular was being talked about as a worker of miracles. The diminutive nun, it was said, could always be found nearby whenever a wondrous event occurred, diligently praying the Rosary. Perhaps she was a saint, they whispered, or one of those traveling mystics who could bend the laws of nature to their will. Jubrail observed how the khawajas competed to offer her their assistance in the hope she might intervene in favor of their businesses, or perhaps cure a family member from sickness. She and her fellow Rosary Sisters had even been given temporary accommodation next door to Hosh Dabdoub by the Mikel family. Jubrail did not know it yet, but his fate had just moved one step closer to that humble nun and her treasured rosary beads. Soon their destinies would be forever intertwined through a momentous offering of quince jam.

CHAPTER 17

OF HYENAS, SERPENTS, AND FRENCH PHILANTHROPISTS

THE VIRGIN HAD LEFT NOTHING to chance. Long before the Rosary Sisters were founded, Marie-Alphonsine already knew every detail of the order, thanks to the Virgin's meticulous instructions: the style and color of the sisters' habits (monastic blue and white); the exact way they would pray the Rosary (kneeling in prostration in front of the altar); which mysteries would be prayed at which precise times of day; when the sisters would hold special fast days for the sake of the Rosary (Mondays and Wednesdays); the names of each of the founding sisters; and even the design of their future convent (a round temple in the form of the Rosary). Everything had been revealed by the Virgin in her visits to Marie-Alphonsine.[1]

Since it was unthinkable for a local Jerusalemite woman to set up her own religious order, Marie-Alphonsine had been obliged to seek the assistance of a local priest in her efforts to form the Rosary Sisters. On this point, too, the Virgin had given specific instructions. In one of her visits to Marie-Alphonsine she had conjured the unmistakable image of her parish priest in Jerusalem, Abouna Yousef Tannous, wearing a brilliant crown of stars above his bearded face. Delighted the Virgin had heard her request that the director be an Arab man, Marie-Alphonsine set about confiding in the priest the mission the Virgin had assigned her.[2] From that moment, Abouna Yousef became one of only three people Marie-Alphonsine ever told about her supernatural visions, the other two being the Latin patriarch of Jerusalem and the Italian priest Antonio Belloni, who ran the orphanage in Bethlehem.[3]

With Abouna Yousef providing unstinting support, Marie-Alphonsine worked tirelessly to enact the Virgin's instructions. Together they recruited the sisters the Virgin had mentioned, found a temporary residence in Jerusalem, and drew up the founding constitution of the order. But there was one instruction the Virgin had not provided: how to deal with the ferocious opposition that would plague Marie-Alphonsine wherever she went. Establishing an Arabic-speaking congregation populated by local women was an affront to the franji nuns who ran the other Catholic orders in Palestine. Worse still was the idea that a woman could take the lead in establishing such an order. For the rest of her life, Marie-Alphonsine would bear the burden of transgressing these boundaries, persecuted by those who sought to preserve the status quo and protect their own privileges.

The first to test her resolve came from her mother superior in the Sisters of Saint Joseph in Bethlehem. Upon hearing of the plan to found the Rosary Sisters, this haughty franji woman immediately ordered Marie-Alphonsine to be sent to live in seclusion in Beirut. When Marie-Alphonsine steadfastly refused to comply, the matter had to be settled by a papal representative dispatched all the way from Rome. They settled on a compromise: Marie-Alphonsine was spared the indignity of banishment to Beirut but had to endure three years of seclusion in Jerusalem, shut up in her father's house while the rest of the Rosary Sisters began their work without her. Her only consolation during those long and tortuous years was the continued presence of the Virgin. "In her compassion she turned my isolation into a paradise, my poverty into happiness, and my torment and weariness into sweetness," she wrote in her notebook, taking growing pleasure in her own pain and suffering.[4]

When her period of seclusion had finally elapsed, Marie-Alphonsine was free at last to join the Rosary Sisters, taking her habit on the feast day of the Rosary in the month of Tishreen al-Awwal in 1883. Setting straight to work, she threw herself into the service of Allah with unswerving devotion, seeking out the poorest women and girls in the most remote regions of Palestine. Living always in the humblest of conditions and never knowing how they would feed themselves from one day to the next, she and her sisters worked tirelessly to alleviate the suffering of those poor creatures and educate them in the true path of the Holy Roman Church.

Before long, her prophetic dream of living among the Bedouin of Transjordania became reality as she journeyed with her sisters in the year 1887 across the River Jordan and into the desert plains surrounding the hill town of al-Salt.[5] Here she found a scattering of tribes who professed to be Catholic but had long since forgotten how to live by the laws of Rome, having adapted instead to the laws of the desert and the habits of their Muslim neighbors. The women of these impoverished tribes were so isolated from the teachings of the church that their only contact with a priest was during their annual visit to al-Salt to participate in the Easter celebrations. Entering the parish church, they would head straight to the Holy Table to take communion, having neither fasted nor confessed. They would then repeat the ritual several times in the same day, the priest helplessly unable to discern who was whom.[6]

Shocked by these rudimentary habits, Marie-Alphonsine sat with the women outside the church and patiently explained the ritual of communion. "Ya banat, you can only receive the Eucharist once during Mass. The flesh and blood of al-Masih cannot be consumed twice in a day!"

The women listened attentively as they puffed on their long clay pipes and sipped their pungent Bedouin coffee, surprised that someone from the church was able to speak Arabic.

"But first you must fast and confess your sins," Marie-Alphonsine continued. "You cannot be in union with Yasu' until you have been absolved."

The women looked confused.

"But what have we done, ya sayyida? We live simple lives in the desert, worshipping our saints and the local fakirs."

"If we say we have no sin, we deceive ourselves, and the truth is not in us.[7] You must have the courage to reflect on your moments of weakness, ya banat."

The next morning Marie-Alphonsine arrived at the church for Mass to find a huddle of Bedouin women waiting for her. All at once they began blurting out the most unspeakable sins committed over the course of their lives. One had tried to hang herself because she could no longer bear to be beaten by her husband. Another had employed a local sorcerer to place a curse on her mother-in-law. One had even killed another woman with her own hands.[8]

"Khalas banat, enough!" the poor nun exclaimed, holding her hands to her ears. "You can only confess to the priest. I am just a lowly handmaid of the church."

The women looked at her in stunned silence.

"Ya sayyida, have you lost your mind?" one of them eventually spoke. "We could never share our secrets with a man!"

From that day onward, a small crowd of women could be found accompanying the Rosary Sisters into the church every morning, tugging on their habits and trying to confess to them before taking communion.[9]

Despite the sisters' dismay and embarrassment at these rudimentary customs, Marie-Alphonsine's unstinting compassion for the poor women produced unprecedented success in reeducating them in the laws of the church. In the space of just a few months, the sisters had attracted 146 girls to study in their school in al-Salt and 86 women to the Confraternity of Christian Mothers they had founded there. Given how far these women had strayed from the true path of Allah, the sisters kept their ambitions limited, teaching them basic catechism and how to venerate the Virgin by thumbing their prayer beads and reciting the Mysteries of the Rosary.

It was true that the women did not always implement these rituals in a strictly Catholic manner, and many were the times Marie-Alphonsine had to admonish them for their superstitious habits.[10]

"Ya ma Soeur, I will add these beads to my collection of amulets—my hjabat and tahwitat," one woman said.[11] "Surely they will help me conjure my ancestors' spirits the next time I visit their tomb. They may also help us cure our sick when we cover them in leaves and give them melted soil from the grotto of the dervish."[12]

"Allah yusamihku. May God forgive you!" Marie-Alphonse would reply. "These beads are not like your amulets and talismans, ya banat. They do not possess magical powers. The church teaches us that there is only one divine power, that of Allah Himself, who alone is capable of bending the laws of nature. The beads are just a way for us to communicate our love for His Holy Mother, the Virgin Mariam."

The women would smile patiently as they puffed on their long pipes, happy to have come into possession of these mysterious new beads. They knew Marie-Alphonsine was a powerful sorceress who could perform miracles with those beads. Acquiring knowledge of how to use the beads might allow them their own access to those powers. In town they had heard stories of how this seemingly unassuming woman had used the beads to bring people back from the dead. In the village of Yafet al-Nasrah in the Galilee, it was said, she had resurrected a young girl who had fallen into a well. Despite everyone proclaiming her dead, Marie-Alphonsine had continued to stand by the well muttering spells with her beads. The local people had scolded and beaten her, blaming her for the incident, as the child had been studying at the Rosary Sisters' school when she had fallen into the well. But the nun had been undeterred, muttering her incantations for hours after the event. To everyone's amazement, the girl later emerged from the well unharmed, recounting how she had seen a string of rosary beads light up under the water like a beacon. The beads had fallen over her neck and pulled her up to the surface.[13]

Marie-Alphonsine would always say her rosary beads were simply a medium of communication with the Virgin and that it was only through years of dedicated recital of the Mysteries of the Rosary that such communication could be established. But wherever she went, rumors followed that she was some kind of saint or sorceress who could enter into the spirit world at will.[14] In total, she performed eight miracles in and around wells and springs. These were the places where water from the interior of the world made its way to the earth's surface, providing crossing points for saints and spirits wishing to enter the land of the living. But such locations had to be treated with extreme care, as they were also used by jinn and ghouls as a point of entrance into the human domains. All over the countryside there were springs and wells where saints of various kinds stood guard to prevent any unpleasant creature from emerging from the underworld.[15]

Marie-Alphonsine, it was said, had acquired the ability to intervene in these aquatic battlegrounds, summoning the assistance of the Virgin to protect humans from the incursions of malignant spirits. But by doing so, she had also placed her own safety in jeopardy. As she made her way around the Palestinian countryside, seeking out the poorest Christian women, she was followed by malignant spirits trying to undermine her work. One night in the village of Beit Sahour, just to the east of Bethlehem, she and two sisters heard a loud banging on the door of the abandoned outhouse where they slept. Opening the latch to peer outside, she saw a huge hyena running around the garden in a frenzy, tearing down the drystone walls that enclosed the school grounds. Hyenas were known to be evil jinn in disguise who could hypnotize people and lure them back to their caves to be devoured.[16] Overcome with fear, Marie-Alphonsine closed her eyes, clasped her beads, and pleaded with the Virgin for protection, as well as to Mar Yousef and Mar Anton, who were known to be workers of miracles in times of great crisis. She could not be sure which of the three saints heard her pleas, but when she opened her eyes and peered nervously out the door, the hyena had miraculously disappeared.[17]

In later years, when she lived once more in Bethlehem, the Devil himself made an appearance one day in a well at the orphans' school where the Rosary Sisters worked. As she was sifting wheat with the children in the schoolyard, she instinctively began to pray the Rosary and make the sign of the cross. Getting up to fetch water, she opened the well to find a fearsome snake writhing in the water, changing its size as it moved and flicked its enormous forked tongue. People gathered from all over town, including a Salesian priest who poured holy water into the well, but nobody could remove the serpent. When the crowds dispersed, Marie-Alphonsine was left by herself to pray all night for the Virgin's protection, clutching her prayer beads as she did so. In the morning, she opened the well to find the snake had miraculously disappeared. For the rest of that summer, the nuns continued to drink from the well until it ran dry. When they finally washed the base of the well, they found no hole from which the snake might have escaped. The only rational conclusion was that it had been al-Shaytan who had appeared that day, writhing in rage at the sound of Marie-Alphonsine reciting the Rosary.[18]

Undoubtedly, these malevolent spirits were the product of the envy that pursued Marie-Alphonsine wherever she went. "Better a lion's bite than the look of the evil eye," people would say, and in the case of Marie-Alphonsine, it was the envy of her own sisters that proved most spiteful. Mother Rosalie Nasr was an elderly nun from Nazareth who had been appointed superior of the Rosary Sisters by Abouna Yousef. Upon her arrival in al-Quds, she quickly developed a furious jealousy toward Marie-Alphonsine, unable to fathom why she enjoyed such exalted status with Abouna Yousef and the other sisters. She embarked on a vicious smear campaign against Marie-Alphonsine, making baseless accusations about her moral rectitude and administering sadistic punishments, such as placing her in isolation and denying her food whenever she protested her treatment. This persecution produced a permanent split among the Rosary Sisters that would eventually lead a group of the sisters to burn Marie-Alphonsine's treasured notebooks in an attempt to destroy evidence of her sainthood. But Marie-Alphonsine's saintly nature could not be suppressed, nor could Mother Rosalie escape divine retribution in the end. By 1895 she had been transferred to Jbeil in Lebanon to help found the Maronite Sisters of the Holy Family. There her harsh methods incurred such resentment that she was clubbed to death over the head by one of the novices.[19]

Meanwhile, Marie-Alphonsine continued on the path of piety and devotion, eventually leading her back to Bethlehem, the town where she had first encountered the Virgin in those rapturous visions in the 1870s and where she still felt closest to her. The trigger for her return was a mysterious donation made to the Latin patriarch of Jerusalem by a certain Madame Picard, the wife of a wealthy Parisian jeweler who enjoyed close relations with the Bethlehem merchants trading in the French capital at that time.[20] In true franji fashion, Madame Picard saw herself as charged with the special task of saving the Christians of Palestine. It was not entirely clear what they needed to be saved from, but she was nonetheless intent on saving them, and in 1892 she donated five hundred francs for the formation of a new orphanage for girls in Bethlehem.[21]

When Marie-Alphonsine was approached by the Latin patriarch to establish the new orphanage, she responded with extreme caution. Not only was she against the interference of the faranja in the affairs of the Rosary Sisters, she was also aware that her old congregation, the Sisters of Saint Joseph, considered Bethlehem their exclusive territory. How incensed they would be to learn that a new congregation of nuns was operating in the town, run by a local upstart who had abandoned their own order![22]

It was only through the interference of her old mentor, the Italian priest Antonio Belloni who ran the boys' orphanage in Bethlehem, that she was eventually persuaded to accept the patriarch's invitation.[23] Taking with her just one other nun from the Rosary Sisters and working initially in utmost secrecy, she set about caring for the poorest girls in the areas where the franji nuns could never reach. In those early days in Bethlehem, the Rosary Sisters had no fixed lodgings and were reliant on the charity of the locals to give them food and shelter. Above all, it was the khawajas of Bethlehem, those very same men who had facilitated Madame Picard's donation in Paris, that supported the Rosary Sisters during those difficult early years in the town. They supplied them with leftover materials from their mother-of-pearl workshops so the sisters could teach bead-making, woodcarving, and embroidery to local orphan girls. They even opened their homes to the sisters, giving them food and shelter when they had nowhere else to go.

In later years, various khawajas would boast that they had hosted Marie-Alphonsine long before she was known to be a saint. Mubarak Dʿeq claimed to have been the first, giving up one of the many bedrooms in his newly built villa. Later, it was the turn of Mubarak's cousin, the khawaja Abdullah, to take them in, before Yousef Lulos intervened and rented them his whole villa so the sisters could finally open a boarding house for orphan girls.[24] When the money from Madame Picard dried up because of a spat between her and the Latin patriarch, it was the khawajas who once again intervened, using their connections with the French consul in Jerusalem to arrange for a two-thousand-franc annual stipend to be paid to the Rosary Sisters by the French government.[25] The stipend was enough to cover the Rosary Sisters' living expenses and teaching supplies, but they continued to rely on the khawajas' hospitality for their accommodation.[26]

For their part, the khawajas were happy to support Marie-Alphonsine. In those days they were busy restoring shrines and funding new municipal projects in an effort to secure their legacy in Bethlehem.[27] They had spent their lives accumulating great fortunes in faraway lands, all thanks to the sanctity of their hometown and the protection its saints afforded them. They were aware of the debt of gratitude they owed Bethlehem, and they never missed a chance to display their philanthropic benevolence, especially when it came to matters of the divine. Marie-Alphonsine was a reminder of the need for piety and modesty at a time when the whole town had become enamored with the accumulation of material wealth. She had sworn to her father she would never leave Palestine, and she lived in self-imposed poverty, working tirelessly to alleviate the suffering of the poor. While the khawajas had been selling rosary beads by the thousands in distant corners of the earth, she had used *her* beads to perform miracles of a different sort, right there on the streets of Bethlehem. She offered them a way to return to their roots and show their devotion to the Virgin. They also knew that those miraculous powers might come in useful one day.[28]

By the beginning of 1909, the town was abuzz with talk of the diminutive nun and the miracles she was performing. Still without permanent lodgings, she and the sisters had found temporary accommodation at the Mikel family mansion on Ras Iftays, right next door to Hosh Dabdoub. Before long, word was circulating about her latest miracle: curing an old woman from the neighborhood, Mariam Giries Kattan, from blindness. Her family had hired a franji doctor named Baker to treat the rapid deterioration of her vision, but he had left shaking his head, declaring she would remain blind for the rest of her life. At that point, it was said, Marie-Alphonsine had quietly slipped into the house, dipped her rosary beads in a cup of water, and invited the family to pray fifteen Hail Marys with her as she sprinkled the droplets into the old woman's eyes. When the old woman awoke the next morning, she had seen spots of light returning to her vision, sending her daughter up the hill to Dar Mikel, where she begged Marie-Alphonsine to return. Marie-Alphonsine repeated the ritual every morning for the next three days, the entire Kattan family dutifully joining her in praying the Rosary. On the following Sunday, the rest of the street looked on in amazement as old Mariam emerged from the house on her own and staggered down to Bab al-Dayr to pray in the church.[29]

"Wallahi that woman is a saint," she could be heard muttering as she zigzagged down the street, blinking at the bright blue sky and bumping into the occasional child as she went. A few days later, she could be seen sat in her customary chair outside the Kattan house, embroidering the intricate wedding dress panels for which she was well known all over town.

The miracle of Mariam Kattan's restored vision produced a wave of excitement on Ras Iftays. The wives of the khawajas queued up at Dar Mikel to ask if there was anything the sisters needed while young children stood outside the window on tiptoe, hoping to catch a glimpse of the saintly woman.

Did Jubrail notice the commotion as he went about his work in Hosh Dabdoub? He was certainly a busy man in those days. Having recently returned from Amerka, he was trying to plot his next business move, wondering whether to invest in Palestine or open a new branch of the family firm somewhere in Amerka. Mostly his attention was focused on the gleaming new palaces appearing all over town, wondering how and where he could build one for himself to keep up with the other khawajas. It was easy to miss Marie-Alphonsine as she ran her errands, so small was her stature and so modest her demeanor. New religious orders were cropping up all around, bringing all manner of nuns, monks, and wild-eyed mystics to the streets of Bethlehem. But if he had looked hard enough, he would have noticed something different about this particular nun. Not only were people following her around town, pleading for her to visit some sickly relative, but there was also something special about her aura and the intensity of her gaze. Her eyes seemed to look right through you, as if focused on some other place beyond the world seen by ordinary people. Some even claimed they had seen her bathed in a white light as she made her way around, incessantly thumbing those prayer beads as she went.

CHAPTER 18

OF THE RESURRECTION OF JUBRAIL DABDOUB

FROM HIS VANTAGE POINT ON the ceiling, Jubrail could see his family gathered around his lifeless body. There was Mariam, his wife, still clutching his limp hand, wailing uncontrollably as his eldest son Yousef struggled to hold her up. His brother Mikhail stood sobbing next to the priest, his head bowed, tarbush held tight to his chest. Meanwhile, his sister Sara was frantically ripping apart her dress in an astonishing outburst of physical strength. Later she would sew up that tear with wide stitches to evidence her mourning.[1]

How long had he been hovering there on the ceiling? He tried to focus his thoughts but could only conjure sporadic fragments of the last few days. Franji doctors coming and going, the word *typhoid* murmured in hushed tones, foul-tasting potions, the sound of Mariam's soothing voice.[2] Above all, the merciless burning of the fever. At one point he had looked up in horror to see his family replaced by a circle of horned jinn, eagerly eyeing his body with fiery eyes.[3] For days he had writhed in and out of consciousness in that sweat-drenched bed. There had been blissful moments when the fever subsided, allowing him to drift into peaceful sleep. But he would quickly awake covered in sweat, the fever more powerful than ever.

"Huwadha hamalu Allahi aladhi yarfaʻu khatiyyata al-ʻalimi."
Behold the Lamb of God who takes away the sins of the world.
The words of Abuna Francis drifted up to the ceiling. Jubrail watched

as the priest hurried through the last rites, struggling to be heard over the wails and sobs.

"Tubaa lil-madʿuwina ila ʿashaʾ ʿursi al-kharufi"
Blessed are those called to the marriage supper of the Lamb.[4]

As the voices below became more distant, Jubrail turned sideways and saw a dark cave open before him. In the same moment he felt the beating and the icy shadow of a pair of enormous wings.[5] Hovering at the cave entrance was a cloaked figure, feathered wings outstretched behind him. Jubrail recognized him as Azrael, angel of death.[6]

"Name?" It was difficult to make out the angel's face under the hood he was wearing. In his left hand he held a scroll with what seemed like a long list of names.[7]

Jubrail opened his mouth but found to his surprise no words would come out.

Azrael let out a sigh and relaxed his wings. "Look, there's no point protesting. I'm just the messenger, acting on instruction from the Lord of the two worlds. You'll have to come with me."[8]

Powerless to resist, Jubrail began to float across the room, following Azrael toward the cave. Looking up as he approached the entrance, he realized he was at the foot of Wadi al-Nar, that great "valley of fire" a few miles to the northeast of Bethlehem where all manner of terrible jinn were said to live in a network of underground tunnels.

Gliding inside the cave, he saw thousands of candles burning on the floor.[9] Above them, a series of images began to flicker before him. Initially they made no sense: a church standing on a cobbled street of giant rosary beads, an enormous wheel spinning high above a white city, a woman's head topped with a crown of spikes. Slowly he realized they were memories, spinning around him like a kaleidoscope, each image merging into the next. He looked closer and saw himself as a young boy, running down to Wadi al-Jamal with Elias, clasping his slingshot as he went. He could see Ammo Hanna sitting out on the riwaq of Hosh Dabdoub gesticulating wildly with his hands. There was his father, old Yousef, bent over one of his mother-of-pearl carvings, painstakingly inscribing the words *Terra Santa* onto the back of the shell.[10]

Turning around, Jubrail found himself looking out over the stern of a ship, the port of Manila looming into view. Casco boats darting all around, he followed the Pasig River upstream as far as Calle del Rosario, where he had once sold his wares as a young man. He looked around, curious to locate his old shop after all these years, but found the memory merging into a new one, this time from the top of the Tour Eiffel, looking down at tiny figures making their way around the exhibition grounds below. Raising his gaze toward the outer edges of the city, he saw his wife, Mariam, playing with his infant daughter, Wardeh, in the garden of a suburban villa. Confused as to why they would be in Paris, he reached out to caress his daughter. The young girl looked up at him and let out a shriek, backing away as she did so.

"Ma tibkeesh habibti, don't cry," Mariam comforted her. "This is your baba."

Jubrail felt a surge of remorse as he saw the sum total of his life laid bare. He had spent so much time away from home that his own daughter did not recognize him. Not only that, but his travels were paving the way for his wife and daughter to move abroad and leave Bethlehem forever.

"Allah yusamihni. I have failed my family!" he cried out, not sure if anyone could hear him.

He was spinning uncontrollably around the cave now, images hurtling past as he went. There was the shop he and Mikhail had founded on Rue Saulnier. The shop that had brought them so much wealth and so much time away from Bethlehem. Standing outside the shop holding a string of rosary beads was a young boy of perhaps fifteen or sixteen years old. Jubrail strained to get a closer look and realized with a gasp it was his brother Murqus, frozen in time at the age of his death. He braced himself for those sunken eyes that had haunted him his entire life, but to his amazement he found that they had been restored to their normal state, looking as they did before the onset of the dreaded cholera.

"Akhoui, I've been waiting for you," Murqus smiled at him.

Jubrail stared at him, still unable to utter any words.

Murqus held his beads out to Jubrail. "Take these, my brother, and turn back. You still have much work to do."

Jubrail took the beads and turned around. The entrance to the cave where he had come in was now bathed in a brilliant white light. In the light he could make out the silhouette of a woman emerging, her hand outstretched toward him. Instinctively he handed her the rosary beads that were still in his hand, and she dipped them into the cup of water she held.

"It is not your time yet," she whispered softly, and sprinkled some drops onto his forehead.

While Jubrail had been levitating on the ceiling, a new delegation had slipped quietly into the room. Three nuns dressed in dark blue habits, their long veils covering tightly fitted coifs, now stood by the bed fingering their rosary beads as they offered prayers to the Virgin.

"It is good so many people are gathered here," one of them muttered to her companion.

"Let us hope the sickness the jinn have brought upon this man can be cast out and diffused among the onlookers."[11]

"Can't you see he's already dead?" screamed Jubrail's sister Sara as she tore her way through her dress.

"I'm afraid our work is done here, Sisters," said the priest, putting his cross back into his satchel with a long sigh.

The third nun now stepped forward, having previously been kneeling in prayer. She placed her hand on the dead man's forehead and stood motionless for several seconds.

Everyone in the room stopped their sobbing and stared at the nun as she leaned forward and whispered in the corpse's ear: "It is not your time yet."

Dipping her rosary beads into a cup of water by the bedside, she began to sprinkle drops on Jubrail's face, chanting a series of Hail Marys as she did so.

"Al-salam ʿalayki, ya Mariam ya mumtiʾalat niʿmah, al-rabb maʿik."
Hail Mary, full of grace, the Lord is with thee.
"Mubarakah anti fi al-nisaaʾ wa-mubarakah thamarat batnik Yasuʿ."
Blessed art thou among women, and blessed is the fruit of thy womb, Jesus.[12]

To everybody's astonishment signs of color were returning to Jubrail's face, and he seemed to be struggling for breath.

"Please," Marie-Alphonsine whispered, "bring him something to eat."

Mariam rushed to the kitchen and came back with a pot of quince jam, which they began to feed gently into Jubrail's mouth. To cries of joy from the onlookers, Jubrail swallowed as the jam passed into his mouth. Barely discernible, but a swallow nonetheless.[13]

"Ya rabb, he's alive!" Sara cried, hugging Mariam in joyous disbelief, her dress in rags around her.

A narrow slit opened at the bottom of Jubrail's closed eyelids. Mikhail dropped to his knees and began sobbing words of gratitude to the Virgin.[14]

Jubrail, eyes open now, looked around him in confusion. Was he dreaming? Where was the woman with the outstretched hand? And where was Murqus? It had seemed like a lifetime had passed since he had followed

Azrael into the tunnel and journeyed into his past. Or had it been just a split second? The only thing he knew for sure was that the Virgin had beckoned him back, restoring him to life so he could fulfill his mission in this world.

Like a modern-day Lazarus, Jubrail had been restored to full health and would go on to live another twenty-two healthy years. From the day of his resurrection onward, he gained a renewed sense of purpose, focusing his energies on maintaining the family base in Bethlehem. He would still travel to Paris from time to time to keep an eye on the shop, but for the first time in thirty years Bethlehem became his home. He made donations to the municipality to carry out improvements around the town, he performed his own renovations on Hosh Dabdoub so the family could live more comfortably together, he spent long hours playing with his daughter, Wardeh, on the terrace, and he trained his younger son, Yousef, to run the family business, teaching him bookkeeping in his father's old office. Eventually he and his brother Mikhail would build their own pink-stone palaces on Hebron Road, standing just a few paces apart, proclaiming the family's combined wealth and providing more space than his sons and daughters would ever need.

Everything Jubrail did in those days was designed to ensure the family remained in Bethlehem. He and his brother Mikhail allowed their elder sons to spend stints running the shop in Paris, but they ran a rotation system where the sons would always be called back after a few months lest they become too acclimated to the franji lifestyle. Jubrail became obsessed with the dangers of living abroad, constantly admonishing his children for any sign they might be planning to relocate to Europe or Amerka. When they pointed out he had spent most of his life overseas, he would quickly retort:

"Ah yes, but I always knew where my home was, and I never dreamed of allowing the women of the family to join me. The shameful customs of Amerka would ruin them!"

Mariam always maintained his incessant pressure would end up pushing their children away. Besides, she would say, half of the Bethlehem khawajas were now living in Amerka with their wives and children. Why should the Dabdoubs be any different?

"Ya mara, this family will always remain in Bayt Lahm!" would come the reply each time, Jubrail banging his fist on the table.

Everybody remarked how Jubrail had changed since his resurrection. He had always been a pious man, but now he prayed more intensely and more zealously than ever before, always focusing his prayers on the Virgin. Back on that fateful day in 1909, he had asked the nun what he could do to repay her. Money was no object, he told her. He could give her a house, a salary, anything she wanted.

"All I wish for, ya khawaja, is that you pray and give thanks to the Virgin every day."[15]

Nobody knew it at the time, but Jubrail's resurrection would be the last of Marie-Alphonsine's miracles. Just a few weeks later she was recalled by her superiors to Jerusalem after fifteen years of service in the sacred town of the Messiah's birth. She lived out the rest of her days in quiet solitude, first in al-Quds, and then finally back in her family's old summer house in Ein Karem, where the presence of the Virgin's favorite spring meant she was never far from her Holy Mother.[16]

She died in a state of sublime peace on the twenty-fifth day of Adhar in the year 1927, reciting the Rosary with her last breath, having fittingly reached the mystery of the Virgin's assumption at the moment of her departure.[17] It was the day of Eid al-Bishara, the feast celebrating the announcement made by the angel Jubrail that the Virgin would give birth to her holy child.

It was only when Marie-Alphonsine's notebooks were discovered upon her death that the Sisters of the Rosary realized she had been ordained with a divine mission, just like the Virgin before her. The sisters had always assumed their priest and mentor, Abouna Yousef, was the founder of their order. Now the truth was revealed in the notebooks: Marie-Alphonsine was a saint who had received direct instructions from the Virgin to establish and lead the order. But she had been rightly cautious to guard this information. When the notebooks were discovered, a bitter war broke out among the sisters. Those of the so-called Nazarene faction would entertain no suggestion that Abouna Yousef was not their founder and quickly set about burning the notebooks. Luckily, for the sake of posterity and the science of history, the charred pages had already been faithfully transcribed by a group of Marie-Alphonsine's followers, as directed by her sister Hanneh. Through these blessed facsimiles, knowledge of the diminutive nun's saintly nature was finally revealed to the world.[18]

In her life experience, Marie-Alphonsine could not have been further apart from the merchants of Bethlehem. She had spent her life in poverty, dedicating herself to the most destitute girls of Palestine, having sworn to her father she would never leave the country. They, by contrast, had spent their lives traveling the world with the aim of accumulating vast fortunes. But despite their differences, their lives collided in those heady days of the new century in ways that neither could have predicted. They were the two forces that nourished Bethlehem's age of miracles, each reliant upon the other. Just as the Rosary Sisters could only maintain their presence in Bethlehem with the support of the khawajas, so too was the khawajas' economic miracle based on the sanctity of their hometown, embodied in the humble figure of Marie-Alphonsine. The sale of all those thousands of rosary beads in every corner of the earth could only be sustained by the redemptive power of Marie-Alphonsine's own beads and the bond with the Holy Virgin they engendered.

Marie-Alphonsine had chosen the path of modesty and poverty where others had pursued celebrity and wealth. Her departure from Bethlehem signaled the end of the time of miracles: the closing of an era where piety and commerce had been held in perfect balance. During her fifteen years of living in Bethlehem she had never found a permanent home, nor did she own any earthly possession except the treasured beads that could always be seen hanging from her woolen belt. All her life, she took pleasure from these physical hardships, reveling in a suffering that only brought her closer to the Virgin.

"Thank you to our beloved mother, who descended and allowed us to partake in her suffering and presence in that town in a humble manger for her abode," read the closing words of her secret notebooks. "Oh, how sweet our life of suffering and poverty. How sweet to partake in the poverty of the Holy Family."[19]

EPILOGUE

BETHLEHEM, 26 AYYAR, 1931

From his bed, Jubrail can hear the sound of motor cars. The fearsome contraptions come hurtling down Hebron Road in a whir of clanging metal and hissing pistons, stirring up clouds of dust as they pass the house. There was a time when the presence of those machines in Bethlehem would have filled him with excitement and wonder. Now they only seem to grate on his nerves. Their growling engines sound like the rumble of thunder announcing the imminent arrival of a storm. He should be used to them. Only a few weeks ago he was in Paris, where every type of mechanical vehicle screeches and grinds its way through the streets. But here in Bethlehem? Tiny Bethlehem, where, in the days of his childhood, no sound other than the ringing of church bells and the muezzin's call to prayer punctuated the stillness of the terraced valleys . . .

"Wake up, Baba, I brought you coffee." His eldest son, Bishara, throws open the shutters. Sunlight comes flooding into the room, revealing geometric patterns weaving their way across the floor.

"Istanbul's finest," Jubrail mutters, remembering the team of artisans he hired back in 1922 to tile the floors.[1] In those days he was looking forward to a glorious retirement, having finally built his own pink-stone mansion to mark his legacy in Bethlehem.

"I need the account books, Baba." Bishara rudely interrupts Jubrail's train of thought. "The lawyer's coming from Jerusalem today to do the bankruptcy evaluation."

Jubrail groans as the indignities of the past few weeks come rushing back. The pain in his chest tightens as he runs through the trauma of seeing his life's work dismantled before his own eyes.

It all started with the crash. From his office in Paris, he received word of the panic gripping the bankers and traders of New York, that great metropolis where he had once lived. Initially he had thought they could withstand the downturn. The French bourse did not plummet as rapidly as in other European countries. But the Paris office was just one center within a global network of clients, suppliers, and distribution partners. The whole business was now predicated on supplying products on credit to the Bethlehem merchants in Central and South America—not only the family's famous Holy Land carvings, but also fabrics, jewelry, glasses, and all manner of other goods produced in Europe and the United States.

If there were two countries where they could ill afford to have their credit lines cut, it was Chile and Bolivia. Yet it was those very two countries that had been the worst affected by the New York crash.[2] In Chile there were more Bethlehemites than anywhere in the world, included among them Jubrail's nephews Zacharia and Khalil Abu-Fheleh, who had opened stores in Santiago supplied by the warehouse in Paris. Bolivia, meanwhile, hosted various outlets of the Dabdoub business, especially in the mountain-ringed city of Cochabamba, where Jubrail's other nephews Anton and Yousef (sons of his younger brother Ibrahim), along with Isa and Yousef (sons of his eldest brother Hanna) had long since set up shop.

Not only did the Bethlehem businesses in those countries see local markets for their products collapse, they were also prevented from transferring their assets out, as a freeze was placed on foreign money transfers.[3] In the space of a few months, virtually all the Dabdoubs' trade between the Paris office and Amerka came to a halt. Frantically had Jubrail sent out letters and telegrams to their debtors in Santiago and Cochabamba, pleading for them to pay back what they had borrowed. But no replies came. Realizing the gravity of the situation, he began selling off all but the most essential assets. The apartments and the shops in Paris, even the orange groves in Jaffa—all had to go in a desperate bid to ward off their own creditors.[4]

The Dabdoubs are not alone in the desperation of their plight. One by one, the business empires built by the Bethlehem families have gone into liquidation. Over the past few weeks, Jubrail has witnessed scenes he would never have believed if he not seen them with his own eyes. Suleiman Jacir, once the richest and most revered of all Bethlehem's merchants, is being subjected to daily humiliations. Just last week Jubrail saw a woman slap him in the face in full public view on Wadi Ma'ali street, screaming at him that his bankruptcy had destroyed her family.[5] Oh, the indignity! Suleiman's family firm, Suleiman Jacir et Frères, was the nearest thing Bethlehem had to a local bank. It not only lent money to merchants but also stored it for them. Suleiman had amassed a fortune through his multiple businesses in France, Haiti, the Philippines, Chile, and the United States. Suleiman, Jubrail, and his brothers had worked closely for decades, partnering in several business ventures and marrying into each other's families. But the crash had sent the whole edifice crumbling, and now there were dozens of merchants in Bethlehem whose livelihoods depended on getting their money back from Suleiman Jacir et Frères.

The day before Suleiman's humiliation in Wadi Ma'ali, an angry mob had gathered around his mighty mansion, just a short distance down Hebron Road from Jubrail's house. They had demanded he repay what they owe him or else face retribution. When the British police had arrived, they immediately saw the potential for violence to erupt and decided to cart poor Suleiman off to Jerusalem to stand trial. It was only through the hard work of Jubrail's nephew-in-law, Issa Basil al-Bandak, that Suleiman had been saved the indignity of a prison sentence. Issa was Bethlehem's most energetic political activist and a champion of the Palestinian Arab struggle against Zionism. His connections with the nationalist leaders in Jerusalem meant he had been able to lobby the mayor there, Raghib al-Nashashibi. Suleiman had been released, but he still had to face the anger of his own people in Bethlehem.[6]

Even Suleiman Jacir's mighty mansion, once a proud symbol of Bethlehem's economic miracle, is being parceled up and sold off at bargain prices. Local merchants, previously of lesser standing, are now competing with franji investors in the scramble to profit from the disintegration of the Jacir empire. The latest to benefit is Hanna Kawwas, returned from Honduras, which escaped the crash relatively lightly. He has already bought shares in the Hirmas mansion, another of Bethlehem's once opulent palaces that has fallen on hard times. Now he has turned his attention to the Jacir palace. People say he is preparing to purchase a one-third share in Suleiman's former abode.[7] How the wheel of fortune turns.

"Is there any good news, Bishara?" Jubrail looks at his son and grimaces. His chest pains are worsening.

"Well, we still have the rent from Hosh Dabdoub," Bishara replies. "But we might have to sell that too to raise enough capital to pay off the debts."

"Abadan, abadan!" Jubrail cries out. Never will he allow the sale of the house of his birth, the cradle of the family business. These days they rent it out to poorer residents—mostly Syriac families that fled Anatolia during the Great War and ended up in Bethlehem. No longer a single household, the hosh has been parceled up into small apartments. The first thing Jubrail did when he arrived back in Bethlehem was pay a visit to the house. Passing through the rusting arched doorway that once proudly bore the insignia of the Dabdoub family shop, he was shocked to find whole families crammed into each room. Where in the past, notable guests from far and wide were served their dinner on silver platters, now the only guests are the chickens and goats that peck at weeds growing in the courtyard.[8]

"It was all so straightforward in the early days," Jubrail begins to reminisce. "Everywhere we traveled, the money kept rolling in. The saints looked kindly on us back then."

Bishara sighs and begins searching for the account books himself. Papers are strewn around the room, mixed with half-opened boxes of unsold merchandise—the result of Jubrail's frantic attempts to track down distant debtors.

"But we always came back," Jubrail continues unperturbed. "We knew our home was in Bethlehem, in the hosh. Not like you lot—raising children all over the world. Soon there'll be no Dabdoubs left here!"

In the past few years, Jubrail has watched his fears become reality. His younger son Yousef is permanently settled in France, where his wife, Afifeh, is now pregnant with their third child. His only daughter, Wardeh, left Bethlehem just a few months ago to start a new life in El Salvador with her husband, Jadallah Batarseh.[9] In the Bolivian city of Cochabamba, he is told, there are now dozens of Dabdoubs. The children of his sister Miladeh recently settled in a Colombian town named San José de Cúcuta. Where will it end? Even Bishara is making noise about joining his cousins in Chile.[10]

"Baba, did we keep accounts during the war years?" Bishara is still rummaging through papers. He spent most of the war in an Ottoman labor battalion and has no idea if there are any books from that period.

"You know, Marie-Alphonsine predicted the whole thing," Jubrail blurts out.

"Predicted what?" Bishara asks, not really listening.

"The war. She saw it coming forty years in advance."

"It wouldn't surprise me. If she could bring you back from the dead, I'm sure she could predict a war."

"Perhaps it was just as well she kept the vision to herself" Jubrail replies. "People would have thought she was crazy if she had told them they'd be sifting through donkey dung in the hope of finding a stray piece of barley to eat."[11]

Jubrail's mind drifts back to that day in the spring of 1915. At first people thought it was a huge rain cloud, making its way over from Jericho to give them a welcome dumping before the dry summer months began. As the cloud drew nearer, they realized to their horror it consisted of billions of ravenous insects come to devour their crops. On top of all the hardship of the war—the closure of ports; the shutting down of banks, newspapers, and postal systems; the food shortages; forced conscription—the Bethlehemites now had to watch as every crop they had planted was decimated, terrace by terrace, by those insatiable locusts.[12]

Jubrail lived through it all. The fear, the starvation, the paralysis of their businesses. Too old to be recruited into the army, he had been rounded up with the other elderly men in the town to work as a garbage collector. Forced to walk through the streets of Bethlehem and Jerusalem shouting "Who has any rubbish?" while the women wept from their windows. He had never felt so humiliated.[13] His daughter, Wardeh, was just eleven years old. What must she have thought, watching her father reduced to such a state? All the grandiose plans he had been hatching—the building of a new mansion in Bethlehem, the expansion of the shop in Paris—had to be put on hold while he collected garbage and struggled to survive. At least he had made it to the end of the war alive. His eldest sister, Mariam, passed away in the spring of 1916, her seventy-year-old body one of many that succumbed to the rampant disease and famine.

"And to think we went through it all just to suffer a new series of calamities," Jubrail mutters.

Bishara has found the books and is making his way out of the house to meet the lawyer.

"I have to go, Baba. I'll be back this afternoon. Sara has come to look after you."

Jubrail looks up at his sister as she sits by the bed and places a wet cloth over his forehead. Twice a widow, she is dressed permanently in black these days, her hair tucked neatly behind her headscarf.

"What's all this talk of calamities? You need to rest now, akhoui," Sara says softly.

Jubrail remembers the long black hair that once flowed freely down her back, left uncut for twelve years as a gesture of thanks to the prophet Ibrahim and his wife, Sara, for bringing her a new child after the death of her first husband.[14]

His thoughts are becoming increasingly disjointed. As the fever worsens, he lets out incoherent cries, interspersed with desperate pleas to the saints.

"Forgive us, nabi Ibrahim. Ya rab, have mercy on us!"

Sara watches over him, helpless to relieve his suffering. She knows it will not be long now. Having seen him die once before, she recognizes the signs.

How strange to see him like this, Sara thinks. For years, Jubrail and their elder brother Mikhail were the dominant forces in her family, directing business operations and casting final judgment over family affairs. With Mikhail passing away last year, Jubrail is the last vestige of that old world of patriarchal authority. Already a new order has arisen, less centralized, more accommodating of individual choice.

Sara recalls when her sons Yousef and Daoud first came back from Amerka after the war. Jubrail had done everything in his power to make them stay, arranging marriages for them with well-respected Tarajmeh families. These were the same sons that had been forcibly separated from Sara after the death of her first husband and placed in the custody of her brother-in-law, Ibrahim, only later to rebel against him by fleeing to Mexico.[15] Now returned to Bethlehem, it had quickly become apparent that they had grown accustomed to doing things their own way in Amerka and would not yield to Jubrail's authority. The elder son, Yousef, had quickly disappeared back to Mexico with his new bride, Hilweh D'ek. Daoud, meanwhile, had vehemently opposed the marriage Jubrail had arranged with his first cousin Marinette. He had fallen in love with a local Orthodox girl, Jamileh Freij. During the war, this Jamileh had been dispatched to Peru at the age of thirteen to marry a Bethlehemite there, only for the journey to be cut short when her chaperone (an uncle from Bethlehem) was caught at the Jaffa docks and conscripted into the Ottoman army. According to Jubrail, the story was a sign from the heavens: not only a warning against marrying an Orthodox girl but also a declaration of the folly of sending women abroad. Young Daoud, however, had other ideas and had soon boarded a ship to Mexico with the young Jamileh.[16]

Looking back now, Sara can see how the authority of the old patriarchs was already crumbling back then. Jubrail and Mikhail did their best to ensure the family remained rooted in Bethlehem, but they were fighting a losing battle. Each of them built his own pink-stone mansion, just a stone's throw apart on Hebron Road, standing as the equal of any merchant palace in town. So proud was Jubrail of his new house when it was completed in 1923 that he had his name engraved in Arabic calligraphy above a stone cross over the front door, as well as in Latin letters on the wrought-iron gates on the road. Like the old Hosh Dabdoub, only a single story could be seen from the road, but to the rear a more grandiose structure revealed itself, consisting of two floors with balustraded balconies looking out across the gardens toward Beit Jala in the west.[17]

At first, the new house was full of people. Guests were entertained in the drawing room while relatives visiting from abroad were hosted in the spare bedrooms. Jubrail persuaded Bishara to stay there during the summer months with his wife and two daughters, inhabiting the lower floor while Jubrail and Mariam lived on the upper level. There was still ample room to accommodate his other son, Yousef, on his visits from Paris. During those times, Jubrail would take his two sons for walks among the olive groves to the rear of the house and recount legends of how the Virgin had once commanded a rock to split open in those very fields, or how Mar Niqula had lived for years in a nearby cave to escape Roman persecution.[18]

"The Amerkan think Mar Niqula is one of their own," Jubrail would giggle. "They call him Santa Claus and worship him during the Christmas feast days." Then he would turn to his sons and fix them with a more serious gaze. "This land is your land, ya awladi, never forget it. One day you'll look out on these fields with your own sons and tell them these same stories."

Watching him now, Sara is not so sure. The house is empty, save for Mariam downstairs, who is mixing remedies from myrtle leaves and the roots of mallow bindweed she hopes will cure her husband's sickness.[19] They have even had to dismiss the maid, so desperate is the state of the family finances. Sara, too, is making plans to leave. She does not have the heart to tell Jubrail, but she has decided to live out her last days in Mexico with her beloved sons. She has lived apart from them for too long, and there is nothing in Bethlehem for her now. Poor Mariam, she thinks. Soon it will be just her in the house. All that space and no one to share it with.[20]

Another motorcar hurtles down Hebron Road, waking Jubrail from his troubled sleep. He bolts upright, sweat pouring from his forehead.

"Wala yhimmak," Sara soothes him. "It was just a car, akhoui, just a car."

Sara coaxes him back into a reclined position, and Jubrail retreats into his thoughts, murmuring something about cars. He is remembering the day Hanna Mansour brought the first motor car to Bethlehem—a shiny white Berliet from France.[21] That was at the beginning of the century, when no one in Bethlehem had ever set eyes on such a thing. The old men sitting in Bab al-Dayr stared in disbelief as the machine came spluttering and bumping into view, plumes of black smoke billowing out from behind it. Some of the men simply got up and ran, crying out in terror that al-Shaytan had arrived in Bethlehem. Their wives later remarked that they had not seen them run so fast since the time the Egyptian troops marched into town to recruit young men into Ibrahim Pasha's army.

Jubrail lets out a burst of laughter, lost in his memories. Sara looks at him, wondering what is going through his mind. Her gaze shifts to the window and she sees an old man leading a donkey down Hebron Road with a boy seated on top. They have probably come from one of the surrounding villages—Battir, perhaps, or al-Walaja—to sell their family's produce at the new market. Suddenly Bishara comes into view, rushing past the donkey with papers tucked under his arm, his franji suit contrasting with the old man's abayeh. Sara lets out a gasp when she sees a priest walking behind Bishara, struggling to keep up.

"Wake up, Jubrail," she tells her brother, hurriedly rearranging the bedsheets. "Bishara has come back to see you."

But Jubrail has already begun his ascent. Rising out of his own body he looks down on Sara and then loses sight of her as he drifts through the ceiling and out across the rooftops of Bethlehem. Eastward he flies, over the fortresslike church, past the village of Beit Sahour and out toward the barren hills of the Wilderness. When he reaches the small settlement of Ubeidiya, he turns northward at the Monastery of Theodosius and descends into the abyss of Wadi al-Nar. At the bottom of the valley, at the entrance to one of the caves, a familiar winged figure awaits him, scroll in hand.

Azrael looks down at his list. "Jubrail Yousef Hanna Yousef Hanna Mikhail Dabdoub?"

"Hayutni!" Jubrail answers proudly in the affirmative at the pronouncement of his ancestral lineage. A long and illustrious line of little bears, stretching all the way back to Hanna, son of Mikhail, born in Bethlehem in 1682.

"You again?" Azrael throws off his hood to reveal a long mane of black hair and a surprisingly friendly face, green eyes shining brightly at Jubrail. He seems pleased to see him. "Mashallah, I remember you from last time! A case of mistaken identity if I recall correctly. We thought we had you on the list, only for the Virgin to inform us otherwise. Guess it just wasn't your time."

"Perhaps she'll come for me again?" Jubrail asks hopefully. "I still have work to do, you see. My business is in a difficult spot. I can't leave my children like this. I need to . . . it just doesn't feel . . ." his voice trails off as he notices Azrael chuckling to himself.

"You're on the list, my friend, no doubt about it. When it's your time, it's your time."

"But what about before? The Virgin came for me."

"Ah, that was different. Back then those things happened all the time, especially around here. The list would change from one day to the next. We used to get all sorts of saints, mystics, and fakirs turning up at the last moment. Doesn't seem to happen anymore. If you're on the list, that's it."

"Have the saints forgotten about us Bethlehemites?" Jubrail ruminates. "They used to keep us safe on our journeys and bless our businesses with success. I remember how common miracles seemed back then. Healing the sick, restoring sight to the blind. The miracle of the fortunes we made—great palaces appearing on the streets of our humble village!" His face clouds over as his mind returns to the struggles of the past year and a half. "Ya 'Adhra, ya Khadr, what did we do to lose your favor? If only Marie-Alphonsine were still with us!"

Azrael lets out a sigh. "Come on, let's get moving. I've work to do."

Powerless to resist, Jubrail floats into the cave behind him. As his eyes adjust to the darkness, he sees the thousands of candles burning on the cave floor. Azrael points to one that has burned right down to the stub, barely flickering.[22] "This is your candle," he says.

So this is how it ends, Jubrail thinks to himself. Taken from his family, his beloved Bethlehem, in the midst of a humiliating business collapse while the British and the Zionists set about dividing up the country. In years to come, will people even know that Bethlehem was once the most prosperous and dynamic town in all Palestine? A town that held the entire world in its gaze; where any number of impossible occurrences could happen daily on its hallowed streets. Will they ever believe that for a few short decades tiny Bethlehem was the scene of such wondrous miracles?

AUTHOR'S COMMENTARY

IN ITS DESIRE TO EXPLORE the porous boundaries between history and fiction, this book sits somewhere in the gray areas of historical writing. One the one hand, trying to write a coherent narrative of Jubrail's journeys around the world required the use of historical imagination. In many cases, the mysterious silences in his life could not be populated with direct empirical evidence. Imitating techniques developed in fictional writing and oral cultures of storytelling, the book consists of scenes from Jubrail's life that are more suggestive of themes and moods than they are exact reproductions.

On the other hand, the narrative is not one conjured from thin air. As with most creative writing, the text is based on real experiences, events, and material evidence woven together from disparate sources into a single narrative. The book is ultimately the work of a historian trained in the methods of empirical academic research. There is hardly a line in the book that is not based on some kind of wider contextual evidence gleaned from over a decade of research carried out in Bethlehem and the various locations to which the Bethlehemite merchants traveled.

This combination of imaginative writing and source-based research requires some further elaboration if the wider goals of the project are to be conveyed. Safely tucked away here at the back of the book so as not to break the flow of the story, this commentary attempts such an explanation: first, in terms of writing techniques, and second, through a more detailed discussion of the source materials.

WRITING PALESTINIAN HISTORY IN A MAGICAL REALIST KEY

An interest in exploring linkages between form and historical meaning sits at the heart of this book. For those of us who deal in the written word, the basic form our work usually takes is that of a narrative: in a essence, a story that develops through familiar plot structures to convey an understanding of some element of past existence. Famously, Hayden White thought narrative so fundamental to the practice of history that he deemed it "a metacode, a human universal on the basis of which transcultural messages about the nature of a shared reality can be transmitted."[1]

Once we embrace storytelling as an essential part of doing history, the questions quickly arise: Which type of story are we telling, and how should that story be constructed? Among the endless array of answers these questions could elicit, one approach has been particularly instructive for this book: the idea that the styles of writing we employ can serve as commentaries on the history itself.

Walter Benjamin was an early exponent of the idea. In his unfinished *Arcades Project* (first conceived in 1927), he tested out a type of writing he called "montage": a technique designed to shine light on life in the age of mechanical reproduction. By juxtaposing long citations with passages of commentary devoid of the historian's explanatory narrative, he was able to convey the fragmentary nature of life under modern capitalism while simultaneously asserting a philosophy of history that saw the historian as reconstructing "flashes" of images from a film roll that has already been played. The point, for Benjamin, was that writing style should reflect subject matter and that this was the most effective way to produce historical meaning: "Method of this project: literary montage. I needn't say anything. Merely show."[2]

Since Benjamin, numerous writers have experimented with different forms of narrative as a way of reflecting on the past. As White once quipped, "If you're going to accept history is an art form, why not make it a *modern* art form?"[3] Various scholars of literature, historical anthropology, and the emerging field of literary anthropology have taken up White's call, providing a rich body of material for exploring the value of creative writing as a route into different understandings of past experience.[4] Those who identify as unhyphenated historians have been a little more reluctant. There are many notable exceptions—the works of Natalie Zemon Davis, Jonathan

Walker, and Sarah Knott have been particularly inspiring for this project—but they remain exceptions within a field that at times seems to be defined by its commitment to a detached, "realist" form of writing.[5]

As with so many aspects of this book, the discovery of Marie-Alphonsine's miraculous salvation of Jubrail in 1909 precipitated a turning point in my own approach to writing. Pondering for the first time Jubrail's faith and piety, I wrote draft chapters and conference presentations about the miracle that explored the nun's relationship with Jubrail and his fellow Bethlehemite merchants. To develop my ideas, I employed terminology borrowed from the anthropology of gift exchange and reciprocity, as well as the sociology of religion and clientelism. I rationalized the merchants' relationship with Marie-Alphonsine as a form of patronage under which the nun's fledgling order received protection and economic support in exchange for the sisters' endorsement and approval of the merchants' profit-making enterprises.

A nagging feeling persisted that something fundamental was missing. The available evidence suggested that all those present at the miracle had understood it as exactly that: the product of divine intervention elicited by Marie-Alphonsine's extreme piety and devotion to the Rosary. In my focus on client-patron relationships and the acquisition of social capital, I was washing over the understandings and assumptions of the historical protagonists themselves. Perhaps the most interesting part of the whole event—the moment where the laws of physics had been suspended—was curiously absent from my writing. As Robert Shanafelt writes in his study of anthropological approaches to miracles, "Our willingness to pass over this 'poof' to consider the results may simply be an example of an overriding focus and obsession with the products of our own concerns."[6]

I began to wonder how I might reconstruct the event in a different way. Slowly, I started to write in a different register, taking for granted that a supernatural event had occurred that day. In the spirit of those anthropologists who embraced the "ontological turn," I forced myself to accept that people experience reality in different ways because they inhabit very different worlds that cannot be explained in terms of universally intelligible symbols.[7] Keeping in mind Eduardo Viveiros de Castro's idea of "a universe peopled by different types of subjective agencies," I returned to the miracle with renewed focus on the "poof factor."[8] It was time to take at face value the assumptions of Ottoman-era Bethlehemites: Marie-Alphonsine was able to invoke the intervention of the Virgin Mary by praying the Rosary, thus bringing Jubrail back from the dead. Full stop. "I needn't say anything. Merely show."

While this seemed like a worthy endeavor, a host of practical and methodological problems quickly presented themselves. The reality is that very few historical sources exist that provide any detail on the subjective agency of people of Jubrail's generation, especially when it comes to their belief in the supernatural. Descriptions abound of the religious habits of Palestinians in the nineteenth century, but few are written by the local people themselves, least of all by the merchants of Bethlehem, a group not prone to autoethnography. Marie-Alphonsine's account of the miracle is elusively brief and matter-of-fact. This in itself seemed revealing of the expectedness of such divine interventions, but trying to write a more detailed description from such fleeting sources would require me to think beyond the empirically verifiable.

There are various responses available to the historian faced with gaps in the sources. Natalie Zemon Davis, for example, explains her recourse to the conditional and the speculative—"would have," "may have," "was likely to have"—in her reconstruction of the life of a sixteenth-century Andalusi diplomat and scholar who traversed the boundaries between Christian Europe and Muslim North Africa.[9] Bryant Simon, meanwhile, presents four different versions of the same story to explore the uncertainties concerning the lynching of two African American men in South Carolina in 1912.[10]

In the case of Jubrail Dabdoub and the merchants of Bethlehem, the pull of sustaining an unbroken narrative, free of analytical interruptions, remained strong. Bethlehem in that period was thrust quite suddenly and unexpectedly into a world of global travel and exchange that was surely difficult to process. In the early days, young men would return from six-month journeys to France, Brazil, or the Philippines, carrying with them stories of strange cities, landscapes, people, and animals. How could those listening be sure what was factual and what was embellished, where the border between reality and dreams lay? And if those at the time inhabited a twilight zone between fact and fiction, why should the historian not try to replicate that uncertainty through a particular approach to writing? As Jonathan Walker explains when employing the form of a tarot reading to write the history of a Venetian spy mystery, "I wanted to make *my* artifice obvious in writing about the artifice of stories told by people in the past."[11]

As explained in the introduction, magical realism seemed the literary genre most adept at capturing the sense of wonder and confusion that greeted the Bethlehem merchants on their initial journeys. I began to experiment by writing in an uninterrupted narrative that imitated the style of classical magical realist fiction. The consequences of following this decision through were at first daunting. First, if I were to sustain the narrative throughout the entirety of the book, I would have to relearn how to make an analytical point. I wanted to discuss the gendered nature of Bethlehem's migration, how the early journeys were seen as a rite of passage for a new form of masculinity emerging in the town. I wanted to make big points about Palestinians' role in globalization and the commoditization of religion. But now this would all have to be done through plot structure, characterization, and dialogue, rather than the tried and tested quote-situate-analyze. Gradually, I trusted in the power of the story, choosing to privilege certain plot lines over others to emphasize these broader societal shifts. Most of all, I came to realize that the style of writing could itself act as a commentary on the history. Deliberately writing in a way that inverted expectations of the "normal" and the "supernatural" became a way of reflecting on the arresting nature of the Bethlehemites' sudden exposure to networks of global trade and travel, as well as their grounding in the agrarian religion (to use James Grehan's phrase) of the Palestinian hill country.[12]

In practical terms, this has involved imitating magical realist authors' tendency to portray encounters with capitalist modernity in the language of wonder, enchantment, and absurdity, while interactions with spirits, saints, and the divine are related using more mundane, quotidian language. I have sought to replicate the genre's disruptions of linear time, emphasizing repetition across generations, recurring dreams, and the persistence of ghostly presences. An example of this is in chapter 7, where Jubrail begins to be visited by his deceased brother, Murqus, in his dreams. I was fascinated by the questions brought up by Murqus's death, which was recorded in the Latin Parish Archive on November, 30, 1868, when Murqus was seventeen and Jubrail just eight. How would Jubrail have processed this event at such a young age, especially given that Murqus was surely on the verge of being sent abroad with his elder brothers? I delved into the realm of pure speculation to convey the persistence of these ghostly presences, imagining Jubrail being haunted by a sense of confusion and guilt over his brother's death, not least because Jubrail was now next in line to continue the family's overseas trading missions.

At times I have directly lifted specific passages of literature and reworked them to fit a particular scene. The closing line of chapter 7, for example, adapts a phrase from Gabriel García Marquez's *One Hundred Years of Solitude* concerning the arrival of the first train in Macondo to describe the paradoxical effects of migration to the Americas: "bringing with it so many new certainties and ambiguities, adventures and calamities." Such cases are discussed in the endnotes, citing the specific passage used. But most of the borrowing has been carried out in a more generic fashion—the regular use of "many years later" to disrupt the linear flow of time, or the employment of phrases like "nobody doubted" to describe saintly interventions—producing a text that is deliberately derivative and imitative.

The overall aim, to paraphrase Michael Wood's analysis of magical realism, is to create an atmosphere in which the history appears drunk but the historian sober.[13] Depicting an inebriated history serves the obvious purpose of underlining the tumult gripping Bethlehem in the late nineteenth and early twentieth centuries—and just how bizarre these journeys would have seemed to the townsfolk. The sobriety of the historian, meanwhile, requires further explanation. A common misreading of magical realism is to focus solely on the "magical" part, forgetting that the "real" is at least half the equation. Magical realism is not fantasy or surrealism. Its power lies in its ability to create scenes that are entirely plausible, realistic, and recognizable to readers, rendering the sudden occurrence of "unrealistic" events all the more arresting. This is why, I believe, the genre holds so much potential for historians and why so much magical realist fiction is fundamentally historical. Magical realist authors situate their plotlines in real-life settings that are often constructed in the most intricate detail. Characters are an integral part of their communities, not the outcasts of fantasy novels. Almost invariably, these communities are intimately connected to the domain of spirits, dreams, and magic, and the tone of writing presupposes that the reader shares these values, producing the matter-of-fact, "sober" observer.[14]

This embeddedness in community points to a sense of mysterious collectiveness so often conveyed in magical realist texts, described by Seymour Menton as the preference for a Jungian over Freudian perspective.[15] My knowledge of Jubrail Dabdoub was limited to fragmentary sources that raise more questions than answers, meaning my intention was always to use his life as a route into exploring a wider zeitgeist gripping Bethlehem—a time when miracles of every kind (economic, supernatural, etc.) seemed to be occurring with great frequency. In this sense, my choice of writing style was an attempt to emphasize the collective over the individual—a deliberate move away from constructions of selfhood, biography, and life writing so favored in social and cultural history today. The decision to focus on one person and his wider family was taken for its narrative value—as a tool to probe the relationship between storytelling and history. Jubrail had stood out to me as the best vehicle to explore this relationship—given his early presence in the Philippines, his participation in the world's fairs, and the miracle of his resurrection—but the goal was never to recreate his life in minute detail or somehow "get inside his head." Rather, it was to construct a kind of composite merchant from the outline of his life story in a similar vein to Marjorie Becker's creation of a "composite priest" in her multisided account of the destruction of Christian icons in a 1930s Mexican village.[16]

As I researched the kinds of contextual sources that could help me put together such a figure, I could not help but notice the surprising yet regular intrusion of religious exclamations. "Oh Reader, regard how he of little faith runs his affairs," writes Jubrail's cousin Ibrahim Yuhanna Dabdoub in his unpublished memoir when describing a family feud over unpaid debts. Despite the memoir's exclusive focus on business matters, it is peppered with phrases like "by the grace of Almighty Allah," "only Allah can judge the reasons," and "thanks to the protection of al-Khadr [Saint George]." This is a trend replicated in the few business letters I came across penned by Jubrail himself. "I offer my prayers to God Almighty to endow you and your beloved family with blessings and good health and to facilitate the smooth running of your mercantile affairs," he writes to a business associate in 1930, a year before his final death.[17]

They may have been ruthless business operators, but Jubrail's generation of merchant-migrants took their faith seriously and applied its logic to their economic affairs. I could have written a long analysis of how business and religion are not mutually exclusive historical categories, relating the example of the Bethlehemites to the historiography that challenges the "rational economic actor" model of transnational merchant networks. But having already committed to a narrative-driven approach meant it made more sense to infuse the story with these religious phrases providing jolting reminders that success as a merchant was closely tied to pious conduct and assistance from saints. This has been done this in a number of ways. Leaving certain religious terms untranslated (Allah instead of God, al-Khadr or Mar Jiryes instead of Saint George) serves to convey the extent to which these seemingly cosmopolitan and mostly Catholic merchants were in fact deeply embedded in the Arabo-Islamic cultural landscape of the Palestinian hill country. I felt a need to emphasize the foreignness of nineteenth-century Bethlehem, especially to readers in English who may be easily fooled by the familiarity of Christian religious terms. I then decided to expand this approach to include snippets of colloquial Bethlehemite Arabic in direct speech—a device increasingly used by authors of diasporic fiction—based on the types of phrases I had encountered in the sources. Most prominently, these include the terms *franji* (pl. *faranja*), a word that technically translates to "Franks" but that was commonly used in Bethlehem to denote western Europeans of any sort; and, of course, Amerka, a word term that stands at the heart of the book's narrative, signifying the realm of possibility that lay beyond the known world of the Bethlehemites.

In addition to underlining the constructed nature of my English-language text, these verbal flourishes serve as further commentary on the relationship between storyteller and audience. Not only am I, the historian, telling a story; I am also describing a society saturated with storytelling. This double-layered story-within-a-story is particularly relevant to the sense of awe, confusion, and misunderstanding provoked in Bethlehem by travelers returning from the other side of the world. I imagined returning émigrés holding court in Bab al-Dayr (the town's central square), spinning yarns to impress their listeners. "By the truth of al-Khadr, I went and came back," Jubrail declares in chapter 13, using a common invocation of Saint George, one of the most important local saints in Bethlehem whom the sources frequently mention as providing protection to the town's merchant-migrants. Or in chapter 14, he exclaims "*Ba'īd 'an is-sāmi'īn!*" echoing a common exclamation used in Palestinian oral folk tales to warn the listener that something abhorrent is coming (in this case, a description of the belly dancers at the Chicago World's Fair).

The lines between fact and fiction were easily blurred in these encounters, and the verbal flourishes help underline this. In their seminal work on Palestinian folk tales, Ibrahim Muhawi and Sharif Kanaana emphasize how the *khurāfiyya* format of storytelling combines the magical and the realistic, grounding tales of the supernatural (jinn, ghouls, etc.) in real-life settings.[18] Their gendered distinction between the *khurāfiyya* ("folk" tales told by women) and the *qiṣṣa* (epic stories told by men in the diwan) seems now a little outdated. The memoirs of Bethlehem intellectual and political leader Issa Basil al-Bandak (b. 1891) are replete with memories of his parents' generation involving social gatherings of both men and women at which folktales would be exchanged. These included the "nights of joy" (*layāli al-faraḥ*) where male representatives from all the town's clans (*ḥamā'il*) would listen to poetry recitals and storytelling with their wives and then celebrate with dancing and revelry into the early hours of the morning.[19] Following this more fluid picture of storytelling in Bethlehem, I have deliberately blurred the distinctions between *khurāfiyya* and *qiṣṣa* in this book. But Muhawi and Kanaana's overall point about the *khurāfiyya* not requiring the audience to suspend its disbelief remained useful in writing about Bethlehem, as it closely resembled magical realism's assumption of the reader's credulity. The result, Muhawi and Kanaana argue, is an inherent ambiguity in the Palestinian *khurāfiyya* (are they real? Have they been deliberately embellished?) that mirrors the ambiguity I wished to portray in the tales of travelers returning to Bethlehem, particularly in describing the years of Jubrail's childhood when the first trickle of emigration began. Consider, for example, the writer Jabra Ibrahim al-Jabra's impression of returning émigrés as a child in 1920s Bethlehem: "Did Miquel come from the far side of the world, from Chile, to carry out the will of the demon [*al-mārid*] living in our fig tree?"[20]

At several points in the book, I have imagined travelers' tales being told within the recognized plot structures of the *khurāfiyya*—for example, a young man leaves his home village in search of faraway riches and has to overcome demons and monsters to find a hidden treasure before returning home (particularly evident in chapter 13 when Jubrail returns from the Philippines). At other times it is the audience's response that pulls us back to the local vernaculars of storytelling. Chapter 14, for example, is told from the perspective of inquisitive townsfolk in Bethlehem's central square after Jubrail returns from the world's fair in Chicago in 1893. Their retorts include accusations that Jubrail is a *khurāfa* (teller of fairytales) at points where he is in fact giving accurate descriptions of the exhibition that nevertheless appear to have transgressed the limits of the listeners' credulity—thus returning to magical realism's playful inversion of the normal and the fantastical.

This type of storytelling is hardly confined to the oral sphere in Palestine. Examples abound of Palestinian—and more broadly, Arabic—writers using the magical as an allegory for history itself. The figure of the *khurāfa* immediately invokes that most mischievous of Palestinian authors, Emile Habibi, and in particular his novel *Saraya, the Ogre's Daughter*, whose original Arabic title, *Khurāfiyyat Sarāyā Bint al-Ghūl*, is a conscious play on the *khurāfiyya* oral tradition. The result is a series of fairy tales whose plot structures serve as commentaries on the Palestinian predicament, insisting that the Nakba cannot be related in purely scientific terms. As Habibi discusses in the introduction: "I have removed *Saraya, Bint al-Ghul* from the class of the long novel from the beginning. What is it, then? I have called it a *khurāfiyya*. I have found that we Palestinian Arabs, whether specialists or not, use the term *khurāfiyya* for every action that catches us by surprise." He goes on to provide an etymological discussion of the term, relating it to the gathering of over-ripe fruit, before linking this to the figure of the *khurāfa*: "A khurafa is a man who offers up—by way of excuse—the claim that he has acted under a genie's spell ... but isn't believed by people, who say he's just 'telling fairy tales'—that is, a fine story but something essentially untrue. Or perhaps senility, kharaf, has distorted his reason."[21] This playful and deliberately ambiguous use of the *khurāfiyya* has been an important influence on my writing of Jubrail Dabdoub's story, and in particular on how the plot structures of Arabic folk tales might be used as a metaphor for Bethlehem's transformation in the late Ottoman period.

Habibi's works might also offer wider potential for the writing of Palestinian history. The unraveling of Palestinian society under Zionism's relentless project of colonization often seems to defy rational explanation. Palestinian historians and those sympathetic to their plight have understandably focused on gathering, recording, and disseminating empirical evidence of this dispossession. But do we also miss fundamental aspects of historical experience by narrating the story in factual, realist terms? Just like the magical realist writers of Latin America who deconstructed the absurdity of nationalist narratives by telling fantastical stories as if they were normal, so too Habibi allows us to grasp the bizarreness of Palestinian existence by maintaining a deadpan tone to convey his farcical and tragic plotlines. Why should historians not do the same to access different elements of Palestinian experience? As the opening lines of Habibi's 1974 novel, *Said the Pessoptimist*, pronounce: "Please tell my story. It is surely as weird as the story of Moses's staff, the resurrection of Jesus, and the election of the husband of a ladybird to the presidency of the United States."²²

ON THE TRAIL OF JUBRAIL DABDOUB (AND OTHERS LIKE HIM)

This book is the story of one man and his journeys around the world. But it is built upon a wider base of source material that has allowed me to imagine snapshots in Jubrail's life. In terms of information relating directly to Jubrail, only broken fragments were available: brief mentions in a cousin's memoir, entries in parish records, the odd Bethlehem-made souvenir still bearing his name, the houses he lived in, and his listings in colonial immigration records and catalogs of international exhibitions. To maintain a narrative flow throughout the whole book, these ghostly traces had to be supplemented with contextual materials that provide clues to how the Bethlehem merchants experienced their journeys and how the townsfolk back home received them upon their return. In the absence of any centralized or exhaustive archive, this was a painstaking task, requiring the collection of an eclectic array of sources, often located in the most unlikely of places.

The connecting thread through much of these sources has been family. A number of recent histories of the region have provided critical perspectives on family, most notably Beshara Doumani's magisterial work on Nablus and Tripoli in which he exhorts us to break down the reductive myths of "the Arab family" and think instead in more fluid, historically contingent terms.²³ This has proved a strong influence on my research on the Bethlehem families of the nineteenth century, causing me to think of them as a constantly changing social and economic construction and even to employ Doumani's notion of the "family firm" to describe the new, deeply patriarchal businesses that had emerged by the 1890s.

Such an approach not only affects the outcome of the research; it also structures how the research itself is carried out. In a project where official, institutional archives prove insufficient, notions of family leave deep imprints on the selection and collection of sources. In Bethlehem, any attempt to access nonofficial collections is quickly directed toward specific family names, which are in turn organized into the town's seven historic clans.²⁴ The researcher is thus invited to trace the town's history through distinctly patrilineal lines of ancestry. Every individual (male or female) is identifiable through their father's name (which serves as a kind of middle name), immediately erasing connections between women who are absorbed into their husband's family upon marriage.

There are ways in which patriarchal notions of family can be circumvented to tease out female agency and experience. At various stages of the research, I pursued different lines of inquiry to avoid women becoming invisible bystanders in these stories. Oral history played a particularly important role here. Through years of tracking down Jubrail's descendants (and those of his siblings), I eventually managed to compile an invaluable collection of interviews that provided the only firsthand glimpses, however vague, of the personal characteristics of Jubrail and his immediate family. These included interviews with female family members who helped disrupt an exclusively male version of the Dabdoub family's rise to prominence. A priceless series of interviews was carried out with Paulette Tissaire (wife of Jubrail's great-nephew, Anton Khalil Dabdoub) and Julia Dabdoub (wife of the grandson of Jubrail's brother Mikhail), as well as correspondence with the descendants of Jubrail's sister Sara, now a resident of Mexico. In addition, some of the male interviewees were descended from female relatives of Jubrail and had thus inherited a set of memories that gave clues to women's experiences of the emigration boom. In Central America, both Edgar Batarse and José Eduardo Siman are descended from Jubrail's daughter and granddaughter respectively, both of whom settled in El Salvador. Collectively, these interviews afforded snippets of information about Jubrail's mother, Rosa, his sister Sara, and his daughter, Wardeh, that allowed me to begin fleshing out these characters in the narrative.

At the same time, I have remained acutely aware of how patriarchal notions of family have encouraged certain lines of inquiry and excluded others. Rather than simply acknowledging this as a limitation, I found it more fruitful to explore how such records are produced by the very social transformations I was researching. The nineteenth century in particular was a time when new notions of family and clan took shape in Bethlehem thanks to the emergence of a novel type of family business in which sons in various corners of the world acted as satellites orbiting the central patriarch in Bethlehem. In this context, tracing paternal lineage in Bethlehem became highly important to the merchant families, as did the drive to produce as many male offspring as possible. As much as they embraced the outside world as a trading zone, those of Jubrail's generation were intent on maintaining their family's status in Bethlehem. It comes as little surprise, therefore, that in this same period families began to draw up their own genealogies and codify their legends of origin, emphasizing rootedness in Bethlehem through male lineage.

Nowhere is this more apparent than in Bethlehem's Latin Parish Archive. This is the place where all Catholic births, baptisms, confirmations, marriages, and deaths are recorded in Bethlehem. Among other things, the archives allowed me to compile a database of every Dabdoub family member born in Bethlehem since the seventeenth century, including dates of birth, baptism, confirmation, marriage, and death for every individual. This in turn meant I was able to glean statistical data on how the emigration boom of the nineteenth century affected things like the average number of children per family and the average age of marriage. Where known, the records also mention births and deaths abroad, allowing me to follow individuals to various countries around the world.

Despite its value in sketching out biographical details, the Latin Parish Archive only allows male lineage to be traced. Every individual's entry is indexed according to their father, meaning women quickly drop out of sight once they marry, or at best can only be understood in relation to fathers and husbands. While the records date back to the early seventeenth century when the Franciscans first began to record systematically their converts to Catholicism, the current cataloging system is a product of the nineteenth century drive by Catholic families to order their heritage according to surnames (*alqāb*), which were adopted for the first time in the seventeenth and eighteenth centuries. These surnames, including *Dabdoub*, were invariably based on some defining characteristic of a male progenitor, as explained in more detail in chapter 3. As the book progressed, it became increasingly clear that focusing on these very masculine conceptions of family, and the male anxieties that arose once ties to Bethlehem began to be broken, was the most productive way to deal with these lopsided sources.

The Latin Parish Archive has been vital in establishing statistical information on the Dabdoubs and on Bethlehem's Catholics more generally. But it is only the tip of the iceberg when it comes to family history in Bethlehem. The real treasures lie in the rich array of memories preserved by families of Bethlehem origin all over the world. Photographs, paintings, letters, telegrams, and devotional objects lovingly inscribed by the carvers of the nineteenth century have all been indispensable additions to the oral history interviews I carried out. Once again, it is family, or a certain conception of family, that has structured how these memories are passed down and preserved. This seems to be especially the case in the kinds of diasporic settings where much of the research for this book took place. When ties across these communities are broken by the passage of time, distance, and colonial erasure, it is often through patrilineal ancestry that attempts are made to rebuild those ties. I was able to follow a lead across countries and continents countless times thanks to a common grandfather, uncle, or male cousin. This resulted in an uneven detective trail that left large areas shrouded in darkness just as much as it shone light on others, reflecting some of the wider challenges Palestinians face in preserving and reconstructing their heritage across far-flung communities.

Nowhere is this process more fraught than in Bethlehem itself, where the daily pressures of occupation render the task of preservation all the more urgent. Of particular importance to this book is the unpublished and handwritten memoir of Ibrahim Yuhanna Dabdoub, kindly shared with me by George al-Aʿma and Anton Shukri Dabdoub. Ibrahim was a distant cousin of Jubrail, and his younger brother married Jubrail's sister Sara in 1884. He also worked as a souvenir carver for Jubrail's father from the age of twelve and later embarked on various overseas business ventures with Jubrail and his brothers. This is the only example I have come across of a close family member writing a memoir or diary that remains intact. At first glance, the memoir frustrates in its almost exclusive focus on recording the business transactions of Ibrahim and his brothers, even providing a ledger of all income and expenditure by way of an appendix at the back of the memoir. This in itself has provided invaluable information on prices, profits, and types of goods. It also illuminates the sheer relentlessness of the Bethlehem merchants' travel itineraries in the late nineteenth century as they hopped from one international exhibition to another. Consider this excerpt describing the movements of Ibrahim's younger brother, Anton (in which Jubrail is mentioned as an "uncle"):

> After he got married [in 1887], Anton traveled in the company of our uncle Jubrail and Ibrahim, as well as Abdullah Dabboura to the exhibition in Copenhagen where they stayed for ten months and brought back a sum of 1,500 French lira, 250 of which went to Anton because the others took a third. Afterward, Anton traveled for a year in the company of Jubrail and Ibrahim,

the three of them earning 150 lira, 35 of which went to Anton. Afterward, he traveled alone to Torino in Italy in 1897, staying for ten months and earning 80 lira. Before that, he traveled to Portugal in the company of Yaqub Sabaat and his cousin Bulus, staying for around four years. He earned a sum of 300 lira. Then, Anton traveled with our nephew Yousef in 1900 to the Paris exhibition, staying abroad for four years, moving from France to Italy and to Germany, for a loss of 90 French lira.[25]

Alongside this wealth of factual information, interesting social dynamics also emerge. Gradually, it transpires that the main motivation behind Ibrahim writing the memoir is to settle an old family score—to prove how his nephews, Yousef and Dawid, borrowed money from him and then disappeared to Mexico without paying their debts. This was a feud that directly impacted Jubrail, as he and his brothers were called upon to mediate the conflict, not least because their sister Sara (the mother of Yousef and Dawid), had become the object of Ibrahim's ire.

But perhaps the most useful part of the memoir was the language itself. I learned to tune in to the memoir's combination of rustic, colloquial Arabic mixed with grandiose exhortations to God, the saints, and various family members. I grasped the extent to which business and faith had become intertwined in the lives of these merchants. I saw how Jubrail was viewed with great reverence and respect among the wider family, supporting impressions provided in the oral history interviews I had carried out. I learned the extent to which business affairs were deemed to be an exclusively male preserve and how the transgression of women into this world produced acute anxieties. I even began using certain words and phrases from the memoir in my own writing as I experimented with different voices and registers. Overall, I can say this has been the single most influential source in the writing of the book.

Alongside the memoir, a host of other sources in Bethlehem have proved invaluable to the task of filling in the gaps in Jubrail's story. Among them are the bricks, mortar, and stone slabs laid down during the late nineteenth and early twentieth centuries that still stand today. I became intimately acquainted with the house in which Jubrail was born and grew up in (still known today as Hosh Dabdoub despite the family long since having moved on), allowing me to situate much of the early chapters of the book in the very building that helped revolutionize Bethlehem's urban design in the

1860s. I also got to know the house Jubrail himself had built in 1923, which still bears his initials on the front gate and was most likely the location of his final death in 1931. Among the many coincidences that seemed to follow me around the town, I discovered this was the very building where I had taken Arabic classes during my first stint living in Bethlehem in 2008, somehow deepening my sense of connection to this man about whom I had so little tangible information. Perhaps more importantly, Jubrail's house was among the last of a wave of new mansions built at the turn of the twentieth century with money flooding in from abroad. Becoming acquainted with these ostentatious, pink-stone palaces became another way of tapping into the great social upheavals produced by the emigration boom, which eventually formed the focus of chapter 17.

Other discoveries lay more hidden from view. A large collection of dusty old cassette tapes, recorded in the 1990s, was discovered in the basement of Bethlehem University. Thanks to the tireless work of Bethlehem historian Adnan Musallam, a group of students had been sent out to record interviews with elderly people in the area, discussing subjects such as "the emigration years," the late Ottoman period, and the First World War. Today there is no one alive who has direct memories of these subjects, making the tapes a unique entry point into a lost world. Listening to the voices of people long since deceased, and reading through the accompanying transcripts compiled by the students, has provided another vital means of imagining the wider world Jubrail inhabited.

Gradually, this disparate trail of fragmentary source materials has come to constitute a kind of archive in itself. I was lucky to obtain a grant from the UK Arts and Humanities Research Council to digitize an initial selection of the materials and create an online repository. Partnering with Bethlehem artist and documentary filmmaker Leila Sansour, we set about compiling the Planet Bethlehem Archive, working with various individuals, families, and institutions in Bethlehem and around the world. The tapes at Bethlehem University were digitized, various family collections cataloged, and individuals identified in hundreds of photographs. Today an openly accessible online archive, the collection contains thousands of items donated from across the Bethlehem diaspora.[26] Very few of them relate directly to Jubrail's life, but collectively they constitute a documentary trail of how the bare bones of his life were fleshed out into a narrative history, however incomplete and imperfect that narrative may be.

The compilation of the Planet Bethlehem Archive reflects the extent to which family collections have been at the heart of this book's research. This in turn signals an attempt to resist defining the people of Bethlehem through the eyes of the state, be that Ottoman, British, or otherwise. Since the beginning of the project, I had a strong impression of a town adept at keeping the state at arm's length. Partly due to its majority Christian population, and partly due to its location tucked away just out of sight from the local seat of imperial power in Jerusalem, the town emanated an unruly presence prior to the twentieth century. There are numerous examples of Bethlehemites chasing tax collectors out of town and launching rebellions against local governors in alliance with local villages.[27] One could well write a history focused on these forms of resistance to Ottoman control, but the subject of this book invited a different approach. Bethlehem's emigration explosion seemed to take place in a parallel universe to the machinations of tax collectors, law courts, and district governors. The only times an Ottoman official would really feature was as a presence to evade in the docks at Jaffa, or as a guarantor of property transactions back in Bethlehem. Of course, there are myriad ways in which Bethlehem's development was contingent upon a complex and dynamic Ottoman context—the improved infrastructure produced by the Tanzimat reforms is one obvious example—but we already have so many histories that focus exclusively on the relationship between subject and state. The aim here is to acknowledge and explore the individual agency Bethlehemites practiced in their daily lives, in which the state played little part.

The deliberate absence of the state does not mean that state records have not proved useful. The Ottoman Archives of the Prime Minister's Office in Istanbul, for example, provided crucial information on how the merchants planned and executed their campaigns at international exhibitions, which were important catalysts for the overseas expansion of their businesses. As a result, chapter 14 is able to document the process by which Jubrail and his brothers attempted to secure a monopoly over the sale of Holy Land souvenirs at the Chicago World's Columbian Exposition of 1893, thanks to correspondence between the Ottoman grand vizier and the governor of Jerusalem that mentions the Dabdoub brothers by name. Likewise, the Ottoman shariʿa court records of Jerusalem show a notable spike in property transactions among Bethlehem's Tarajmeh merchant families in the mid to late nineteenth century. These records reveal how changes resulting from the 1858 Ottoman Land Code combined with the emergence of Bethlehem's new merchant elite to produce a rush to claim ownership of land outside the borders of the old town in the 1860s, '70s, and '80s. The competition was particularly intense on Ras Iftays, where Jubrail's parents were the first to build their residence in the late 1850s, constituting an important step toward the overseas expansion of their business—something explored in detail in chapter 4.

This book has also benefited from the copious documentation of the Catholic Church's activities in Bethlehem. Among Arabic-speaking regions, the town has a unique relationship with Catholicism thanks in large part to the Franciscan presence there since the fourteenth century. In terms of conversions to Roman Catholicism, the Franciscans enjoyed more success in tiny Bethlehem than in any other city or town in the entire region.[28] As a result, there is an abundance of material recorded by the friars and their superiors that documents their interactions with the local population. A major resource for accessing this material is the Custodia di Terra Santa Archive in Jerusalem, which has provided key information on how the Catholic community to which Jubrail belonged gradually built up the skills and social capital required to launch their overseas ventures in the nineteenth century. Equally useful in this task was the Propaganda Fide archive in Rome, which contains sporadic glimpses of the tensions that existed between the friars and the local population in Bethlehem, particularly regarding the Franciscans' deliberate attempts to stop the Bethlehem artisans from traveling abroad to sell their produce. Collectively, these sources help situate the nineteenth-century emigration boom as the culmination of a much longer-running process that stretches back at least as far as the seventeenth century rather than a sudden, inexplicable eruption.

Despite the usefulness of these institutional records, the driving force behind the book's narratives remain the personal stories of local actors in Bethlehem. Nowhere was this more apparent than in the life of Marie-Alphonsine, the Jerusalemite nun who lived in Bethlehem for many years and eventually performed the miracle on Jubrail in 1909. Thanks to Mother Praxede Raja Salem Sweidan, I was introduced to a fascinating collection of materials in the Beit Hanina convent of the Rosary Sisters that relates to Marie-Alphonsine's life. These include paintings of her miracles commissioned in the 1980s (among them a depiction of Jubrail's resurrection) and, most importantly, the original notebooks that Marie-Alphonsine kept that document her life, visions, and miracles. Although the account of Jubrail's miracle is brief, when viewed within the wider array of sources held at the Beit Hanina convent, it has opened a vital window into a spiritual landscape in which Jubrail and his fellow merchants were still firmly grounded.

Looking back, so many of those who have contributed to this book have now passed on. As with each passing of a generation, there is an acute feeling of sadness that accompanies the realization that certain times and places no longer exist within living memory. It fills me with regret that Mother Praxede will not be able to read these lines. Nor will Dr. Michel Dabdoub, Julia Dabdoub, Paulette Tissaire, or Milia Rishmawi. I can only feel blessed to have been able to hear their stories and hope that in some small way the narrative I have produced will help those stories live on.

ACKNOWLEDGMENTS

WRITING A BOOK LIKE THIS would be unthinkable without the generous support of a wide cast of characters across multiple locations. In Bethlehem, George al-Aʿma and Khalil Showkeh were my mentors in understanding the intricacies of the town's history. I remain in awe of their knowledge and dedication to preserving Bethlehem's precious urban heritage, and I am immensely thankful for their openness in sharing materials. At Bethlehem University, Adnan Musallam and Walid Atallah kindly gave me access to the university's resources, and at the Centre for Cultural Heritage and Preservation, the late Nada Atrash guided me through the town's architectural history. Meanwhile, at the Bethlehem Latin Parish Archive, Victor Babun responded to my incessant requests with unending patience and grace.

The openness of members of the Dabdoub family still based in Bethlehem has been equally important. Dr. Michel Abdallah Dabdoub, Julia Dabdoub, Christiane Dabdoub-Nasser, Pauline Anastas, Anton Shukri Dabdoub, Paulette Tissaire, Andre Dabdoub, and Carol Sansour all welcomed me into their family stories with open arms. Various other contributors around Bethlehem and the neighboring towns of Beit Sahour and Beit Jala must be mentioned. In particular, George Sammur, Mitri Raheb, Milia Rishmawi, Lilian Keraʿa, Nabil Qawwas, Nabil Bandak, Echlas al-Azzeh, Carol Abu Akleh, Fadi Abu Hamameh, Hanna Musallam, Abuna Mario Murru, Samir Salem, Elen Eloussie, Jihan al-Aʿma, and Ghadeer Najjar provided valuable input through their knowledge and expertise. I also owe a huge debt of gratitude to Fadi and Abeer Rishmawi and to Salah and Amal Abdrabbu for their warm, open-ended hospitality, and to Mother Praxede Raja Salem Sweidan in nearby Beit Hanina.

Further afield, the participation of people from various areas of Bethlehem's diaspora was invaluable. My thanks in particular go to Alice Siman (granddaughter of Jubrail Dabdoub), José Eduardo Siman (Alice's son), Edgar Escolán Batarse (great-grandson of Jubrail), Peter Dabdoub, Antonio Dabdoub Escobar, Jack Nicola Kattan, Arthur Hazboun, Kathy Saade Kenny, William Victor Kattan, Julie Mazour de Daboub, Gabriela Daboub Morales, Mariela Kawas, Jacobo Kattan, Enrique Yidi Daccarett, and Odette Yidi David.

The genesis of this book took root during my time as a postdoctoral researcher at the University of Cambridge, where I received crucial support from Tim Harper, Chris Bayly, Kate Fleet, Andrew Arsan, John Slight, and Ambrogio Camozzi Pistoja. I have since moved on to the University of Sussex, where my colleagues Feras Alkabani, Martin Evans, Fawzia Haeri Mazanderani, Vinita Damodaran, Darrow Schecter, Eric Schneider, Anne-Marie Angelo, Tom Davies, Melissa Milewski, Sharon Webb, James Drew, and Freja Howat contributed both intellectual and moral sustenance. From this base, I was lucky enough to receive input from inspirational scholars all over the world. Particular thanks go to Salim Tamari, Carol Khoury, Akram Khater, William Gervase Clarence-Smith, Beshara Doumani, Nadim Bawalsa, Cecilia Baeza, Camila Pastor, Ian Coller, Ben Fortna, Eliseo Fajardo Madrid, Alexander Zeron Alvarado, Arlene Clemesha, Linda K. Jacobs, Rodolfo Pastor Fasquelle, Yasemin Avçi, and Yener Bayar.

From 2017 to 2019 I received a research fellowship from the UK Arts and Humanities Research Council (AHRC), whose generous support allowed me to tie the various strands of research together and begin writing the narrative. Most recently, I have become hugely thankful for (and reliant upon) the dedication, efficiency, and incisive feedback provided by the editorial team at Stanford University Press, particularly Kate Wahl, Cat Pavel, and Adriana Smith.

I finish by thanking three people who have been a constant source of inspiration. Leila Sansour has always been on hand to shine light on Bethlehem's bewilderingly diverse social fabric and to provide priceless sparks of creativity. Gerardo Serra has heroically read through multiple drafts, never failing to offer his astute and unique brand of feedback and allowing me to situate the book within wider debates on the writing of history. Finally, Layla Zaglul Ruiz has been my editor in chief, artistic inspiration, and rock of support all rolled into one, reading endless versions of the text and giving me the belief to keep going through the moments of doubt and exasperation. Thank you Laylita for your love and patience.

GLOSSARY OF ARABIC TERMS

GENERAL TERMS
abayeh: Woolen cloak worn by rural men in Palestine
akhoui: My brother
Allah: God
Amerka: The Americas (alternatively, anywhere overseas)
Ammo: Colloquial form of ʿ*amm* (uncle)
Baba/Yaba: Dad
Bayt Lahm: Bethlehem
bilad al-faranja: Western Europe (lit. "lands of the Franks")
franji (pl. *faranja*): Western European (lit. "Frankish")
al-Khadr: Saint George/al-Khidr
khawaja: Honorific commonly used in Bethlehem for male merchants of high standing
latini (pl. *latin*): Catholic
Mama: Mom
mar: Saint
al-Quds: Jerusalem
qumbaz: Long-sleeved cotton coat worn by Bethlehemite men
rumi (pl. *rum*): Greek Orthodox Christian
al-Shaytan: The Devil
tawb: A dress, especially the distinctive embroidered dress with square chest panels worn by women in Bethlehem
Yasuʿ/al-Masih: Jesus

MONTHS OF THE YEAR
Kanun al-Thani: January
Shubat: February

Adhar: March
Nisan: April
Ayyar: May
Huzayran: June
Tammuz: July
Ab: August
Aylul: September
Tishrin al-Awwal: October
Tishrin al-Thani: November
Kanun al-Awwal: December

CURRENCY

ghurush: Silver coins often called "piastres" in European sources. One hundred ghurush made up one Ottoman lira.

lira fransawi (or "French lira"): Term used by Bethlehemites for French francs

LENGTH AND WEIGHT

ayak: Unit of length, equivalent to 378 millimeters or about 15 inches

uqiyya: Unit of weight that varied from region to region. In the district of Jerusalem, it was equivalent to 240 grams or about half a pound.

NOTES

INTRODUCTION

1. Jubrail Dabdoub to Anton Dabdoub, Paris, February 10, 1930, private collection of Peter Dabdoub.

2. Marie-Alphonsine's notebooks are reproduced in full in Sister Praxede Sweidan, *Kalimat al-'adhra' al-mukarrama al-umm Marie-Alphonsine Danil Ghattas* (Jerusalem: Latin Patriarchate Press, 2004). This quote comes from the second manuscript, p. 17.

3. Benedict Stolz, *A Handmaid of the Holy Rosary: Mother Mary Alphonsus of the Rosary, First Foundress of an Arab Congregation, 1843–1927*, trans. Natalie Bevenot (New York: Benziger Brothers, 1938), 97.

4. Ibrahim Yuhanna Dabdoub, "Mukhtasar tarikh 'ilat al-marhum Yuhanna Yaqoub al-Dabdoub" (unpublished memoir, 1923, private collection of Anton Shukri Dabdoub). I have drawn extensively upon this memoir in writing this book. My thanks to Anton Shukri Dabdoub for sharing it with me.

5. Brenda Cooper, *Magical Realism in West African Fiction* (London: Routledge, 1998), 1. For a broader discussion of magical realism's popularity among writers in the Global South, see Mariano Siskind, "The Global Life of Genres and the Material Travels of Magical Realism," in *The Palgrave Handbook of Magical Realism*, ed. Richard Perez and Victoria A. Chevalier (London: Palgrave Macmillan, 2020), 21–66.

6. Salim Barakat, *Fuqaha' al-zalām* (Nicosia: Majallat al-Karmel, 1985), 16.

7. This relationship is explored in my article, Jacob Norris, "Dragomans, Tattooists, Artisans: Palestinian Christians and Their Encounters with Catholic Europe in the Seventeenth and Eighteenth Centuries," *Journal of Global History* 14, no. 1 (2019): 68–86.

8. See Penne L. Restad, *Christmas in America: A History* (Oxford: Oxford University Press, 1996).

9. See Ben Highmore, *Cultural Feelings: Mood, Mediation and Cultural Politics* (London: Routledge, 2017).

10. See, for example, Hayden White, "The Value of Narrativity in the Representation of Reality," *Critical Inquiry* 7, no. 1 (Autumn, 1980): 5–27.

11. Salman Rushdie, *Midnight's Children: A Novel* (1981; reprint, London: Random House, 2006), 1–2.

12. This refers to criticism leveled by John Paul Ghobrial in "The Secret Life of Elias of Babylon and the Uses of Global Microhistory," *Past and Present* 222, no. 1 (2014): 59.

13. Kemal Karpat, "The Ottoman Emigration to America, 1860–1914," *International Journal of Middle East Studies* 17, no. 2 (May 1985): 185.

14. For more detail, see Jacob Norris, "Exporting the Holy Land: Artisans and Merchant Migrants in Ottoman-Era Bethlehem," *Mashriq and Mahjar: Journal of Middle East and North African Migration Studies* 1 no. 2 (2013): 17–45.

15. A vivid account of the trade is given in Ameen Rihani's celebrated novel, *The Book of Khalid* (1911; reprint, New York: Melville House, 2012), 16.

16. *Le Matin*, 1911 (describing the arrival of Syrians in the early 1890s), cited in Roger Gaillard, *Les Blancs debarquent. La Republique exterminatrice. Premiere partie: Une modernisation manqueé, 1880–1896* (Port-au-Prince, 1991), 275–76.

17. Alix Naff, *Becoming American: The Early Arab Immigrant Experience* (Carbondale, IL: Southern Illinois University Press, 1985), 103.

18. Philip Forzley, ed., *Autobiography of Bishara Khalil Forzley*, memoir, August 2, 1953, Immigration History and Research Center, University of Minnesota, 8, cited in Gregory Orfalea, *Before the Flames: A Quest for the History of Arab Americans* (Austin: University of Texas Press, 1988), 81.

19. Notable examples include Sarah Gualtieri, "Gendering the Chain Migration Thesis: Women and Syrian Transatlantic Migration, 1878–1924," *Comparative Studies of South Asia, Africa and the Middle East* 24, no. 1 (2004), 67–78; and Akram Khater, *Inventing Home: Emigration, Gender, and the Middle-Class in Lebanon, 1870–1920* (Berkeley: University of California Press, 2001).

20. See Jacob Norris, "Mobile Homes: The Refashioning of Palestinian Merchant Homes in the Late Ottoman Period," *Jerusalem Quarterly*, no. 83 (2020): 9–33.

21. For more detail, see Jacob Norris, "Return Migration and the Rise of the Palestinian Nouveaux Riches, 1870–1925," *Journal of Palestine Studies* 46, no. 2 (2017): 60–75.

22. Examples of this type of literature include Yehoshua Ben-Arieh, *Jerusalem in the 19th Century: Emergence of the New City* (Jerusalem: Yad Izhak Ben-Zvi, 1986); Ruth Kark and Michal Oren-Nordheim, *Jerusalem and Its Environs: Quarters, Neighborhoods, Villages, 1800–1948* (Detroit, MI: Wayne State University Press, 2001); and Mark LeVine, *Overthrowing Geography: Jaffa, Tel Aviv, and the Struggle for Palestine, 1880–1948* (Berkeley: University of California Press, 2005).

23. *Falastin*, August 27, 1913, 2.

24. See Saleh Abdel Jawad, "Landed Property, Palestinian Migration to America and the Emergence of a New Local Leadership: Al-Bireh, 1919–1947," *Jerusalem Quarterly*, no. 36 (2009): 13–33.

CHAPTER 1: OF A LAND CALLED AMERKA, OR HOW AMMO HANNA WAS SAVED BY AL-KHADR

1. Hanna Khalil Morcos (b. 1824, d. 1900), or Ammo Hanna, as I have imagined him to have been known—was the earliest example I have found of a Bethlehemite traveling to the Americas and returning to tell the tale. He was recorded as arriving in Brazil in 1851. See Majid Radawi, *Al-hijra al-ʿarabiyya ila al-Barazil 1870–1986* (Damascus: Dar Tlas, 1989), 48. His journey to Brazil led to further trips to the Americas among his family members, as shown in the Morcos family record books in the Bethlehem Latin Parish Archive. For example, his eldest son, Khalil, is recorded as having died "in America" in 1883.

2. The construction of Hosh Dabdoub around 1860 is explored further in chapter 4. Its location appears to have been deliberately chosen to attract visitors to its shop as they caught their first glimpse of Bethlehem. The excitement around this location was captured by the English reverend James Kean in the 1890s, possibly while standing on the roof of Hosh Dabdoub itself: "Seated on this perch, you gaze south across the valley upon Bethlehem, the eye dwelling especially on the vast confused conglomeration of lofty buildings at the east end. These cover and contain the cave wherein our Lord was born. A certain whiteness seems to add majesty to the general aspect of Bethlehem." See Rev. James Kean, *Among the Holy Places: A Pilgrimage through Palestine* (London: T. F. Unwin, 1895), 114. I also discuss the house's architectural innovation in Jacob Norris, "Mobile Homes: The Refashioning of Palestinian Merchant Homes in the Late Ottoman Period," *Jerusalem Quarterly*, no. 83 (2020): 9–33.

3. The *khamasin* is a dry hot wind from the Sahara that brings dust storms to Bethlehem and the surrounding area every spring. It takes its name from the fifty-day period in spring in which it usually arrives. In European sources, the *khamasin* is often referred to as a *sirocco*. The 1860s and '70s was the period in which package tours of the Holy Land began in earnest, sending a greater variety of visitors to Bethlehem from Europe and North America, alongside the more traditional array of pilgrims, clergy, and mystics. Among the newer visitors was a greater number of European women whose styles of dress frequently invoked bemusement from the local population. See, for example, Mary Eliza Rogers, *Domestic Life in Palestine* (London: Poe & Hitchcock, 1865), 43. For the birth of modern tourism in Palestine, see Timothy Larsen, "Thomas Cook, Holy Land Pilgrims, and the Dawn of the Modern Tourist Industry," *Studies in Church History*, no. 36 (2000): 329–42.

4. The term *burnayṭa* is used in Bethlehem to denote any type of Western-style hat. This contrasts with the turban or *ʿamāmeh* worn by most men in Bethlehem during the time of Jubrail's childhood. The *tarbush*, or fez, meanwhile, only began to be adopted in Bethlehem in the early twentieth century, but by then many of the younger generation were already wearing Western-style hats they had picked up abroad. Early photographs taken in Bethlehem in the late nineteenth and early twentieth centuries often show a contrast between younger men wearing these stiff-brimmed Western hats and the older generation of men, who still wore the turban or sometimes a *tarbush*. Numerous examples of such photographs have been collected in the Planet Bethlehem Archive at the following link: http://planetbethlehem.org/ (see especially the William Victor Kattan and Katrina Saʾade collections).

5. In interviews with descendants of Jubrail and his peers, pocket watches featured consistently in stories of new objects brought back to Bethlehem by merchants in the mid to late nineteenth century. Pocket watches began to gain popularity among the elites of big cities in the late eighteenth century but were still relatively rare in provincial, rural areas like Bethlehem up until the late nineteenth century. In these areas, the standard way of measuring time remained sundials, which captured "seasonal hours" that varied in length according to the season. For example, a daytime hour in the summer was longer than a nighttime hour to ensure high noon was always at six o'clock and sunset always at twelve o'clock. For this reason, I have imagined that Bethlehemites viewed a European-style or *franji* pocket watch in the 1860s as having little practical use given the agricultural day revolved around a fixed time for noon and sunset, as well as for times of prayer.

The ringing of church bells was officially permitted for the first time in the Ottoman Empire under the Reform Edict of 1856, shortly before Jubrail's birth in 1860. But travelers' accounts frequently mention the ringing of bells for ceremonies prior to that date, indicating how the town's majority Christian population was able to preserve an exceptional status for itself on certain religious matters. Meanwhile, the town's small Muslim population was granted its own mosque in 1860 (discussed in chapters 2 and 5), bringing the sound of the muezzin's call to prayer to Bethlehem for the first time in a regular fashion.

It was not until the beginning of the twentieth century that the Ottoman state embarked on its famous building spree of clock towers in cities across the empire, including the one completed in Jerusalem in 1908. Even then, most mechanical clocks and watches were set to Islamic time (referred to in European sources as *alla turca*), whereby the day would be divided into two segments to ensure prayer times were structured around the changing time of the setting sun. The first of these segments would begin at sunset and run for twelve hours, followed by a second segment that would run until sunset.

For further discussion of these shifting ways of measuring time, and the sociopolitical meanings attached to them, see Ron Fuchs and Gilbert Herbert, "A Colonial Portrait of Jerusalem: British Architecture in Mandate-Era Palestine," in Nezar AlSayyad, *Hybrid Urbanism: On the Identity Discourse and the Built Environment* (Westport, CT: Praeger, 2001), 89–91; Avner Wishnitzer, *Reading Clocks, Alla Turca: Time and Society in the Late Ottoman Empire* (Chicago: University of Chicago Press, 2015); Mehmet Bengu Uluengin, "Secularizing Anatolia Tick By Tick: Clock Towers in the Ottoman Empire and the Turkish Republic," *International Journal of Middle East Studies* 42, no. 1 (2010): 17–36; and A. Bir, Ş. Acar, and M. Kaçar, "The Clockmaker Family Meyer and Their Watch Keeping the *alla turca* Time," in *Science between Europe and Asia*, ed. F. Günergun and D. Raina, vol. 275, *Historical Studies on the Transmission, Adoption and Adaptation of Knowledge*, Boston Studies in the Philosophy of Science (Dordrecht: Springer, 2011).

6. Throughout the book, western Europeans are referred to as *faranja* (*franji* in the singular). This is the local Arabic term widely found in sources from Bethlehem at that time, derived from the Crusader-era term *Franks* or *Frankish*, which denoted western Europeans generally, rather than French-speakers in particular. In Arabic, the verb *tafarnaja* (تفرنج) also carries the meaning "to become Europeanized."

7. The story of Abdallah Hazboun and his career with Napoleon's "Mamelouks de la Garde" is recounted in Ian Coller, *Arab France: Islam and the Making of Modern Europe, 1798–1831* (Berkeley: University of California Press, 2011), 131–32, 148–50.

8. Andrea Dawid's death is recorded in Latin Parish Archive, September 7, 1796, with the sole note, "Morto in Latin America."

9. In interviews with descendants of Bethlehemites who traveled to the Americas in the nineteenth century, stories of saintly interventions during perilous journeys were frequently told. These were not stories witnessed firsthand, but rather tales passed down through the generations. The idea here is to recapture that sense of listening to those tales as travelers returned to Bethlehem and to explore the extent to which they were understood through a world view in which saints and miracles were an expected part of life. I have been greatly influenced by the work of James Grehan, whose concept of agrarian religion explores how the religious practices of Christians, Muslims, and Jews in nineteenth-century Palestine and Syria often strayed wildly from textual orthodoxy. These religious beliefs cut across sectarian boundaries and were rooted in the turning of the seasons, more visceral forms of worship, and belief in the miraculous power of local saints, dervishes, and mendicants. Grehan also emphasizes the extent to which this religious culture was not unique to the countryside but was also embedded in towns and cities. See James Grehan, *Twilight of the Saints: Everyday Religion in Ottoman Syria and Palestine* (Oxford: Oxford University Press, 2016), especially 14–19.

The most common figure in Bethlehemites' tales of saintly interventions during the early journeys to the Americas is Saint George, or al-Khadr ("the green one"), who enjoys a particular veneration in the Bethlehem area. As in many parts of Bilad al-Sham, local traditions in the Bethlehem area have merged the Muslim saint/angel al-Khadr with the Christian figure of Saint George (Mar Jiryes in Arabic). This holds special significance due to the nearby shrine (which is today a church) in the village of al-Khader, named because of its association as the site of Saint George's imprisonment by the Romans and venerated for centuries by Muslims and Christians alike for the healing powers of its relics (the chains in which Saint George was bound). Al-Khadr thus appears in Bethlehem tradition as a green-robed figure able to fly long distances who offers protection, fertility, and prosperity to local residents. For more on this local tradition, see William Dalrymple, *From the Holy Mountain: A Journey among the Christians of the Middle East* (London: Flamingo, 1998), 339–44.

10. In Arabic, the phrase is "Btintwi al-ard ilhun." See Tawfiq Canaan, *Mohammedan Saints and Sanctuaries in Palestine* (London: Luzac, 1927), 123.

11. The former Syrian consul in São Paulo, Majid Radawi, lists Hanna Khalil Morcos as the first migrant from Syria and Palestine to arrive in Brazil in 1851. See Radawi, *Al-hijra*, 48.

12. For a discussion of the transformation of Brazil's economy under Dom Pedro II in the mid-nineteenth century, see Robert H. Mattoon Jr., "Railroads, Coffee, and the Growth of Big Business in São Paulo, Brazil," *Hispanic American Historical Review* 57, no. 2 (1977): 273–95.

13. The arrival of the first train in Jerusalem in 1892 is described in chapter 13. The first railway in Brazil opened in 1854, around the time Ammo Hanna was recorded as entering the country. See Mattoon Jr., "Railroads."

14. According to the celebrated Palestinian novelist Emile Habibi, "A khurafa is a man who offers up—by way of excuse—the claim that he has acted under a genie's spell . . . but isn't believed by people, who say he's just 'telling fairy tales.'" See Emile Habibi, introduction ("Oration") to *Saraya, the Ogre's Daughter: A Palestinian Fairy Tale*, trans. Peter Theroux (Lake Worth, FL: Ibis, 2006), 8–9.

15. This description is inspired by Jabra Ibrahim Jabra's account of his visits to Rachel's Tomb when he lived in Hosh Dabdoub as a young boy in the 1920s. See Jabra Ibrahim Jabra, *Al-bi'r al-ula: fusul min sirah dhatiyah* (Beirut: al-mu'assisah al-'arabiyah lil-dirasat wa al-nashr, 2001), 89.

CHAPTER 2: OF THE HALLOWED RIDGE, OR HOW JUBRAIL LEARNED TO PROFIT FROM CHRISTMAS

1. Precise population figures by town or village in the late Ottoman period are notoriously difficult to gauge, as the Ottoman censuses were collected by region (*kaza*) rather than by specific town or village. Most travelers' accounts from the 1860s estimate the population of Bethlehem to be around four thousand. The American writer Ellen Clare Miller estimated the population to be between three thousand and four thousand in 1867, the year of Jubrail's seventh birthday. See Ellen Clare Miller, *Eastern Sketches: Notes of Scenery, Schools and Tent Life in Syria and Palestine* (Edinburgh: William Oliphant and Company, 1871), 148.

2. This description of Bethlehem's changing architectural makeup is based primarily on photos and drawings of the town's skyline in the mid- and late nineteenth century. Some examples are collected in the Planet Bethlehem Archive at http://planetbethlehem.org/ (see especially the Library of Congress collections). Also of use was Catherine Weill-Rochant's research on Bethlehem's urban evolution. See Catherine Weill-Rochant, "Histoire et évolution urbaine," in *Maisons de Bethléem*, ed. Philippe Revault, Serge Santelli, and Catherine Weill-Rochant (Paris: Maisonneuve et Larose, 1997), 7–30.

3. For the gradual emergence of settled Bedouin communities in that period, including among the Taʿamreh tribes, see D. H. K. Amiran and Y. Ben-Arieh, "Sedentarization of Beduin in Israel," *Israel Exploration Journal* 13, no. 3 (1963): 161–81.

4. Numerous sources describe the Saturday markets in Bethlehem in which men, women, and children from the neighboring Taʿamreh villages descended on the town. A particularly colorful description of the market in the 1920s is provided in Jabra Ibrahim Jabra, *Al-biʾr al-ula: fusul min sirah dhatiyah* (Beirut: al-muʾassisah al-ʿarabiyah lil-dirasat wa al-nashr, 2001), 67–68.

5. Bethlehem was unique in its intensive exposure to Catholicism. Since at least the early seventeenth century, it has contained the largest Roman Catholic population in the Custody of the Holy Land—a custody that included all of modern-day Syria, Lebanon, Jordan, Palestine/Israel, and Cyprus. Already by 1764 the Catholic population of the Bethlehem parish numbered over a thousand people, which likely constituted a majority of Bethlehem's Christian population. The principal reason for the town's high proportion of Catholics was the success of the Franciscan friars in converting the local population. They did this by offering a series of financial incentives that included the allocation of a wide range of jobs as well as more direct bribes. I have described in more detail this mutually beneficial but often tense relationship between the Bethlehemite Christians and the Roman Catholic Church in Jacob Norris, "Dragomans, Tattooists, Artisans: Palestinian Christians and Their Encounters with Catholic Europe in the Seventeenth and Eighteenth Centuries," *Journal of Global History* 14, no. 1 (2019): 68–86.

6. *Rumi* is the Arabic term for the local Orthodox church under the wider authority of the "Greek" Orthodox Church with its patriarchate in Ottoman times in Istanbul. For examples of excommunication, see Norris, "Dragomans," 68–86.

7. Throughout the centuries, travelers of various kinds to Bethlehem have remarked how Muslims have prayed alongside Christians in the Church of the Nativity. For an example of a seventeenth-century Muslim account, see ʿAbd Al-Ghani Al-Nabulusi, *Al-haqiqa wa-1 -majaz fi-rihlat bilad al-sham wa misr wa-1 -hijaz* (Damascus: Dar al-Maʿrifa, 1989), 365. The current Mosque of Omar was built in its initial form in 1860 and renovated in 1958. It is not clear if the town's Muslims had a fully-fledged mosque within the town's boundaries before 1860. Famously, the first Muslim conqueror of Palestine, Caliph Omar ibn al-Khattab, instructed his Muslims followers in 637 CE to not demolish the church in Bethlehem to make way for a mosque but instead to pray individually in a preexisting "arc" (*ḥaniyya*) that faced in the Muslim direction of prayer (*qibla*). This place of prayer is sometimes associated with an entirely separate building but is more commonly thought to have been an apse in the church itself where Muslim pilgrims and local residents carried out their prayers for centuries. This latter interpretation of the arc as an apse is summarized in Dionigi Albera, "Mary and Multi-Faith Pilgrimages," in *The Oxford Handbook of Mary*, ed. Chris Maunder (Oxford: Oxford University Press, 2019), 623. Whatever the exact nature of Omar's instructions in 638 CE, it is clear that Muslims regularly prayed in the main nave area, even after the construction of the mosque in 1860. For a summary, see Claudio Alessandri, *The Restoration of the Nativity Church in Bethlehem* (Boca Raton, FL: CRC Press, 2020), 356. For a detailed study of how the Muslim residents of the neighboring Faghur village gradually moved into Bethlehem during the Ottoman period, eventually forming the distinct Fawaghreh Quarter by the end of the eighteenth century, see Khalil Showkeh, *Qariyat faghur wa-harat al-fawaghreh fi bayt lahm* (Bethlehem: self-pub., 2009). Showkeh documents how two of the Fawaghreh families, the Shakhur and the Showkeh families, were routinely appointed by the Ottoman district governor as the town shaykhs (*shuyūkh*), acting as mediators between the imperial state and the local population on issues such as tax collection, military service, and land sales. See pp. 86–102.

8. This scene took place on December 29, 1831, and was described in the travel memoir of the man who made the dramatic intervention—the German Trappist monk Ferdinand von Geramb. Here I have retold the story from the perspective of the local inhabitants, imagining it to be the day of Jubrail's mother's confirmation. Born in 1826, it is possible she would have completed her confirmation in the chapel of Santa Caterina around that time. See Ferdinand von Geramb, *A Pilgrimage to Palestine, Egypt and Syria*, vol. 1 (London: Henry Colburn, 1840), 134–35.

9. These processions were not rituals of time immemorial but the product of Ottoman reforms in the nineteenth century that allowed a more visible Christian

presence in Jerusalem and the surrounding area. This particularly impacted the Catholic community, which was permitted to reestablish the Latin Patriarchate in 1847, therefore facilitating the annual procession to Bethlehem on December 24. Likewise, the 1856 Ottoman Reform Edict awarded Christians the right to build new churches, to hold crosses in processions, and to ring church bells. For details of the wider impact of these reforms on Palestine, see Alexander Scholch, *Palestine in Transformation, 1856–1882: Studies in Social, Economic, and Political Development* (Washington, DC: Institute for Palestine Studies, 1993), 242, 270.

10. The language used to describe the entourage has been loosely adapted from Gabriel García Marquez's famous description of a pilgrimage entourage in *Love in the Time of Cholera*, trans. Edith Grossman (1985; repr., London: Penguin, 1989), 235–36.

11. I have adapted the description of the Christmas celebrations from various eyewitness accounts of the Catholic ceremonies in Bethlehem in the late nineteenth and early twentieth centuries, especially from the account of H. H. Kitchener, who attended the celebrations in Bethlehem in 1875. See Lord Kitchener, "Kitchener in Bethlehem," *Palestine Exploration Fund Quarterly Statement* 49 (1917), 36–39. I have also used the account in Jabra, *Al-bi'r al-ula*, 80–82.

CHAPTER 3: OF THE TOILS OF YOUSEF AND ROSA, OR HOW THE BETHLEHEMITES ACQUIRED THEIR NAMES

1. Multiple stories are told about the origins of the Dabdoub name, which conveys in Arabic the sense of "little bear," or even "teddy bear." Various versions of these stories are collected in Peter Dabdoub's short book on the family, Peter Dabdoub, *The Little Bear: Origins of the Dabdoub Family* (Mexico City: Endora, 2010). See also the website Dabdoub.PS (The Bethlehem Chronicle), accessed January 15, 2022, http://www.dabdoub-ps.com/397849332.

2. Among Arabic-speaking regions of the Ottoman Empire, Bethlehem was unique in having a long-standing Roman Catholic population. The Tarajmeh clan played a central role in the initial emergence of this community, acting as a key intermediary between the Franciscan friars and the wider population. This is evidenced in the Franciscan conversion records, which begin in the early seventeenth century and show a core list of initial converts hailing from the "dragoman" (*turcimanni* in Italian) families. Indeed, in the case of Bethlehem, the standard role of *turcimanni* took on a particular meaning to denote a whole community of families (including women and children) working for the Franciscan friars, rather than the usual individual translator or guide attached to a European consul. Rendered in local Arabic as *tarājmeh*, this role gave the clan in Bethlehem its name. For lists of the community of *turcimanni* in Bethlehem from the early seventeenth century onward, see Archivio Storico della Custodia di Terra Santa (ASCTS), Jerusalem,

Archivi delle parocchie, Betlemme S. Caterina, Registri sacramentali, 1/2: Liber confirmatorum.

Some stories in the oral tradition of the Tarajmeh families, meanwhile, assert that the Tarajmeh presence in Bethlehem goes back much further than the seventeenth century to the initial arrival of the Franciscans in the town in 1347. This tradition recounts how the Tarajmeh dispersed (either through conversion or relocation) upon the friars' imprisonment in Damascus by the Ottoman governor during 1537–40, only to later reestablish themselves once the friars were allowed back. The Franciscan conversion registers give some credence to this narrative, as the early entries of the *turcimanni* in the seventeenth century are all described as "reconciliato fattosi Greco" (reconciled having turned Orthodox), whereas later conversions are listed as "abbracciò la religione Cattolica" (embraced the Catholic faith). See ASCTS, Sacramenti: Riconciliati e convertiti (3).

3. The Tarajmeh's long history of close relations with the Franciscan friars led to numerous episodes of tension involving sexual affairs. In 1769, for example, a friar named Serafino at the Franciscan convent was found to be harboring an unnamed local widow in his cell at night. Having initially been dismissed from his position, Serafino convinced the Franciscan guardian in Jerusalem to give him a second chance. According to the curate in Bethlehem, the same woman was later found to be pregnant, causing her family to threaten to kill both her and the friar, "following the Arabic law always practiced here." This time Serafino was immediately dispatched to Verona and the woman sent "far away." Meanwhile the woman's family had to be placated in the Ottoman law courts to the tune of "at least fifteen thousand piasters." See Archives of the Sacred Congregation of the Propaganda Fide (SCPF), Rome, Scritture Riferite nei Congressi (SC), Terra Santa e Cipro, vol. 12, 89–90. This was clearly not an isolated incident at the convent in Bethlehem, as evidenced by a nearly identical case occurring in 1783. See Hogget-Attestato, December 1, 1783, no. 1058, in *L'Archivio storico della Custodia di Terra Santa*, ed. Andrea Maiarelli (Jerusalem: Terra Santa, 2012).

4. The origin stories of the Tarajmeh clan are numerous and varied. They usually involve a pair of brothers of noble European stock (French or Italian) who settled in Bethlehem and married into local society. From this point, two branches of the clan are said to have formed: *awlād ḥārat al-fawqa* (children of the upper floor) and *awlād ḥārat al-taḥta* (children of the lower floor), in reference to the two brothers living on two floors of the same house. Within the Dabdoub family, a particular version of this story has long circulated that specifies that two noble brothers from the Italian Monteforte family were sent by Pope Innocent III to capture and guard the Church of the Nativity as part of the Fourth Crusade in the early thirteenth century. This story, and various legends attached to it, are recounted in Dabdoub, *Little Bear*, 27–36, 66–69. Other oral traditions in the Tarajmeh clan, however, contradict this story of noble Italian origins.

An alternative version of the story is affirmed by Anton Mansour, whose family descends from the Abu Khalil family—the oldest recorded Tarajmeh family in the Bethlehem Latin Parish Archive. In this version, the clan's ancestor was a local mercenary soldier from the Galilee who joined the crusading Venetian forces of Simon V/VI de Montfort (of French, not Italian, origin) upon their landing in Jaffa in the 1240s. The descendants of this soldier maintained close relations with the Venetians and by the fourteenth century had taken up residence in Bethlehem, where they worked as translators at the newly opened Franciscan convent (dated to 1347). From this point, the same story about two brothers living on different floors of the same house is told. Anton's account is based on his family's oral tradition and his research in the Latin Parish Archive, as well as on extensive Y-DNA testing he has carried out on Tarajmeh family members. He maintains that none of these Y-DNA tests have revealed any European ancestry. My thanks to Anton for sharing his findings with me.

Stepping back from the details, the two versions reveal interesting aspects of Tarajmeh identity and collective memory. The most commonly told story—that of the two Italian noblemen—provides a powerful foundational myth for a group of families who have long based their identity on connections to Catholic Europe, rooting this identity in a genealogical and biological connection to noble Italian stock. This fits with the stereotype still held by other Bethlehem clans today that the Tarajmeh are haughty and obsessed with the idea of their European heritage. In Anton Mansour's alternative version, the Tarajmeh appear much more rooted in local society, albeit originating from further north, in the Galilee. I have tried to map these alternative versions of the Tarajmeh origins onto local rivalries in mid-nineteenth-century Bethlehem to explore the clan's sense of difference due to their close relations with the Franciscan friars.

5. The Franciscan Friars Minor developed some of Europe's earliest credit and banking systems in the fifteenth century in the form of the Monti di Pietà—essentially, charitable pawn shops where poor people could obtain loans at modest interest rates. See Annabel Jane Wharton, *Selling Jerusalem: Relics, Replicas, Theme Parks* (Chicago: University of Chicago Press, 2006), 120–25; and Ariel Toaff, "Jews, Franciscans, and the First *Monti di Pieta* in Italy (1462–1500)," in *Friars and Jews in the Middle Ages and Renaissance*, ed. Steven J. McMichael and Susan E. Myers (Leiden: Brill, 2004), 239–54.

6. Bernardino Amico served the Franciscan Custody of the Holy Land between 1593 and 1597 and produced the first scale drawings of many of the major Christian shrines of the area, including the Church of the Holy Sepulchre in Jerusalem and the Nativity Church in Bethlehem. The impact of his work on the Bethlehem souvenir industry is described in Bellarmino Bagatti, "L'Industria della madreperla a Betlemme," in *Custodia di Terra Santa 1342–1942* (Jerusalem: Tipografia dei Francescani, 1951), 133–52; and in Michele Piccirillo, *La nuova Gerusalemme: Artigia-*

nato Palestinese al servizio dei luoghi santi (Bergamo: Edizioni Custodia di Terra Santa, 2007), 28–29.

7. Artisans in Bethlehem trained in the abstract traditions of Islamic and Byzantine art had a long history of clashing with the more "realist" demands of western European patrons. For discussion of the Crusader period, see Lucy-Anne Hunt, "Art and Colonialism: The Mosaics of the Church of the Nativity in Bethlehem (1169) and the Problem of 'Crusader' Art," *Dumbarton Oaks Papers* 45 (1991): 69–85.

8. Franciscan scholar Michele Piccirillo provides a detailed inventory of over thirty surviving examples of these models, documenting their circulation around churches, palaces, and museums all over Europe, from the Palazzo Ducale in Venice to the Royal Danish Kunstkammer in Copenhagen. See Piccirillo, *La nuova Gerusalemme*. Numerous accounts written by travelers and pilgrims describe how the Franciscans commissioned local artisans in Bethlehem to make these models. Some of these accounts reveal the high prices they fetched among pilgrims. For example, a 1674 account written by a Jesuit priest, Michel Nau, stated that "the models of the Holy Sepulchre vary from 15 to 20 scudi." See Michel Nau, *Voyage de Terre-Sainte* (Paris: Pralard, 1679), 397. With an exchange rate into local piastres (or ghurush) of roughly 1 scudo to 1 and a half piastres, this means a single cross could fetch the equivalent of the annual per-capita rate of the jizya tax levied on non-Muslims (4 and a half piastres in 1679), although it should be remembered this is the amount the Franciscans received, not the artisans themselves. For the annual jizya rate, see Jerusalem Shari'a Court Sijill, Center for Palestinian Heritage, Abu Dis, Occupied Palestinian Territories, 181, p. 100, 1092 H/1681 CE. The conversion rate to the scudo is based on the assumption that a scudo was equivalent in value to a Venetian ducat, whose conversion rate of 1 and a half Ottoman ghurush is cited in Dror Ze'evi, *An Ottoman Century: The District of Jerusalem in the 1600s* (Albany, NY: SUNY Press, 1996), 144.

While tracing the precise identity of the artisans who made the models is a near impossible task, it is clear the Tarajmeh had specialized in this work by the early seventeenth century, as specified in the single reference Piccirillo was able to find to an artisan—"fatto da Giorgio nostro turcimanno" (made by our dragoman Jiryes)—from 1638 (see Piccirillo, *La nuova Gerusalemme*, 36).

For a detailed study of the composition and historical context behind two particular models held in the British Museum, see Jonathan Williams, Philip Kevin, Caroline Cartwright, and Jacob Norris, "Sacred Souvenir: The Holy Sepulchre Models in the British Museum and Their Material Historical Contexts," *British Museum Technical Research Bulletin* 8 (2014): 29–38.

9. This process is described in Corneille le Bruyn, *A Voyage to the Levant: Or, Travels in the Principal Parts of Asia Minor*, trans. W. J (London: Jacob Tonson,

1702), 200. The trade is a reminder that local women were deeply engaged in the encounter with Catholic Europe, even when the surface-level contact more visibly involved men. The Milk Grotto has long been revered as a distinctly female shrine—a place where local women, both Christian and Muslim, gathered in prayer and extracted powder from the cave walls to mix with water and make into small cakes, either for their own consumption or for sale to pilgrims.

10. In the eighteenth and nineteenth centuries, a Holy Land tattoo was a staple souvenir option for European pilgrims visiting Bethlehem and Jerusalem, with perhaps the most famous recipients being King Edward VII of the United Kingdom in 1862 and his sons, Princes Albert and George, in 1882. While the practice has a much longer history among Christians in the region, the Tarajmeh of Bethlehem appear to have specialized in the practice by the seventeenth century, as testified in numerous pilgrims' accounts. For examples that describe the specific "pricking" technique employed by the Bethlehem Tarajmeh, see Le Bruyn, *Voyage to the Levant*, 201–2; and *A Journey to Jerusalem: Or, A Relation of the Travels of Fourteen Englishmen, in the Year 1669* (London: T. M. for N. Crouch, 1672), 23–24.

11. This is the story of Scottish traveler William Lithgow, whose account of his visit to Bethlehem in 1612 describes how he managed to persuade a local artist he named "Elias Areacheros" to give him a distinctly Protestant tattoo featuring the crown of King James, paying the man two piastres—a large sum of money, considering that the annual rate of the jizya tax paid by non-Muslims *per person* was four and a half piastres in 1679. Lithgow reports how his Franciscan hosts subsequently became "greatly offended" upon seeing the tattoo. For this description and Lithgow's drawing of his tattoo (reproduced here in the main text), see William Lithgow, *Travels and Voyages through Europe, Asia, and Africa for Nineteen Years* (London: J. Meuros, 1770), 268–70. Lithgow's later misfortune of having the tattoo forcibly removed by the Spanish Inquisition in Malaga in 1620 is recounted in Clifford Edmund Bosworth, *An Intrepid Scot: William Lithgow of Lanark's Travels in the Ottoman Lands, North Africa and Central Europe, 1609–21* (London: Ashgate, 2006), 89.

12. Sources suggest that the Franciscans erred on the side of overproduction to ensure maximum levels of overseas demand could be met. This led to frequent episodes of friction with local artisans when sales abroad were temporarily saturated. European travelers' accounts, such as that penned by Swedish writer Frederik Hasselquist in the 1750s, state how the Bethlehemites would "attack and force [the friars] to buy a quantity of Paternosters, models of the grave of Christ, crosses, and other ware of this kind." See Fredrik Hasselquist, *Voyages and Travels in the Levant in the Years 1749, 50, 51, 52* (London: Royal Society, 1766), 148–49.

From the perspective of local artisans, the Franciscans had cultivated a sense of expectation that a steady stream of Catholic buyers was available. Some of them had taken out loans or bought property based on an assumed income from the souvenir trade—commitments they could no longer maintain when the Franciscans cut off the supply chain (see, for example, Hogget-Attestato, October 27, 1733, no. 895, in *L'Archivio storico*, ed. Maiarelli). As Hasselquist himself reported at the time of his visits in the early 1750s, there were fifteen-thousand-piastres-worth of Bethlehem-made devotional objects in the Franciscans' Jerusalem warehouse awaiting export to Europe (see Hasselquist, *Voyages and Travels*, 217).

13. The incident occurred in the 1760s and is described in Giovanni Mariti, *Viaggi per l'isola di Cipro e per la Sorìa e Palestina, fatti da Giovanni Mariti fiorentino dall'anno 1760 al 1768*, vol. 4 (Florence: Stamperia di S. A. R., 1770), 31–33.

14. The description of the courtyard is based on the description of a Bethlehem house in Mary Eliza Rogers, *Domestic Life in Palestine* (London: Poe & Hitchcock, 1865), 44. As discussed in chapter 5, it is likely Rogers was describing the Dabdoub house.

15. The advent in the mid-nineteenth century of mother-of-pearl waste extracts from the button industry in Europe and the United States is documented in a number of sources. A US Department of Commerce report from 1913 documents the sale of this waste product to Palestine in some detail, stating that the United States previously dominated the export sales but at that time England and Austria were increasing their share of the market with a superior quality of mother-of-pearl waste. The report even gives exact prices of pearl waste used in the Bethlehem trade at that time, ranging from eighteen cents to $3.20, depending on the provenance and quality of the product. See US Dept of Commerce, *Daily Consular & Trade Reports*, nos. 16 and 81, April 8, 1913, p. 136. Meanwhile, a study of excavations carried out in Jaffa and Jerusalem by Israeli archaeologist Inbar Ktalav has revealed further detail on the import of mother-of-pearl waste extracts into Palestine from Austria in the late nineteenth century. Out of 313 fragments of oyster shells found at the excavation sites, 258 were shown to be button waste. Ktalav concludes these imports were mainly destined for use in the Bethlehem souvenir industry. See Inbar Ktalav, "Button Waste and Religious Souvenirs in the Holy Land, during the 19th and Early 20th Centuries," *Quaternary International* 390 (2015): 133–45.

16. The effect of the import of Australian shells (via British empire trade routes) on carving in Bethlehem is documented in Enrique Yidi Daccarett, Karen David Daccarett, and Martha Lizcano Angarita, *El arte palestino de tallar el nacar* (Barranquilla: self-pub., 2005), 44–46.

17. Daccarett, Daccarett, and Angarita, 43–46.

18. The confirmation of "Elias il dottore" is recorded in the Franciscan records, as are the subsequent conversions, baptisms, and confirmations of his wife and descendants. The records show that this family formed the nucleus of the new Cath-

olic community in Bethlehem. See ASCTS, Jerusalem, Archivi delle parocchie, Betlemme S. Caterina, Registri sacramentali, 1/2: Liber confirmatorum.

19. The available sources speak almost exclusively of male-to-male encounters between local Bethlehemites and European pilgrims (the vast majority of whom were men until the late nineteenth century). This does not mean women did not play important roles as producers of souvenirs (examples of the Milk Grotto stone are discussed above), but contact with pilgrims was almost always between men. Indeed, the specialization of the Tarajmeh men as souvenir sellers seems to have put particular pressure on women to perform agricultural and domestic work in a town (or large village) that was still greatly reliant on subsistence agriculture for its food supplies until the late nineteenth century. For example, the Greek traveler L. S. Kosmopolites wrote upon visiting Bethlehem in 1753: "The wives [of the Catholic men] are employed in fetching wood, and providing victuals, tilling the field, looking for their cattel [sic], and carting their husband's work for Jerusalem, for sale." L. S. Kosmopolites, *A Series of Letters, Addressed to Sir William Fordyce*, vol. 2 (London: Payne and Son, 1788), 190–91. Meanwhile, a Franciscan report from as early as 1634 emphasized how the more urban women of nearby Jerusalem were excluded as marriage prospects for Bethlehem's Catholic men: "The men of Bethlehem have no need for women [from Jerusalem] who are always indoors, but rather for those who are out working in the vineyards and fields" (quei di Bettelemme non han bisogno di donne, che se ne stiano sempre in casa ritirate, ma sì bene, che si vadino fuori alle vigne e campi a lavorar). See Leonhard Lemmens, ed., *Acta S. Congregationis de propaganda fide pro Terra Sancta*, vol. 1 (1622–1720) (Quaracchi: Collegio di S. Bonaventura, 1921), 78.

20. All biographical details concerning the Dabdoub brothers' marriages and the ages of their brides are contained in the Dabdoub family records of the Bethlehem Latin Parish Archive.

21. The Franciscan inventories, held in the Archives of the Sacred Congregation of the Propaganda Fide (SCPF) in Rome, document a remarkable flow of riches into the Franciscan monasteries of Bethlehem and Jerusalem from the sixteenth century onward. These items mostly consisted of liturgical and decorative items sent from Catholic nobility all over Europe. A particularly detailed inventory of the Holy Land convents from the 1630s includes donations to the Bethlehem monastery of Saint Catherine's from the patriarch of Venice and the grand duke of Tuscany. See SCPF, Scritture Riferite, Terra Santa, vol. 1, 112–15. Megan Armstrong explores how this flow of goods reflected a renewed engagement with the Holy Land on the part of early modern Catholics seeking spiritual and political legitimacy in the context of the Counter-Reformation. See Megan Armstrong, *The Holy Land and the Early Modern Reinvention of Catholicism* (Cambridge: Cambridge University Press, 2021).

22. I have documented the frequent instances of theft from the Franciscans' monasteries in Jerusalem and Bethlehem, and the resulting security measures taken by the Franciscans, in Jacob Norris, "Dragomans, Tattooists, Artisans: Palestinian Christians and Their Encounters with Catholic Europe in the Seventeenth and Eighteenth Centuries," *Journal of Global History* 14, no. 1 (2019): 68–86.

CHAPTER 4: IN WHICH BETHLEHEM GETS A NEW STREET

1. The folktale of the wasps is described by Toine Van Teeffelen at https://palestine-family.net/the-wasps/

2. Palestinians have long associated the striped hyena with these demonic traits and practices. For an early academic discussion, see Tawfiq Canaan, *Mohammedan Saints and Sanctuaries in Palestine* (London: Luzac, 1927), 243–35. Striped hyenas and jackals still inhabit the Dead Sea wilderness today, albeit in smaller numbers, and continue to be hunted due to their association with evil jinn.

3. Numerous paintings, etchings, and early photographs testify to the fact that virtually no buildings existed beyond Qoos az-Zarara until the 1860s. For examples, see figures 1 and 2.

4. For the historic role of the Abu Ghosh family in controlling the road from Jaffa to Jerusalem and their clash with the Ottoman state during the mid to late nineteenth century, see Mustafa Abbasi, "'Guardians' of the Road: Abu Ghush Family in the Jerusalem Mountains during the Eighteenth and Nineteenth Centuries," *Jerusalem Quarterly* 78 (2019): 38–53. Abbasi describes how the Ottoman governor arrested Mustafa Abu Ghosh and imprisoned him in Cyprus between 1846 and 1853. After his release, he came under increasing pressure to yield to Ottoman authority (see pp. 47–49).

5. The construction of the new Dabdoub family home, dated between 1858 and 1860, arrived at a critical juncture in Ottoman land policy. The 1858 Ottoman Land Code made it obligatory for ownership of all lands to be registered, creating new categories of ownership in the process. As the lands around Ras Iftays fell outside Bethlehem's built-up urban area, they came under the *miri* category: state-controlled land that was leased out indefinitely to occupants who were given usufruct rights. Importantly, these rights included heritable right to possession of the land, as well as its profits. In Bethlehem, this appears to have led to a rush to establish possession of the land on Ras Iftays as the town's newly emerging merchant elite jostled for land and access to visiting pilgrims. As detailed below, the Dabdoubs appear to have been the first to have done so, but they were followed by a stream of other merchant families in the 1870s and '80s. The scramble among the Tarajmeh families to secure the title deeds to the lands at Ras Iftays is documented in the Jerusalem Shari'a Court records, which contain dozens of entries registering their occupancy of the land. See Jerusalem Shari'a Court Sijill, Center

for Palestinian Heritage, Abu Dis, Occupied Palestinian Territories, pp. 322–380, 1291–1308H/1874–1890 CE. These include disputes involving the Dabdoub family home and the limits of its lands (see endnote 12, below). More broadly, the land rush on Ras Iftays fits a wider pattern of land being increasingly marketized in Ottoman Palestine after the promulgation of the 1858 Land Code. Most historians agree that, while the code was designed to increase state revenue from taxation of land, it had the unintended effect of creating a de facto private land regime. This was particularly the case with *miri* lands, which made up the majority of land in Palestine and could now be bought, sold, and bequeathed by individuals, even though such lands were officially the property of the state. See Kemal H. Karpat, "The Land Regime, Social Structure, and Modernization in the Ottoman Empire," in *Studies on Ottoman Social and Political History: Selected Articles and Essays*, ed. Kemal H. Karpat (Leiden: Brill, 2002), 349; Haim Gerber, *Ottoman Rule in Jerusalem 1890–1914* (Berlin: Klaus Schwartz, 1984), 217–18; and Doreen Warriner, "Land-Tenure Problems in the Fertile Crescent in the Nineteenth and Twentieth Centuries," in *The Economic History of the Middle East 1800–1914*, ed. Charles Issawi (Chicago: University of Chicago Press, 1966), 72.

6. Evidence suggests Hosh Dabdoub was the very first residence built beyond Qoos az-Zarara. First, the memoir of Jubrail's cousin Ibrahim Yuhanna Dabdoub (b. 1853) states that he was sent to work at Hosh Dabdoub at the age of twelve (i.e., in 1865). Second, a property registration document from 1867 shows the land at Hosh Dabdoub was already registered in the name of Yousef Dabdoub's four sons (see endnote 8, below). Third, it appears that the construction of houses on the road began at the top of the hill and worked its way down. Hosh Dabdoub is at the highest point on the hill and is therefore likely to have been built slightly earlier than the Dawid house (1859), on the other side of the street, and Dar Mikel (1878), further down on the same side. These two houses can be dated more confidently due to inscriptions on their facades.

7. I have not been able to obtain specific information on the architects who designed the new Dabdoub residence. With its mixture of European influences (the long, linear shape of the house) and Ottoman-Islamic designs (the pointed archways of the main door at street level and the riwaq arched arcade), the house represented a breakthrough in architectural design in Bethlehem and most likely involved input from prominent architects outside of Bethlehem, possibly including Europeans. For this reason, I have kept the descriptions of the building team deliberately vague, imagining the scene from the perspective of people in the old town looking at the planning team and wondering where they had come from. The stonemasons, meanwhile, would almost certainly have been local to the Bethlehem area, as the town had a longstanding reputation for stonecutting and stonemasonry due to its proximity to large limestone deposits. Most of the new

houses in Jerusalem in the late nineteenth and early twentieth centuries were built by Bethlehem stonemasons, as reported in Yehoshua Ben-Arieh, *Jerusalem in the Nineteenth Century: The Emergence of the New City* (New York: St. Martin's Press, 1986), 400; and Ruth Kark and Michal Oren-Nordheim, *Jerusalem and Its Environs: Quarters, Neighborhoods, Villages, 1800–1948* (Detroit, MI: Wayne State University Press, 2001), 126.

8. An 1867 document from the Bethlehem waqf records shows that the land on Ras Iftays was registered in the name of Yousef and Rosa's four surviving sons: Hanna, Mikhail, Jubrail, and Ibrahim. This document is reproduced in Khalil Showkeh, appendix A, *Tarikh bayt lahm fi-1 -'ahd al-'uthmani* (Bethlehem, 2005).

9. A description written in the early 1890s by an English reverend named James Kean describes an encounter that quite possibly took place on the roof of Hosh Dabdoub, just past the Wells of David (Biyar Daoud) at the top of Ras Iftays. Written in the second person, the description gives a sense of how appealing this view was to pilgrims' sensibilities:

> You step on to the roof of a newly built cottage by the roadside, and sit down. The back wall is towards the road, and no higher than an ordinary fence: the ground in front is deeper. Conversation on the roof reaches the ears of the inmates, who begin to come out and look up to see what is the matter. . . . Seated on this perch, you gaze south across the valley upon Bethlehem, the eye dwelling especially on the vast confused conglomeration of lofty buildings at the east end. These cover and contain the cave wherein our Lord was born. A certain whiteness seems to add majesty to the general aspect of Bethlehem.

See Rev. James Kean, *Among the Holy Places: A Pilgrimage Through Palestine* (London: T. F. Unwin, 1895), 114.

10. For a more detailed discussion of the innovative architecture of the new Dabdoub residence, see my article, Jacob Norris, "Mobile Homes: The Refashioning of Palestinian Merchant Homes in the Late Ottoman Period," *Jerusalem Quarterly* 83 (2020): 9–33.

11. A letterhead used by Yousef and Rosa's eldest child, Hanna (Jubrail's eldest brother), dated December 9, 1899, used this design as the company logo (private collection of George al-A'ma). I have imagined this to be the original design used on the first shop front erected by Yousef. The new Dabdoub residence is thought to have been one of the first houses in Bethlehem to incorporate a fully-fledged store and warehouse into its design. It is likely it would have included some sort of sign visible to potential customers from the street. For the explosion of public signs and lettering in Palestine during this period, see Yair Wallach, *A City in Fragments: Urban Text in Modern Jerusalem* (Stanford, CA: Stanford University Press, 2020);

and Ami Ayalon, *Reading Palestine: Printing and Literacy, 1900–1948* (Austin: University of Texas Press, 2010).

12. The dispute was recorded on January 26, 1888. See Jerusalem Shari'a Court Sijill, Center for Palestinian Heritage, Abu Dis, Occupied Palestinian Territories Sijill, 378, p. 135, 1306 H/1888 CE. Al-Commandari's claim was made against Jubrail's eldest brothers, Hanna and Mikhail, who were in charge of the Dabdoub family business by that time. The entry states that the brothers were disputing a wider piece of *miri* land on Ras Iftays that included olive and fig orchards occupied by some of Bethlehem's most successful merchants at that time, including Hanna Mansour and Hanna Nassar. Interestingly, it is noted that al-Commandari's brother, Francis, is "absent abroad" (*ghā'ib 'an al-waṭn*), denoting the extent to which these disputes played out in the context of overseas business ventures that led to increased competition among merchant families.

13. A number of the new houses built on Ras Iftays in this era incorporated their own chapels. See Ghadeer Najjar, *Bethlehem: The Historic Center and Bethlehemites in Jerusalem* (Bethlehem: Diyar, 2017), 42. I am grateful to Ghadeer for informing me that Hosh Dabdoub included such a chapel and that these chapels were built to compensate the prophet Musa (Moses) for the trees cut down in the construction of the houses.

14. These descriptions are based on interviews with Jubrail Dabdoub's great-nephew, Dr. Michel Dabdoub (Bethlehem, March 15 and 17, 2011), and email correspondence with Anton Mansour, great-great-grandson of Hanna Mansour.

15. These mansions all still stand today, a little lower on the hill than Hosh Dabdoub. A number of them still bear the family name and date of construction on their facades. Today the road is known as Star Street and is part of Bethlehem's UNESCO World Heritage pilgrimage route.

16. The Abu Fuad bakery was formed in 1886 and is still in operation today. The Sabbagh café is described in Najjar, *Bethlehem*, 43. The monkeys and performing bears on Ras Iftays appear in a slightly later period (the 1920s), in the childhood autobiography of Jabra Ibrahim Jabra, *Al-bi'r al-ula: fusul min sirah dhatiyah* (Beirut: al-mu'assisah al-'arabiyah lil-dirasat wa al-nashr, 2001), 84–85.

17. The mosaics and cemetery were discovered in 1895, prompting largely unfounded speculation that this might be the site of King David's burial. See Bellarmino Bagatti, *Gli antichi edifici sacri di Betlemme in seguito algli scavi e restauri praticati dalla Custodia di Terra Santa, 1948–1951* (Jerusalem: Franciscan Printing Press, 1952), 248–55. The site had long attracted tourists and pilgrims before the 1895 discovery due to the local belief that these were the Wells of David, but the new excavations clearly increased the site's popularity among visitors. Compare, for example, the Baedeker guide to Palestine and Syria from 1876 and 1912 (p. 242 and p. 178, respectively).

18. The practice of employing servants in Palestinian homes has largely been overlooked by historians. Caroline Kahlenberg's article "New Arab Maids: Female Domestic Work, 'New Arab Women,' and National Memory in British Mandate Palestine," *International Journal of Middle East Studies* 52 (2020): 449–67 is a breakthrough in this regard, charting the employment of maids in mandate-era Palestine as an essential component of the construction of the "new Palestinian woman." Prior to the mandate period, knowledge of this area is limited. Oral tradition in Bethlehem frequently states that maids from the Taʿamreh villages began to be employed in the new houses of the Tarajmeh on Ras Iftays at the end of the Ottoman period. But there is clearly a longer history of servants and even slaves still to be uncovered, not least in Bethlehem, given the existence there of an archway named Qoos al-Abid (Arch of the Slaves). In the Beersheba District, meanwhile, Salman Abu Sitta describes how several African families had been working for generations by the 1930s as servants in his household in the village of al-Maʾin. See Salman Abu Sitta, *Mapping My Return: A Palestinian Memoir* (Cairo: American University in Cairo Press, 2016), 6–7. Kahlenberg also documents how British Mandate officials investigated the practice of selling girls of former black slaves of Bedouin tribes to wealthy families in Nablus and Jenin as *abid* (slaves/servants). See Kahlenberg, "New Arab Maids," 466.

19. Kahlenberg describes the circulation of women's magazines among bourgeois households in Palestine in the 1920s and '30s. Magazines such as the Beirut-based women's magazine *Al-marʾa al-Jadida* (The new woman) and the Palestinian radio program *Al-bayt al-ʿarabi al-jadid* (The new Arab home) gave advice on how women should interact with their maids in an even-tempered, professional manner. Kahlenberg describes how this was largely in line with western European discourse at that time, suggesting that some Palestinian housekeepers treated their maids and servants with harsher methods, including physical punishment. See Kahlenberg, "New Arab Maids," 455–59.

20. The Aftimos market was a new market in late nineteenth-century Jerusalem where the finest fabrics in Jerusalem could be purchased. It was founded on land in the west of the Old City bought by the Greek Orthodox patriarch in 1837. See Sylvia Auld, Robert Hillenbrand, and Yusuf Natsheh, *Ottoman Jerusalem: The Living City, 1517–1917*, vol. 1 (London: Altajir World of Islam Trust, 2000), 230.

21. The 1860s through the 1880s was a period of unprecedented growth in the numbers of pilgrims visiting Jerusalem, Bethlehem, and the wider "Holy Land." For the birth of western European and North American package tours in this period, see Timothy Larsen, "Thomas Cook, Holy Land Pilgrims, and the Dawn of the Modern Tourist Industry," *Studies in Church History* 36 (2000): 329–42. For the growth in numbers of Russian pilgrims, see Derek Hopwood, *The Russian Presence in Syria and Palestine 1843–1914* (Oxford: Clarendon Press, 1969).

22. Based on Jabra's account in *Al-bi'r al-ula*, 48.

23. Jabra describes how he would carry out these tasks as a young boy for a local carver named Khalil Zmairiyya. See *Al-bi'r al-ula*, 100.

24. These items commonly appear in the inventories of Bethlehem businesses by the end of the nineteenth century. For example, a business card of Jubrail Dabdoub's younger brother Ibrahim from around the turn of the twentieth century lists "stones from the Dead Sea and Mecca fruit beads" among his shop's items for sale (private collection of George al-A'ma). As early as 1817, the English traveler and clergyman Edward Daniel Clarke describes the "Mecca fruit" beads he was sold, made from "a very hard kind of wood whose natural history we could not learn." The beads, he goes on, were "dyed yellow, black or red." See Edward Daniel Clarke, *Travels in Various Countries of Europe, Asia and Africa*, vol. 4 (London: Cadell and Davies, 1817), 305. The Bethlehemites' sale of the black bitumen rock from the Dead Sea (known locally in Arabic as *hajar musa*) was described in 1867 by M. Louis Lartet in the London-based scientific journal *The Intellectual Observer*: "The Christians of Bethlehem make religious symbols out of it that they sell, under the name of Dead Sea stones, to the numerous pilgrims who flock every year to Jerusalem." See "Lartet on the Asphalt of the Dead Sea," *Intellectual Observer* 10 (1867): 63.

25. Such cards were widely sold in Bethlehem souvenir shops by the end of the nineteenth century. They are listed as one of the items in the shop of Jubrail's brother Ibrahim (see previous note).

26. Edward Daniel Clarke's description of Mecca fruit beads from 1817 gives an interesting account of why pilgrims bought these locally available goods despite seemingly being aware of the large markup applied by the local merchants: "This sort of trumpery is ridiculed by all travelers: but we cannot say it was scouted by any of them; for there has not been one who did not encourage the manufactories by the purchases he made. It offers an easy method of obtaining large quantities of acceptable presents, which occupy little space, for the inhabitants of Greek and Catholic countries." See Clarke, *Travels in Various Countries*, 305–6.

27. The prices of the goods are based on sales of similar items listed in Ibrahim Yuhanna Dabdoub, "Mukhtasar tarikh 'ilat al-marhum Yuhanna Yaqoub al-Dabdoub" (unpublished memoir, 1923, private collection of Anton Shukri Dabdoub), 50–52. The sum of two hundred ghurush was equivalent to the monthly salary of an Ottoman policeman around that time (1870s). See Akram Khater, *Inventing Home: Emigration, Gender, and the Middle Class in Lebanon, 1870–1920* (Berkeley: University of California Press, 2001), 56.

28. Translated from the Arabic proverb اخطب لابنتك ولا تخطب لابنك.

29. I have carried out a statistical survey of all the Dabdoub marriages recorded in the Latin Parish Archive in Bethlehem between 1715 (the year of the first recorded marriage) and 1948. This constitutes a total of fifty-five marriages. Across these re-

cords, the average male age at marriage was 26.3 years old, while the average female age was 16.6 years old. Hanna and Mikhail's marriages in 1867 and 1873 conform remarkably closely to these averages, both for bride and groom. Overall, the average ages remained fairly constant over the course of the eighteenth, nineteenth, and early twentieth centuries. The most noticeable variation is a drop in the average age of female marriage in the twentieth century (prior to 1948) to 15.6 years. This might suggest that the consolidation of the family firms in the late nineteenth and early twentieth centuries pushed the Dabdoubs to seek out ever-younger brides to produce the maxim number of male sons for new overseas ventures.

CHAPTER 5: OF UNRULY MARKETS AND UNDERWATER SHIPS

1. These rooftop games are described in Jabra Ibrahim Jabra, *Al-bi'r al-ula: fusul min sirah dhatiyah* (Beirut: al-mu' assisah al-'arabiyah lil-dirasat wa al-nashr, 2001), 49–50, 61.

2. In her description of the Franciscan school in Bethlehem in the late 1850s, English traveler Mary Eliza Rogers writes how the boys showed her their Italian exercises and translations and "sang a Latin hymn to the Virgin, giving a peculiarly Oriental twang to the last sounds of every line." Mary Eliza Rogers, *Domestic Life in Palestine* (London: Poe and Hitchcock, 1865), 42–43.

3. Elias Suleiman Dabdoub (1857–1916) went on to become one of the most celebrated of Bethlehem's master carvers in the late nineteenth and early twentieth centuries. I have imagined he and Jubrail, as cousins of a similar age, to have been playmates as children. Among the mother-of-pearl masterpieces Elias later produced are models of the Dome of the Rock and the Jerusalem clock tower commissioned by Sultan Abdulhamid II around 1906. The Dome of the Rock model is today on display in the Topkapi Museum in Istanbul. Such was the fame of Bethlehem's mother-of-pearl carvers by then that royalty and political dignitaries around the world purchased their work or received it as gifts. This was especially the case with the brothers Bishara Zougbi (1863–1934) and Yousef Zougbi (1878–1964). See Enrique Yidi Daccarett, Karen David Daccarett, and Martha Lizcano Angarita, *El arte palestino de tallar el nacar* (Barranquilla: self-pub., 2005), 68–73.

4. This description of the old Dabdoub residence and the people in it is based on the description of a Bethlehem house provided in Rogers, *Domestic Life in Palestine*, 43–48. Rogers visited the house with her brother in the late 1850s, stating that it was the residence of a mother-of-pearl carver her brother had met on a previous visit. She describes the house in detail, as well as her encounter with the carver's wife, Mariam, their baby, and Mariam's mother. She also states that Mariam's first son is named Elias. She does not give the carver's name but states that he was an orphan at that time and that he was known in Bethlehem as one of the most skilled mother-of-pearl carvers. Based on these details, I have deduced the man was Su-

leiman Ibrahim Dabdoub (1813–1876), the first cousin of Jubrail's father, Yousef. Suleiman was an orphan in the early 1860s and was married to a woman named Mariam Abu-Fheleh (1836–1915), the daughter of Hanneh Souadi (1816–1900). Suleiman was renowned as one of Bethlehem's best carvers and was the father of Elias Dabdoub (described above), who features prominently in this chapter and went on to become a renowned mother-of-pearl artist. I have adapted Rogers's description to imagine Jubrail visiting his cousin Elias's house in the 1860s. The details of the house, the people's dress, the grandmother's tattoos, the baby's cradle, and the relic of Saint Joseph (Mar Yousef) all come from Rogers's description.

5. The new mosque built in 1860 was a small, modest building, standing at the far side of Nativity Square, opposite the church. See Khalil Showkeh, *Tarikh bayt lahm fi-1 -'ahd al-'uthmani* (Bethlehem, 2005), 273–75; and Nada al-Atrash, "World Heritage Site in Bethlehem and Its Potential Reflections on Tourism," in *The Politics and Power of Tourism in Palestine*, ed. Rami K. Isaac, C. Michael Hall, and Freya Higgins-Desbiolles (London: Routledge, 2015), 83. The mosque was then rebuilt by the Jordanian government in the 1950s with a far taller minaret. Before the construction of the mosque, a designated space for Muslim prayer existed within the Nativity Church complex, as related by the Muslim scholar Yaqut during the Crusader period. See Moshe Sharon, *Corpus Inscriptionum Arabicarum Palaestinae*, vol. 2: B–C (Leiden: Brill, 1997), 181. Despite the existence of specific sites of Muslim prayer, numerous travelers' accounts from the eighteenth and nineteenth centuries relate how Muslims prayed alongside Christians in the main nave of the Nativity Church. See, for example, Giovanni Mariti, *Viaggi per l'isola di Cipro e per la Sorìa e Palestina, fatti da Giovanni Mariti fiorentino dall'anno 1760 al 1768*, vol. 3 (Florence: Stamperia di S. A. R., 1770), 44.

6. The origins of the Fawaghreh clan lie in the nearby village of Faghur and the migration of people from that village to Bethlehem beginning in the sixteenth century. The migration increased after a conflict with the neighboring village of Beit Suweir in the mid-eighteenth century that destroyed Faghur. The two most prominent families within the clan were (and still are) the Shakhur and Showkeh families, who always assumed the Ottoman-appointed role of town shaykh. Generally, however, the Fawaghreh were quite a poor clan in Bethlehem due to their peasant origins, and they did not profit from the mother-of-pearl trade to the same degree as the town's Christians. Indeed, in the nineteenth century many of them left Bethlehem to settle as cattle farmers in nearby villages such as Wadi Rahhal, Jurat ash-Sham'a, and Wadi al-Nis. See Khalil Showkeh, *Qariat faghur wa-harat al-fawaghreh fi bayt lahm* (Bethlehem, self-pub., 2009), 86–91, 110–120, 143–47; and Ruth Kark and Michal Oren-Nordheim, *Jerusalem and Its Environs: Quarters, Neighbourhoods, Villages, 1800–1948* (Detroit, MI: Wayne State University Press, 2001), 272–73. The reverence in which Bethlehem's Muslims hold the Virgin Mary

results from the prominent position afforded to her and the story of Jesus's birth in Muslim scripture and subsequent traditions. Famously, the Quran devotes more space to Jesus's conception and birth than the New Testament does. In much subsequent Muslim tradition, especially in Sufi practices, the Virgin and Jesus assume various kinds of saintly status. For further discussion, see Tarif Khalidi, *The Muslim Jesus: Sayings and Stories in Islamic Literature* (Cambridge, MA: Harvard University Press, 2001).

7. Hanna and Mikhail's participation at the Paris Exposition Universelle in 1867 was related to me in conversations with Mikhail's grandson, Dr. Michel Dabdoub (interviews in Bethlehem, March 15 and 17, 2011). Their presence at the Paris exhibition, alongside others from Bethlehem, such as the Atik and Mubarak families, is confirmed in the official exhibition catalog, which lists several Bethlehem mother-of-pearl and olive-wood carvers with these family names in the Ottoman section. See *Catalogue général: Exposition Universelle de 1867 à Paris. Oeuvres d'art: Groupe I, Classes 1 à 5*, vol. 1 (Paris: Dentu, 1867), 197.

8. The Ottoman *ayak* was a unit of measure equivalent to 378 mm, meaning 114 *ayak* is equal to 43 meters. The submarine in question, *Le plongeur*, famously inspired Jules Vernes to write *Twenty Thousand Leagues under the Sea* after he saw it exhibited at the Paris Exposition Universelle of 1867.

9. Reference is made to "les petits ouvrages en bois d'olivier de Jérusalem" in the official Ottoman report of the exposition. See Salaheddin Bey, *La Turquie à l'Exposition universelle de 1867* (Paris: Hachette, 1867), 138. For a description of the various components of the so-called Turkish Village, as well as the visit of Sultan Abdülaziz, see Zeynep Çelik, *Displaying the Orient: Architecture of Islam at Nineteenth-Century World's Fairs* (Berkeley: University of California Press, 1992), 60–61.

10. The Ottoman disappointment at not being included within the main exhibition hall alongside the European nations is expressed in Salaheddin Bey, *La Turquie à l'Exposition*, 29–30.

11. A third-class fare on a steamship from Alexandria to Marseille in the late 1860s cost around 140 francs (the equivalent of 685 Ottoman ghurush). Once the cost of hotels, railway tickets, and touts was factored in, the journey would have cost well over 700 ghurush. This was a huge sum of money in Bethlehem at the time, as evidenced by the sale prices of mother-of-pearl carvings. In the memoir of Ibrahim Yuhanna Dabdoub (a cousin of Jubrail), top-end mother-of-pearl works (that could take weeks to produce by teams of carvers) would fetch between 5 and 10 ghurush. See Ibrahim Yuhanna Dabdoub, "Mukhtasar tarikh ʿilat al-marhum Yuhanna Yaqoub al-Dabdoub" (unpublished memoir, 1923, private collection of Anton Shukri Dabdoub), 13, 15.

12. Antonio Belloni was an important figure in the expansion of the Bethlehemite souvenir businesses into western Europe and appears several times in this

book, including in chapter 18 as a spiritual mentor to Marie-Alphonsine, the nun who saved Jubrail's life in 1909. Belloni, known locally as "Abulyatama" (Father of the Orphans), established an orphanage in Bethlehem in 1864 with an adjoining technical school that trained the orphans in mother-of-pearl and olive-wood carving. Over time, he bought increasing quantities of souvenirs from local artisans as sale and gift items to his benefactors in Europe. Unlike the Franciscans, he also actively helped and encouraged local merchants to sell their products abroad, providing them with access to his wide network of benefactors, especially in France, Belgium, Germany, and Italy. This produced considerable opposition among the Franciscan friars but also ensured his legacy in Bethlehem as a hero of the town's wealth creation in the late nineteenth century. Local historian George Sammur, for example, attributes his grandfather's step up from Manger Square hawker to workshop owner in the 1880s to the sales contacts Belloni helped him establish. See George Sammur, *Bayt lahm 'abr al-tarikh* (Bethlehem: Wiam, 2007), 76–77. The Franciscans' lengthy condemnations of Belloni's activities in Bethlehem are held in the Archives of the Sacred Congregation of the Propaganda Fide (SCPF), Rome, Scritture Riferite nei Congressi (SC), Terra Santa e Cipro, vol. 29, 611–703.

By 1891 Belloni had incorporated his orphanage into the Italy-based Salesian Society, providing greater financial security and eventually a gleaming new church—the Church of the Sacred Heart—constructed in 1902. The records held by the Salesian Society in Bethlehem document the regular flows of devotional objects from the orphanage to benefactors and dignitaries all over Europe. A number of bulletins in the society's newsletter show how Belloni used these connections to promote local Bethlehem souvenir businesses. For example, he sent regular shipments to the Roman Catholic Cathedral in Tournai, Belgium, of "objets de piété et de fantaisie fabriqués à Bethléem." These included "toutes sortes de chapelets" (all kinds of rosaries) and "crucifix en nacre pour oratoire" (mother-of-pearl crucifixes for use in prayers), which were then sold at a certain "dépôt de ces objets chez M. Decallonne-Liagre" in Tournai's Grand Place. See Collection of the Bethlehem Salesian Church, *Bulletins de Tournai sur l'Oeuvre de Bethléem, de 1873 à 1880*. See, for example, the entry for May 15 through June 15, 1873, p. 5. I am grateful to Don Mario Murru for allowing me access to these records.

Hanna Mansour is frequently mentioned in Bethlehem oral tradition as the "right-hand man" of Antonio Belloni, who trained him in bookkeeping and various forms of merchant trading. Mansour's status as one of the most successful Bethlehem merchants is attributed to this relationship. My thanks to Anton Mansour, great-great-grandson of Hanna Mansour, for sharing many of his family stories with me. I have also mentioned Abdallah Atik here, as he is listed as one of the Bethlehemite displayers of mother-of-pearl wares in the *Catalogue général* (p. 197) of the Paris exhibition of 1867.

CHAPTER 6: OF SUNKEN EYES IN A CASKET, OR HOW BETHLEHEM CAME TO BE COVERED IN DUST

1. This criticism is based on Jabra's recollections of his father's view of Catholics in the town. Jabra's family was from Bethlehem's small Syriac Orthodox community. See Jabra Ibrahim Jabra, *Al-bi'r al-ula: fusul min sirah dhatiyah* (Beirut: al-mu'assisah al-'arabiyah lil-dirasat wa al-nashr, 2001), 97.

2. The earthquakes of 1868 occurred on January 24, February 19, and October 7. See Thomas Chaplin, "Observations on the Climate of Jerusalem," *Palestine Exploration Fund Quarterly* 15, no. 1 (1883): 32.

3. The *khamasin* began in September. The majority of the olive-picking season takes place later, toward the end of October. But some varieties of olives in the Bethlehem area are harvested at the end of September or at the beginning of October, depending on rainfall and temperatures that year. The harvest of 1868 was preceded by a wet winter and hot summer, meaning the harvest would have begun early. See Chaplin, "Observations," 17, 22.

4. Chaplin describes the *khamasin* of 1868 as a freak event. See Chaplin, "Observations," 17.

5. Chaplin records a temperature drop of 35 degrees Fahrenheit in the four days between the *khamasin* ending on October 30 (88 degrees Fahrenheit) and the end of the subsequent rainstorms beginning on November 3 (53 degrees Fahrenheit). He also notes the two clouds drifting over from a westerly direction on the morning of October 30. See Chaplin, "Observations," 17.

6. The Bethlehem Latin Parish Archive records that Jubrail's brother Murqus died on November 30, 1868, at the age of seventeen. The reason for his death is unknown, but I have imagined it here to have been caused by cholera. Between the years of 1865 and 1870, the area around Jerusalem (including Bethlehem) was struck by various waves of a cholera epidemic. This was part of the global pandemic of 1865–75, which was transmitted from the Indian subcontinent to the Middle East via Hajj pilgrims returning from Mecca. See Alexander Scholch, *Palestine in Transformation, 1856–1882: Studies in Social, Economic, and Political Development* (Beirut: Institute for Palestine Studies, 1993), 32–33; and E. Schwartz, D. Bar-El, and N. Schur, "The History of Cholera Epidemics in Israel," *Harefuah* 144 no. 5 (May 2005): 363–70.

7. This is a reference to the saint's shrine in the church of the nearby village of al-Khadr. Pledging gifts as votive offerings as a way of inducing the assistance of saints was common practice in Palestine. For Christians, this was particularly the case with al-Khadr. The specific offerings described here, as well as the placing of the plate on the sick child's head, are taken from Tawfiq Canaan, *Mohammedan Saints and Sanctuaries in Palestine* (London: Luzac, 1927), 134, 257.

8. Jubrail's traumatization upon seeing his brother's dead body at the wake is

adapted from the much later experience of his granddaughter, Alice-Madeleine Dabdoub, who was forced to attend the wake of her cousin when staying at her grandfather's house as a young girl in the 1930s. Alice describes how the sight of the dead body traumatized her and how from that day on, she never attended funeral wakes again. Here I have imagined a similar reaction being provoked in the young Jubrail upon seeing his brother's dead body, especially due to the effect of cholera on the eyes. My thanks to Alice's son, José Eduardo Siman, for sharing his mother's experiences with me.

9. The description of the preparation of Murqus's body is based on conversations with elderly people in Bethlehem today, as well as on information provided in H. H. Spoer and A. M. Spoer, "Sickness and Death among the Arabs of Palestine," *Folklore* 38, no. 2 (1927): 135–39.

CHAPTER 7: OF MECHANICAL WONDERS ON NEAR AND DISTANT SHORES

1. The white donkey, green robe, and digging of canals are symbols of prosperity in classical Arabo-Islamic dream interpretation, as described most famously by the seventh-century scholar Ibn Seerin. See Ibn Seerin, *Ibn Seerin's Dictionary of Dreams according to Islamic Inner Traditions*, trans. Shaykh Muhammad al-Akili (Philadelphia, PA: Pearl, 2004), 67, 124, 184. The digging of the canal also doubles as an omen of Jubrail's future voyage to the Philippines via the Suez Canal. The use of generic dream symbols is an attempt to replicate magical realism's interest in Jungian psychology with its emphasis on dream symbol archetypes and myths. See Seymour Menton, *Magic Realism Rediscovered, 1918–1981* (Philadelphia, PA: Art Alliance Press, 1983), 13–14.

2. For the general surge in Western tourism and pilgrimage to the Holy Land in the late 1860s and 1870s, including to Bethlehem, see Naomi Shepherd, *The Zealous Intruders: The Western Rediscovery of Palestine* (New York: Harper and Row, 1987), 187–94.

3. A sizeable literature exists on the subjugation and violence that underpinned representations of colonial subjects at the world's fairs of the late nineteenth century and how this subjugation inaugurated a Western engagement with colonial peoples as objects of visual consumption—the world conceived as though it were an exhibition. For a classic rendering of this argument, see Timothy Mitchell, "The World as Exhibition," *Comparative Studies in Society and History* 31, no. 2 (1989): 217–36.

4. As much as the world's fairs were sites of colonial subjugation, they also opened up economic opportunity for a wide range of noncolonial actors seeking to profit from the colonial gaze. This was clearly the case with the Bethlehem merchants, who targeted the world's fairs with remarkable intensity in the expansion

of their businesses. I take my cue here from the growing literature that brings out the agency of Ottoman and Egyptian actors who sought to manipulate the orientalist stereotypes of the world's fairs to their economic advantage and also reshape them according to their own notions of cultural heritage. For examples, see Julia Phillips Cohen, "Oriental by Design: Ottoman Jews, Imperial Style, and the Performance of Heritage," *American Historical Review* 119, no. 2 (2014): 364–98; and Zeynep Çelik, *Displaying the Orient: Architecture of Islam at Nineteenth-Century World's Fairs* (Berkeley: University of California Press, 1992), 10–11.

5. This is vividly demonstrated in the memoir of Jubrail's cousin Ibrahim Yuhanna Dabdoub, who describes how he and his brothers circulated the European exhibitions in the 1880s and 1890s. In one passage, he lists four exhibitions visited by his brother Anton in the space of as many years (Copenhagen, Torino, Lisbon, and Paris). See Ibrahim Yuhanna Dabdoub, "Mukhtasar tarikh 'ilat al-marhum Yuhanna Yaqoub al-Dabdoub" (unpublished memoir, 1923, private collection of Anton Shukri Dabdoub), 8–9.

6. A specific passage in Ibrahim Yuhanna Dabdoub's memoir describes how he and his brother Anton were arrested and held for four hours by police at an exhibition in London in 1880 because they didn't have a permit to sell ("ma kān maʿna amr lil-biiʿ"). Dabdoub, "Mukhtasar," 5.

7. The success of the Bethlehemites at the Vienna exhibition is described in "Orientals at Vienna," *Popular Science Monthly* (August 1873): 493–97. The memoir of Ibrahim Yuhanna Dabdoub also documents the profits made by various Bethlehem merchants at the exhibition. See Dabdoub, "Mukhtasar," 4. The model of Jerusalem was made by Stephen Illés, a Hungarian bookbinder who lived in Jerusalem and later displayed the model all over Europe, beginning at the 1873 Vienna Exhibition. It was built from zinc on a scale of one to five hundred. See Rehav Rubin, "Stephan Illes and His 3d Model-Map of Jerusalem (1873)," *Cartographic Journal* 44, no.1 (2007): 71–79. Today the model is held in the Tower of David Museum in Jerusalem.

8. A description and illustrations of the Ottoman Pavilion at Vienna are provided in Zeynep Çelik, *Displaying the Orient*, 63–67.

9. See, for example, the article "Orientals at Vienna," *Popular Science Monthly* 3 (Aug 1878): 493–97. The article includes a reference to "the carved olive-wood from Jerusalem [that] recalls the pedlers' hawking goods made for sale at the doors of the Holy Sepulchre" (497).

10. This detail on Yaqub Giacaman is provided in the French National Archives from when he was one of four Bethlehem merchants lobbying the French Foreign Ministry to establish an Arabic-speaking Melkite church in Paris. See Archives Nationales (AN), Pierrefitte-sur-Seine, Paris, ministère de l'Instruction Publique to Prefecture de Police, May 15, 1886, F/19/5590.

11. A number of histories of Arab immigration to Brazil cite the Zakhariyya brothers as the first migrants from the region to establish a presence in Brazil. For the most detailed account, see Jorge S. Safady, "A Imigração Árabe no Brasil (1880–1971)" (PhD diss., Universidade de São Paulo, 1972), 78. Safady states that the Zakhariyya brothers opened a shop in 1874 selling Holy Land curios on Rua da Alfandega in the center of Rio de Janeiro. This was a busy commercial area at the time, set back a short distance from the city's port, popular among immigrants opening small businesses. Transatlantic postal services to Jerusalem were still highly unreliable in the early 1870s; hence, I have imagined that news of the Zakhariyya brothers was carried back to Bethlehem via the regular flow of Franciscan friars into the town, many of whom had also served their order in Latin America. My thanks to Arlene Clemesha for her help tracking down the references to the Zakhariyya brothers in Brazil.

12. These early postal services in Jerusalem are discussed in Johann Büssow, *Hamidian Palestine: Politics and Society in the District of Jerusalem 1872–1908* (Leiden: Brill, 2011), 450–51.

13. Plans to construct the Jaffa–Jerusalem Railway went back at least as far as 1873, nine years before its eventual completion. See Anthony Travis, *On Chariots with Horses of Fire and Iron: The Excursionists and the Narrow Gauge Railroad from Jaffa to Jerusalem* (Jerusalem: Hebrew University Magnes Press, 2008), 27–32.

14. The participation of the Banayut brothers at the Philadelphia Centennial International Exhibition of 1876 is recorded in the City of Philadelphia Archives, as cited in Eric Davis, "Representations of the Middle East at American World Fairs," in *United States and the Middle East: Cultural Encounters*, ed. Abbas Amanat and Magnus T. Bernhardsson (New Haven, CT: Yale University Center for International and Area Studies, 2002), 359.

15. Linda K. Jacobs discusses how Mikhail (rendered "Michel" in English) and Beshara Dabdoub are recorded in the Philadelphia City Archives as the owners of one of two Bethlehem bazaars (the other belonging to the Banayut brothers) at the Centennial International Exhibition of 1876. These records also show how the Dabdoubs had gained prior approval from the Ottoman authorities and paid customs duties prior to their arrival in Philadelphia. See Linda K. Jacobs, "Palestine at the Centennial Fair of 1876," *Jerusalem Quarterly* 80 (2019): 81–83. For more discussion of the success of the Bethlehem bazaars in Philadelphia, see Davis, "Representations of the Middle East," 359; James D. McCabe, *The Illustrated History of the Centennial Exhibition* (Philadelphia, PA: National Publishing Company, 1876), 617; Louise Seymour Houghton, "Syrians in the United States," *The Survey: A Journal of Constructive Philanthropy* 26 (1911): 480–95; and Adele L. Younis, *The Coming of the Arabic-Speaking People to the United States* (New York: Center for Migration Studies, 1995), 144–48.

16. The phrasing of this sentence is an adaptation of Gabriel García Marquez's description of the arrival of the first train in the fictional village of Macondo, which has inspired the general tone of this chapter. Marquez writes: "El inocente tren amarillo que tantas incertidumbres y evidencias, y tantos halagos y desventuras, y tantos cambios, calamidades y nostalgias había de llevar a Maconodo." Gabriel García Marquez, *Cien años de soledad* (1967; repr., Madrid: Espasa-Calpe, 1982), 266.

CHAPTER 8: IN SEARCH OF AMERKA

1. This chapter introduces part 2 of the book by stepping back from the individual story of Jubrail Dabdoub to look more broadly at Bethlehem's emigration explosion in the late nineteenth century. By the early 1880s, the initial trickle of migrants out of the town had turned into a surge as hundreds of young men set off for the Americas.

2. The famous Lebanese writer, Ameen Rihani, who made the journey to New York as a young man in the 1880s, described the samasira as "rapacious bats" who would "hover around the emigrant." See Ameen Rihani, *The Book of Khalid* (1911; repr., Brooklyn, NY: Melville House, 2012), 29–32.

3. For more detail, see Jacob Norris, "Across Confessional Borders: A Microhistory of Ottoman Christians and Their Migratory Paths," in *Minorities and the Modern Arab World: New Perspectives*, ed. Laura Robson (Syracuse, NY: Syracuse University Press, 2016), 39–60.

4. The family record books in the Bethlehem Latin Parish Archive are littered with epitaphs such as "morto in America" or "morto in Marsiglia" from the late nineteenth and early twentieth centuries, without any further details provided.

5. The incident is documented in Archivo General del Ministerio de Asuntos Exteriores y Cooperación, Madrid, H 2698, Turquia, Politica, 1880, set of letters and telegrams, January 2, 1880, to February 13, 1881. The shipwrecked travelers are referred to only as "Turcos" (the most common appellation for Arabic-speaking Syrians at that time in Latin America), so I am only speculating they were from Bethlehem. My thanks to William Clarence Smith for sharing this reference with me.

6. The request of Giries (Don Jorge) Kattan was made on March 19, 1883, and is recorded in the Havana City Hall archives. See Rigoberto Menendez Paredes, "Los árabes en Cuba," in *Los árabes en América Latina: Historia de una emigración*, ed. Abdeluahed Akmir (Madrid: Siglo, 2009), 382.

7. In Jamaica, the Bethlehem families that had established trading bases by the end of the nineteenth century included the Handal, Sem'aan, Shamie, and Milady families. In Santo Domingo, the Sem'aan and Deek families were prominent, alongside a growing number of traders from Nazareth who had followed the Bethlehemites' example and begun settling there in the 1890s. In Cuba, meanwhile, a

small community of Bethlehemites had made the island their base by the 1890s. Families like the Babun and the Abad families imported luxury goods from Spain as well as from the American mainland. These families can be found in Najib Abdou's 1907 business directory. See Nagib T. Abdou, *Dr. Abdou's Travels in America and Commercial Directory of the Arabic Speaking People of the World* (Raleigh, NC: Moise A. Khayrallah Center for Lebanese Diaspora Studies Archive), 372, 381, 391–92, 394–95, accessed August 21, 2018, https://lebanesestudies.omeka.chass.ncsu.edu/items/show/13912.

8. This process is described by Brenda Gayle Plummer, who cites US consular reports on the early Syrian merchants in Haiti. See Brenda Gayle Plummer, "Race, Nationality, and Trade in the Caribbean: The Syrians in Haiti, 1903–1934," *International History Review* 3, no. 4 (October 1981): 519.

9. For example, Najib Abdou's business directory estimated the Syrian population in Cuba to be 2,500 in 1907. See Abdou, *Dr. Abdou's Travels*, 388.

10. Documented in Joseph Miller Wilson and Edward Strahan, *The Masterpieces of the Centennial International Exhibition*, vol.3, *History, Mechanics and Science* (Philadelphia: Gebbie and Barrie, 1876), 171. There were even reports of hawkers selling Holy Land goods in an Irish accent. See Eric Davis, "Representations of the Middle East at American World Fairs," in *United States and the Middle East: Cultural Encounters*, ed. Abbas Amanat and Magnus T. Bernhardsson (New Haven, CT: Yale University Center for International and Area Studies, 2002), 359.

11. Sources in numerous countries across the Americas describe this phenomenon. In the late nineteenth century, it seems to have been particularly pronounced in the United States and the Caribbean region. For examples, see Alix Naff, *Becoming American: The Early Arab Immigrant Experience* (Carbondale, IL: Southern Illinois University Press, 1985), 10; Louise Fawcett and Eduardo Posada-Carbo, "Arabs and Jews in the Development of the Colombian Caribbean, 1850–1950," in *Arab and Jewish Immigrants in Latin America: Images and Realities*, ed. Ignacio Klich and Jeff Lesser (London: Frank Cass, 1998), 70; and Luz Maria Martinez Martiel, "The Lebanese Community in Mexico," in *The Lebanese in the World: A Century of Emigration*, ed. Albert Hourani and Nadim Shehadi (London: I.B. Tauris, 1992), 382.

12. These sales techniques are documented in Gregory Orfalea, *Before the Flames: A Quest for the History of Arab Americans* (Austin: University of Texas Press, 1988), 81; and Naff, *Becoming American*, 81, 103, 170.

13. As reported in much of the Haitian press at the time, which vilified the Syrian immigrants. See Roger Gaillard, *Les Blancs Debarquent. La Republique Exterminatrice. Premiere Partie: Une Modernisation Manqueé, 1880–1896* (Port-au-Prince, 1991), 275–76.

14. The scapegoating of the Syrian traders in Haiti is documented in Plummer, "Race, Nationality and Trade." In Cuba, a handful of Syrians actually joined the

revolutionary forces in the War of Independence of 1895–98, including two Bethlehemites from the Abad family. But the Syrians were nonetheless accused of collaborating with the Spanish colonial government. See Paredes, "Los Arabes en Cuba," 372.

15. The "sweet waist of Amerka" is a reference to Pablo Neruda's 1950 poem "La United Fruit Co." on the United States' economic exploitation of Central America.

16. Charles L. Stansifer, "E. George Squier and the Honduras Interoceanic Railroad Project," *Hispanic American Historical Review* 46, no. 1 (1966): 1–27.

17. The role played by the banana plantations as an entry point for Bethlehemites (and Syrians more generally) trading in Central America (especially in Honduras) is discussed briefly in Roberto Marín Guzmán, "Los árabes en Centroamérica," in Akmir, *Los árabes*, 450–51; and Nancy Gonzáles, *Dollar, Dove, and Eagle: One Hundred Years of Palestinian Migration to Honduras* (Ann Arbor: University of Michigan Press), 68–69.

18. Two of Salameh's brothers, Suleiman and Damasio, had settled in the town of Pimienta by 1910 and were soon to be joined by the sons of their elder brother Daoud. My thanks to Jacobo Kattan, Luisa Fernanda Kattan de Castellanos, and Rolando Kattan Paredes for this information. I have also used the 1930 Honduran business directory, *Propaganda Pro Honduras* (Havana: Molina y Cia, 1930), San Pedro Sula Municipal Archives, 290, 330, 360.

19. The United Fruit Company.

20. Peter Chapman, *Bananas: How the United Fruit Company Shaped the World* (Edinburgh: Canongate, 2007), 102.

21. The introduction of company stores run by the American-owned plantations, as well as the opposition of the Bethlehemites to them, is documented in Dario Euraque, *Reinterpreting the Banana Republic: Region and State in Honduras, 1870–1972* (Chapel Hill: University of North Carolina Press, 2000), 33–35. The methods of adaptation employed by the Bethlehemites, including selling wholesale to the plantations and importing products from the United States using the banana boats, was related to me by descendants of the Kattan family, which played a leading role in this process. Interviews conducted with Jacobo Kattan, Luisa Fernanda Kattan de Castellanos, and Rolando Kattan Paredes, San Pedro Sula, Honduras, October 27 and 29, 2018.

22. The population of San Pedro Sula grew from around 600 in 1860 to around 1,200 in 1875 to 5,000 in 1900 and then to more than 10,000 by 1920. For detailed analysis of the rapid expansion of San Pedro Sula from the 1870s onward and its connection to the banana industry, see Euraque, *Reinterpreting*, 21–40; and Rodolfo Pastor Fasquelle, *Biografía de San Pedro Sula: 1536–1945* (DIMA, 1990), 340–78.

23. The Kattan family claims to have introduced the first postcodes, and it still owns the address PO Box 1 in San Pedro Sula. My thanks to Jacobo Kattan for this information.

24. The factories opened by the Bethlehemites in the 1920s and 1930s were the predecessors of today's maquila industry in San Pedro Sula, which is a major supplier of clothing to US retailers. Jacobo Daoud (David) Kattan established the first known clothing factory, named La Sampedrana, in San Pedro Sula in 1923. Using machinery imported from the United States, the factory specialized in making shirts, trousers, and underwear. By the early 1930s, it was employing over one hundred workers and had changed its name to President Paz in honor of the former Honduran president, Miguel Paz Parahona, who was also a doctor and cured Jacobo's son, Juan Kattan, from polio. My thanks to Jacobo Kattan, grandson of Jacobo Daoud Kattan, for sharing this information with me. For wider discussion of the Bethlehemites' shift in northern Honduras to manufacturing, see Euraque, *Reinterpreting*, 33.

25. From baptismal records of the Catedral de San Pedro Apóstol, San Pedro Sula, Honduras. The earliest entry of a Bethlehemite family baptism is that of José Handal, son of Regina and Yusef, born on May 15, 1902, and baptized on August 17, 1902.

26. Today, around 250,000 people of Bethlehem origin live in Honduras—the second largest population in the Bethlehem diaspora and the largest by proportion of population (Honduras has a total population of 9.5 million).

27. Oral tradition in Bethlehem frequently cites the prevalence of Lebanese migrants in the major port cities of Brazil, Uruguay, and Argentina as the reason why the Bethlehemites made their way to the western side of South America, particularly Chile and Bolivia. Scholars of Palestinian migration to Chile have also cited this as a factor in the migrants' choice of destination. For examples, see Nicole Saffie Guevara and Lorenzo Agar Corbinos, "A Century of Palestinian Immigration to Chile: A Successful Integration," in *Latin American with Palestinian Roots*, ed. Viola Raheb (Bethlehem: Diyar Publishers, 2012), 60–62; and Cecilia Baeza Rodriguez, *Les Palestiniens d'Amerique Latine et la Cause Palestinienne: Chile, Bresil, Honduras, 1920–2010* (PhD diss., Sciences Po, 2010), 81.

28. By the 1870s, steamship companies were running regular passenger service from western Europe that docked first at Monte Video and/or Buenos Aires (Rio de Plata) before continuing around Cape Horn and eventually calling at the major ports along the western coast of South America. These companies included Lavarello Line (with routes from Genoa to Buenos Aires to Valparaiso to Callao) and the Pacific Steam Navigation Company (with routes from Liverpool to Bordeaux to Lisbon to Cape Verde to Rio de Janeiro to Montevideo to Punta Arenas to Valparaiso to Arica to Mollendo to Callao). Details of the routes are provided on the Ships List website. See "Lavarello Line / G.B. Lavarello," The Ships List, updated July 21, 2009, http://www.theshipslist.com/ships/lines/lavarelloline.shtml; and "Pacific Steam Navigation Company," The Ships List, updated April 11, 2009, http://www.theshipslist.com/ships/lines/pacific.shtml.

29. Some families in both Bethlehem and Chile maintain that the first migrants to arrive in Chile made their way across the Andes on muleback. This is backed up in academic studies such as Saffie and Agar, "A Century," 64; and Lorenzo Agar Corbinos, "Inmigrantes y descendientes de árabes en Chile: Adaptación social," in Akmir, *Los árabes*, 113.

30. Numerous nineteenth-century travelers' accounts provide descriptions of crossing the Camino de los Andes before the opening of the Transandine Railway in 1910. None of these were written by Middle Eastern travelers, but they provide a sense of the harshness of the conditions, as well as the specific geographical features of the route. For examples, see Peter Schmidtmeyer, *Travels into Chile, over the Andes, in the Years 1820 and 1821* (London: Longman, 1824); Francis Bond Head, *Rough Notes Taken during Some Rapid Journeys across the Pampas and among the Andes* (1826; repr., Cambridge: Cambridge University Press, 2009); and Robert Proctor, *Narrative of a Journey across the Cordillera of the Andes, and of a Residence in Lima, and other Parts of Peru, in the Years 1823 and 1824* (London: Robinson and Co., 1825).

31. In her account of her journey from Bethlehem to Chile in 1924, Victoria Kattan de Hirmas recounts the legends of such miracles (involving saints, French companions, and cognac) said to have occurred during the early journeys of the Bethlehemites across the Andes. See Victoria Kattan de Hirmas, *Mis 100 años de vida: Chileña nacida en Belen* (Santiago de Chile: A&V Comunicaciones), 58–59.

32. This tale is related in the autobiography of Victoria Kattan de Hirmas when describing the arrival in Valparaiso of her father-in-law, Saleh (Pacifico) Hirmas, and his brother Giries (Jorge) in the late nineteenth century. See Kattan de Hirmas, *Mis 100 años*, 49–50.

33. The Valparaiso–Santiago Railway opened in 1863.

34. It is a common trope in oral tradition that migrants from Bethlehem and Beit Jala chose to settle in Chile's Central Valley because the landscape reminded them of home. For more detailed discussion, see Nadim Bawalsa, *Palestinian Migrants and the Birth of a Diaspora in Latin America, 1860–1940* (PhD diss., New York University, 2017), 176–77.

35. These two men are listed as the first recorded Palestinians to reside in Chile in the Jordanian historian al-Badawi al-Mulaththam's 1956 history of Palestinians in South America. See al-Badawi al-Mulaththam, *Al-natiqun bi-1 -dad fi amrika al-janubiyya* (Beirut: Dar Rihani, 1956), vol. 1, 107.

36. This is a reference to the llamas, alpacas, and guanacos reared by the Quecha and Aymara peoples of the Altiplano in the Andes—a region crossed by many Bethlehemite migrants in the late nineteenth century who settled in Bolivia, Peru, and Chile. In early colonial writings, llamas were mistakenly assumed to be a relative of the European sheep within the ovine family. See Daniel W. Gade,

"Llamas and Alpacas as 'Sheep' in the Colonial Andes: Zoogeography Meets Eurocentrism," in *Journal of Latin American Geography* 12, no. 2 (2013): 221–43. These animals have since been reclassified within the camelid family. The similarity with camels would likely have been more apparent to Arab travelers.

37. For the Peruvian cities, see Leyla Bartet, "La inmigración árabe en Perú," in Akmir, *Los árabes*, 171–73. For the Bolivian cities, see Marc J. Osterweil, "The Economic and Social Condition of Jewish and Arab immigrants in Bolivia, 1890–1980," in *Arab and Jewish Immigrants in Latin America: Images and Realities*, ed. Ignacio Klich and Jeff Lesser (London: Frank Cass, 1998), 146–66.

38. In Spanish, the proverb is "En cada pueblo en Chile, hay un sacerdote, un policía y un Palestino." Chile today holds the largest Bethlehemite population, with around 500,000 tracing their origin to the Bethlehem area (including Beit Jala). This population is far greater than in Bethlehem itself and constitutes the largest Palestinian community anywhere in the world outside the Middle East.

CHAPTER 9: OF TROUBLES ON THE TROCADÉRO

1. The presence of Jubrail and his brothers at the exhibition was related to me by Dr. Michel Dabdoub (interviews in Bethlehem, March 15 and 17, 2011) and is noted in Ibrahim Yuhanna Dabdoub, "Mukhtasar tarikh 'ilat al-marhum Yuhanna Yaqoub al-Dabdoub" (unpublished memoir, 1923, private collection of Anton Shukri Dabdoub), 4.

2. For a description of the success of their Bethlehem bazaar and the efforts of other vendors to mimic them (including those who did so in an Irish accent), see Linda K. Jacobs, "Palestine at the Centennial Fair of 1876," *Jerusalem Quarterly* 80 (2019): 81–83; and Eric Davis, "Representations of the Middle East at American World Fairs," in *United States and the Middle East: Cultural Encounters*, ed. Abbas Amanat and Magnus T. Bernhardsson (New Haven, CT: Yale University Center for International and Area Studies, 2002), 359.

3. Johann Büssow has determined that by the early 1890s, more than one steamship a day was docking in the Jaffa port. See Johann Büssow, *Hamidian Palestine: Politics and Society in the District of Jerusalem 1872–1908* (Leiden: Brill, 2011), 442. The specific routes between Jaffa, Beirut, and Marseille during that period, as well as the price of tickets, is recorded in *Appleton's European Guidebook for English Speaking Travelers*, vol. 2 (New York: D. Appleton and Co., 1880), 828.

4. Ottoman restrictions on emigration, and the reversal of the policy in the 1890s, are discussed in Kemal Karpat, "The Ottoman Emigration to America, 1860–1914," *International Journal of Middle East Studies* 17, no. 2 (May 1985): 186–89. It is unlikely that Jubrail would have had a passport, as these were still relatively rare in the 1880s. A full discussion on the official paperwork required to leave the empire legally is provided in Christoph Herzog, "On Migration and the State: Ottoman

Regulations concerning Migration since the Age of Mahmud II," in *The City in the Ottoman Empire: Migration and the Making of Urban Modernity*, ed. Ulrike Freitag, Malte Fuhrmann, Nora Lafi, and Florian Riedler (London: Routledge, 2010), 129. Will Hanley, meanwhile, provides an interesting discussion of how passports were still relatively rare in the Ottoman Empire up to the turn of the twentieth century. See Will Hanley, "Papers for Going, Papers for Staying: Identification and Subject Formation in the Eastern Mediterranean," in *A Global Middle East: Mobility, Materiality and Culture in the Modern Age, 1880–1940*, ed. Liat Kozma, Cyrus Schayegh and Avner Wishnitzer (London: I.B. Tauris, 2014), 179–85.

5. I have estimated the cost of the journey using Akram Khater's calculations of how much it cost to travel from Mount Lebanon to the United States or South America in that period. The first parts of those journeys followed the same routes to western Europe as Jubrail and his brothers took in 1878. See Akram Khater, *Inventing Home: Emigration, Gender, and the Middle Class in Lebanon, 1870–1920* (Berkeley: University of California Press, 2001), 56.

6. The late 1870s and early 1880s in Paris was the so-called bustle era for women's dresses, in which the fabric was gathered at the back, creating an exaggerated, shelf-like appearance. See Deborah Mancoff, *Fashion in Impressionist Paris* (Merrell, 2012). The comparison to an ostrich would have made sense for someone from Palestine and Bilad al-Sham in the nineteenth century, where the Arabian Ostrich was still prevalent in eastern areas until the mid-twentieth century.

7. This is the famous concert organ designed by the renowned French organ builder Aristide Cavaillé-Coll.

8. The street was the so-called Rue des Nations. For an artist's panorama of the layout of the 1878 exhibition, see "Panorama des palais," L'Histoire par l'image, December 2007, https://www.histoire-image.org/fr/comment/reply/5831.

9. The Tunisian Pavilion, where the Bethlehemites displayed their goods at the exhibition, was located along with the Moroccan tent in front of the Trocadéro Palace, which housed the official displays of France. According to Zeynep Çelik, this positioning was designed to represent French colonial patronage over the North African territories. See Zeynep Çelik, *Displaying the Orient: Architecture of Islam at Nineteenth-Century World's Fairs* (Berkeley: University of California Press, 1992), 69. The official exhibition report describes how "Christians from Jerusalem" and other Levantine merchants bought up exhibition space, which they used to sell Holy Land souvenirs at the Tunisian bazaar. It was common for such reports to use "Jerusalem" as a catchall term when in fact the traders were from Bethlehem. The report also states that these activities had been inspired by the success of similar merchants at the Vienna exhibition of 1873. See *Rapport administratif sur l'Exposition Universelle de 1878 à Paris*, vol. 1 (Paris: Imp. Nationale, 1881), 411–12.

10. For the complex processes and motives that informed the way Ottomans

"dressed up" for the world's fairs exhibitions, see Linda K. Jacobs, "'Playing East': Arabs Play Arabs in Nineteenth Century America," *Mashriq and Mahjar Journal of Middle East Migration Studies* 2 (2014): 79–110; Julia Phillips Cohen, "Oriental by Design: Ottoman Jews, Imperial Style, and the Performance of Heritage," *American Historical Review* 119, no. 2 (2014): 364–98; and Ray Hanania, *Arabs of Chicagoland* (Chicago: Arcadia, 2005), 9–11. The sources (photographic and textual) I have encountered that relate to the Bethlehemites' presence at the world's fairs suggest that they did not go to the same lengths as many other participants to exoticize their dress. In general, they aspired to be part of a global cosmopolitan elite and their dress tended to reflect this (Western-style suits and hats). But this does not mean that they were not prepared to don more Middle Eastern–looking clothes if it was good for business.

11. The exhibition report describes how the "Christians from Jerusalem" began subletting their stalls in the Tunisian bazaar to other Middle Eastern traders until the Trocadéro was "invaded by porters and sellers of unregulated junk [*pacotilles innommés*]." There is no mention of Bethlehemites or the Dabdoub family, but here I have imagined the scheme was devised by Jubrail, given that various members of the Dabdoub family state the brothers were present at the exhibition. See *Rapport administratif*, 411–12.

12. The head and torch-bearing arm of the Statue of Liberty was completed by Frédéric Auguste Bartholdi before the rest of the statue was designed, and it was displayed at various exhibitions around the world, including the Paris exhibition of 1878, where the head was a major attraction. See Edward Berenson, *The Statue of Liberty: A Transatlantic Story* (New Haven, CT: Yale University Press, 2012), 52–54.

13. This description of going inside the head is based on the account written by Rudyard Kipling, who visited the head at the Paris exhibition of 1878. Cited in Berenson, *Statue of Liberty*, 52.

14. For Jubrail's arrival in New York in 1892, see chapter 14.

15. The demonstration of Alexander Graham Bell's telephone and Thomas Eddison's phonograph and megaphone at the Paris exhibition of 1878 are described in Robin Boast, *The Machine in the Ghost: Digitality and Its Consequences* (London: Reaktion, 2017), 28–29. The demonstration of Yablochkov's famous electric candles at the Paris exhibition is described in Sandy Isenstadt, *The Electric Light: An Architectural History* (Cambridge, MA: MIT Press, 2018), 4–5.

16. The official exhibition report describes how the exhibition commissioner ordered the evacuation of the stalls that had been sublet and imposed stricter regulations. See *Rapport administratif*, 411–12.

CHAPTER 10: OF THE DECLINE OF HOSH DABDOUB, OR HOW JUBRAIL'S SCHOOLING CAME IN USEFUL

1. Rosa died in Bethlehem on October 29, 1878.

2. In Dabdoub family memory, Rosa is remembered as a strong personality who contributed to the running of the family business as well as to the maintenance of the household. This is based on interviews with Rosa's great-grandson, Dr. Michel Abdallah Dabdoub, on March 15 and 17, 2011, and with Paulette Tissaire Dabdoub, who was married to the grandson of Rosa's son Mikhail, on August 14, 2015, in Bethlehem.

3. Ibrahim Yuhanna Dabdoub describes in his memoir how he and his brothers journeyed to France and Belgium in 1880 "in the service of our uncle Yousef." Given the relatively low budget Yousef had assigned them ("130 French lira") and the lack of visits to any major international exhibitions, these do not appear to have been major ventures for the family business. See Ibrahim Yuhanna Dabdoub, "Mukhtasar tarikh 'ilat al-marhum Yuhanna Yaqoub al-Dabdoub" (unpublished memoir, 1923, private collection of Anton Shukri Dabdoub), 4–5.

4. These are some of the first families to be mentioned trading in Cuba, Haiti, and Santo Domingo in the late 1870s and early 1880s. More detail is provided in chapter 8.

5. These families had well-established businesses in Paris by the early 1880s. For more detail, see Jacob Norris, "Across Confessional Borders: A Microhistory of Ottoman Christians and Their Migratory Paths," in *Minorities and the Modern Arab World: New Perspectives*, ed. Laura Robson (Syracuse, NY: Syracuse University Press, 2016), 39–60.

6. I have found no evidence of Jubrail or his brothers carrying out overseas trips between 1878–81, despite this being the point at which merchant families in Bethlehem were embarking on trips to the Americas in ever-greater numbers. This has led me to imagine the Dabdoub business experiencing a period of decline following the death of Jubrail's mother, Rosa, in October 1878 and the mishap at the Paris exhibition that same year. This in turn serves as a vehicle for imagining how Jubrail's trip to the Philippines in the autumn of 1881 came about.

7. Imagining the guilt Jubrail felt surrounding the Paris trip and his desperation to prove his worth in the family business, I explore how these early overseas trips served as a kind of rite of passage for young men in Bethlehem. Sources such as the family books in the Latin Parish Archive and the memoir of Jubrail's cousin, Ibrahim Yuhanna Dabdoub, show the strikingly young age of most of the merchants who traveled abroad in the late 1870s and early 1880s—they were typically between seventeen and twenty-five. As explored in other chapters of the book, sending out their youngest men on these risky voyages to faraway locations was clearly a tactic families used. The memoir of Ibrahim Yuhanna Dabdoub gives glimpses into the

fear and intense desire to prove their worth that this dynamic produced among the young merchants. For example, he describes his feelings when he traveled abroad for the first time in 1880, working for Jubrail's father, Yousef: "In 1880 fate decreed I should travel with our brother Anton with our capital being only 130 French lira from the house of our uncle Yousef for travel expenses. We didn't know how to speak a single word except what we drew from Arabic. When we got off at Marseille we were overwhelmed and running out of time to the point of being in tears, asking God to make things easier for us." See Dabdoub, "Mukhtasar," 4.

8. The concept of the *sarha* (pl. *sarhat*) as a form of meditative retreat into the countryside is discussed by Raja Shehadeh in the context of his grandfather's habits. See Raja Shehadeh, *Palestinian Walks: Notes on a Vanishing Landscape* (London: Profile, 2010), 1–5.

9. Adnan Musallam documents how Hanna Khalil Morcos (referred to here as "Ammo Hanna") ended up living in Mexico in the 1880s. See Adnan Musallam, *Folded Pages from Local Palestinian History in the 20th Century: Developments in Politics, Society, Press and Thought in Bethlehem in the British Era, 1917–1948* (Bethlehem: WIAM, 2002), 44.

10. The import of shells from the Philippines for use in the Bethlehem souvenir industry is documented in Enrique Yidi Daccarett, Karen David Daccarett and Martha Lizcano Angarita, *El arte palestino de tallar el nacar* (Barranquilla: se, 2005), 42–43.

11. For an exploration of how the opening of the Suez Canal produced new forms of mobility between the Mediterranean Sea, the Red Sea, and the Indian Ocean among certain merchant communities while limiting it for others, see Valeska Huber, *Channelling Mobilities: Migration and Globalisation in the Suez Canal Region and Beyond, 1869–1914* (Cambridge: Cambridge University Press, 2013).

12. These are the families that went on to establish a presence in the Philippines in the 1880s and 1890s. This is documented in more detail in chapter 12. Given that Jubrail Dabdoub was the first recorded name from Bethlehem to appear in the Philippines, I have imagined in this chapter the process whereby these other families may have been providers of credit for his initial voyage. The importance of credit networks among Bethlehemite and Syrian/Lebanese merchants in the Philippines in the late nineteenth century is discussed in William Clarence-Smith, "Lebanese and Other Middle Eastern Migrants in the Philippines," in *Population Movement beyond the Middle East: Migration Diaspora and Network*, ed. Akira Usuki, Omar F. Bajunid, and Tomoko Yamagishi (Osaka: National Museum of Ethnology, 2005), 115–43.

13. Issa Anton Sa'di accompanied Jubrail on his first voyage to the Philippines in 1881 and appears in the Spanish colonial immigration records of that year. See chapter 11 for more detail on Issa and Jubrail's journey.

CHAPTER 11: OF A STREET NAMED ROSARIO

1. Jubrail Dabdoub and Issa Sa'di are recorded in the Spanish colonial records in Manila as arriving in the Philippines on the *Francisco Reyes* steamship. See the National Archive of the Philippines (NAP), Manila, SDS 1716, Radicación de Extranjeros, Otomanos, October 17, 1881.

2. Valeska Huber describes the Suez Canal's route through the Egyptian desert as a "frontier of the civilizing mission," describing the highly unequal new relationships the canal forged between Bedouin caravans and European colonial actors. She also describes the sense of spectacle the desert caravans produced for those on board the steamships. See Valeska Huber, *Channelling Mobilities: Migration and Globalisation in the Suez Canal Region and Beyond, 1869–1914* (Cambridge: Cambridge University Press, 2013), 141–71.

3. The shipping routes, ports of call, and journey times between Cadiz and Manila (via Port Said) in the 1880s are usefully laid out in Resil B. Mojares, "The Traveling Filipino," chap. 12 in *Isabelo's Archive* (Mandaluyong City: Anvil, 2013).

4. Spanish colonial immigration records show the *Reyes* docked in Singapore on route to Manila. See NAP, SDS 1716, Radicación de Extranjeros, Otomanos, October 17, 1881. Based on the routes provided in Mojares, *Isabelo*, the ship is likely to have docked in Galle prior to Singapore.

5. The encouragement of migrant labor, particularly Chinese, in Singapore under British colonial rule in the mid to late nineteenth century produced an exponential expansion of the city and created a model for British colonial immigration policies across South Asia, the Indian Ocean, and the Caribbean. See Stan Neal, *Singapore, Chinese Migration and the Making of the British Empire, 1819–67* (Rochester, NY: Boydell Press, 2019). For the ways in which British control over Singapore's urban environment was contested by the local population in the late nineteenth century, see Brenda Yeoh, *Contesting Space in Colonial Singapore: Power Relations and the Urban Built Environment* (Singapore: NUS Press, 2003), 28–47.

6. In conversations and written accounts describing the early journeys of Bethlehem merchants, the desperate recourse to prayer on the steamships is often mentioned, as well as stories of sightings of saints. This was related to me in interviews with Dr. Michel Abdallah Dabdoub, grandson of Jubrail's brother Mikhail, on March 15 and 17, 2011, as well as in Ibrahim Yuhanna Dabdoub, "Mukhtasar tarikh 'ilat al-marhum Yuhanna Yaqoub al-Dabdoub" (unpublished memoir, 1923, private collection of Anton Shukri Dabdoub), 4–6.

7. October 17, 1881, is the date of Jubrail's arrival in the Philippines as recorded in NAP, SDS 1716, Radicación de Extranjeros, Otomanos, October 17, 1881.

8. A useful guide for describing Manila's system of waterways and the increasing concern with the pollution and putrefaction of its waters in the late nineteenth

century has been Xavier Huetz de Lemps, "Waters in Nineteenth Century Manila," *Philippine Studies* 49, no. 4 (2001): 488–517.

9. These shifts in the Spanish colonial government's economic policies from the 1850s up to the 1880s, and their effect in bringing new international traders to the Philippines, are described in William Gervase Clarence-Smith, "Middle Eastern Migrants in the Philippines: Entrepreneurs and Cultural Brokers," *Asian Journal of Social Science* 32, no. 3 (2004): 431.

10. My descriptions of Binondo in the paragraphs that follow are drawn from various academic works and literary sources, as well as from conversations with local residents of the area. Particularly useful were Manuel A. Caoili, *The Origins of Metropolitan Manila: A Social and Political Analysis* (Manila: University of the Philippines Press, 1999), 40–43; Lorelei D. C. De Viana, *Three Centuries of Binondo Architecture, 1594–1898* (University of Santo Tomas Publishing House, 2001), 45–58; Richard Chu, *Chinese and Chinese Mestizos of Manila: Family, Identity, and Culture, 1860s–1930s* (Leiden: Brill, 2010); and Jose Rizal, *Noli Me Tangere*, trans. Soledad Lacson-Locsin (1887; repr., Honolulu: University of Hawaii Press), esp. chap.1, which is set in Binondo.

11. There is evidence that artisans in Bethlehem were using mother-of-pearl imported from the Philippines. See Enirque Yidi Daccarett, Karen David Daccarett, Martha Lizcano Angarita, *El arte palestino de tallar el nácar* (Barranquilla: self-published, 2005), 45–48. It is therefore possible that part of Jubrail's mission in the Philippines was to see if they could buy mother-of-pearl shells directly from the fisheries there, but there is no evidence that they ever achieved this. William Clarence-Smith has been tracing the pearl export routes from the Sulu islands (especially Jolo) to Singapore (which cut out Manila altogether) in the Centre des Archives Diplomatiques, La Courneuve, Paris. My thanks to William for sharing this information with me.

12. Simon Semora appears in the Spanish colonial records as a merchant from Jerusalem receiving a residency permit in Manila on December 9, 1881. This was four days before Jubrail and Issa received their own residency permits using the same guarantor (*fiador*)—a local employee at the port called Mariano Rodriguez (described later in this chapter). It's therefore very likely that Jubrail and Issa met Semora in Manila. Semora's Sephardic Jewish name makes it likely that Ladino (a form of Spanish) would have been his first language. Few Sephardic Jews in Jerusalem spoke Arabic as a first language in that period. For Semora's residency application, see NAP, SDS 1716, Radicación de Extranjeros, Otomanos, December 9, 1881.

13. In the approval of Jubrail's application for a residency permit in Manila, the Spanish governor noted he had a shop in Binondo selling "efectos de su pais." See NAP, SDS 1716, Radicación de Extranjeros, Otomanos, December 13, 1881. Based

on the more detailed information about the shops of those Bethlehemites who followed Jubrail to Binondo, it is likely his store was on Calle del Rosario.

14. NAP, SDS 1716, Radicación de Extranjeros, Otomanos, December 13, 1881.

CHAPTER 12: BY THE TRUTH OF AL-KHADR, I WENT AND CAME BACK!

1. The Arabic expression is "U-haqq el-Khadr el-akhdar inni ruHt u-jit!" Tawfiq Canaan cites this expression as an exclamation used by Palestinian Christians when someone doubts an element of a story they are telling. See Tawfiq Canaan, *Mohammedan Saints and Sanctuaries in Palestine* (London: Luzac, 1927), 125–26.

2. The *khurāfiyya* is a type of Palestinian folktale that typically grounds magical, supernatural characters and events in settings that would be very realistic to the listeners. The plotline of a young male hero traveling to faraway lands to prove his worth and make his fortune is a standard trope of these tales, as discussed briefly in Ibrahim Muhawi and Sharif Kanaana, *Speak, Bird, Speak Again: Palestinian Arab Folktales* (Berkeley: University of California Press, 1989), 41.

3. Photographic evidence suggests sofas, largely imported from Europe, had already become commonplace among affluent Bethlehem families by the turn of the twentieth century. For a study of how Paris led the way in the global rush to buy sofas in the late nineteenth century and how this transformed interior living spaces, see Joan DeJean, *The Age of Comfort: When Paris Discovered Casual and the Modern Home Began* (Bloomsbury, 2009), 144–64.

4. A reference to *mansaf*, a traditional Bedouin dish, usually eaten on the night of the *khutbah* in Palestine.

5. The description of the various wedding ceremonies is taken from accounts provided in memoirs from Bethlehem from that time. In particular, see Ibrahim Yuhanna Dabdoub, "Mukhtasar tarikh 'ilat al-marhum Yuhanna Yaqoub al-Dabdoub" (unpublished memoir, 1923, private collection of Anton Shukri Dabdoub), 19–21; and the published memoir of Issa Basil al-Bandak, *Issa Basil Bandak: hayatuhu, a'maluhu, mudhakkaratuhu, 1898–1984*, ed. Adnan Musallam (Bethlehem: Diyar, 2013), 49. The *hadda* singing tradition at weddings is described in Amatzia Bar-Yosef, "Traditional Rural Style under a Process of Change: The Singing Style of the 'Ḥaddāy,' Palestinian Folk Poet-Singers," *Asian Music* 29, no. 2 (1998): 57–82.

6. A *tawb* is a long-sleeved robe, and a *hatta* is a headdress, both worn by Bedouin Arabs and popular in late nineteenth-century Palestine as the groom's attire at wedding ceremonies.

7. Yousef Giries Handal is held to be the first Bethlehemite to have settled on the Caribbean coast of Honduras at some point in the mid to late 1880s. He is thought to have traveled there from an earlier base on the Caribbean islands.

By 1902, Yousef and his wife, Regina, were baptizing their son, José, in the town of San Pedro Sula. José's baptism is thought to be the earliest entry for a Syrian-Palestinian baptism in Honduras. See baptismal records of the Catedral de San Pedro Apóstol, San Pedro Sula, Honduras, August 17, 1902.

8. These trips and the earnings they made are documented in Dabdoub, "Mukhtasar," 6, 50. The arrival in Manila of Hanna Dabdoub in 1883 and a later trip made there by his brother Mikhail is recorded in the National Archives of the Philippines (NAP), Manila, Radicación de Extranjeros, Otomanos, SDS 1755.

9. Ibrahim Dabdoub equates the 250 French "lira" to 27,250 ghurush, a huge sum of money in Bethlehem at the time. See Dabdoub, "Mukhtasar," 6, 50.

10. The Philippines is referred to as "Filibina bilad al-hind" in Dabdoub, "Mukhtasar," 6. The list of Bethlehem family names in the Philippines is compiled from the records of the National Archives of the Philippines in the 1880s and 90s. See NAP, Radicación de Extranjeros, Otomanos, SDS 1716, 1732, 1751, 1755, 1756, 1763.

11. The dispersal of peddlers from Ottoman Syria around the Philippine islands and their reliance on credit networks is documented in William Gervase Clarence-Smith, "Middle Eastern Migrants in the Philippines: Entrepreneurs and Cultural Brokers," *Asian Journal of Social Science* 32, no. 3 (2004): 431.

12. Elias Abu Hamameh was recorded by the Spanish authorities as arriving in Manila on October 17, 1889, while Basil and Khalil (Carlos) were "radicated" in 1890 (although the documents mention Khalil had already been trading in Manila in 1889). See NAP, Radicación de Extranjeros, Otomanos, SDS 1756.

13. The records in NAP Radicación de Extranjeros, Otomanos, SDS 1716, 1732, 1751, 1755, 1756, and 1763 show the regularity with which the Abu Hamameh family acted as *fiadores* (guarantors) for newly arriving Syrian migrants.

14. Ten thousand Filipino pesos was equivalent to around 5,000 US dollars. In terms of spending power, this is worth around 120,000 US dollars in 2022. To give a sense of how wealthy the Abu Hamamehs had become, the total capital of one of the young immigrants they vouched for as guarantors was recorded as 150 pesos. NAP, Radicación, SDS 1755, September 6, 1889.

15. The Syrian community, including the Bethlehemites, was temporarily threatened during the revolutionary turmoil that gripped the Philippines between 1896 and 1898. Having previously relied on the Spanish regime to keep their imported goods moving through the islands' ports, the Syrians were now placed in a delicate position, as much of the local population viewed them as an unwanted foreign presence whose cheap imported goods undercut local traders. Reports of attacks on Syrians became common by 1897, and on February 6, 1898, the Abu Hamameh brothers' shop, El Belen (Bethlehem), in Manila was burned down. By the summer of 1898, the French consul was arranging the evacuation of Syrians on French cruise ships. This would all prove a temporary blip for the Syrians, however,

as they soon returned in large numbers once the American military occupation was established at the end of 1898. For Chinese merchants, the American occupation was a disaster, as the new regime implemented newly racialized laws designed to restrict Asian immigration, just as in the United States itself. But for the Syrians and the Bethlehemites it was a boon, as they were largely successful in convincing the American authorities that they should be classified as "free white persons." In the ensuing decades, many Bethlehem families made the islands their long-term home, and it was not until the Japanese occupation of World War II that the community was severely depleted. Information on the attacks on Syrians in 1897 and the French evacuation the following year was kindly shared with me by William Clarence-Smith based on his research at the Instituto de Historia, Consejo Superior de Investigaciones Científicas, Madrid, and the Centre des Archives Diplomatiques, La Courneuve, Paris. The fire at the Abu Hamameh shop in 1898 is reported in NAP, Radicación de Extranjeros, Otomanos, SDS. The American restrictions placed on Chinese merchants and the classification of Syrians as "free white persons" is documented in Clarence-Smith, "Middle Eastern Migrants," 434–41.

16. These features of Bethlehemites' lives in the Philippines were related to me by Samir Elias Salem in interviews held in Bethlehem on September 23 and 24, 2011. Samir's father, Elias, grew up in Manila in the 1920s, speaking Tagalog as a first language with the family maid and visiting the cockfights against his mother's orders. The Salem family was one of the most well-established Bethlehem families in the Philippines, trading all over the islands in cloth and jewelry. See National Library of the Philippines (NLP), Manila, Rosenstock's Directory, Manila Firm Names (1927–28, 1935, and 1938).

17. The *kristo* is the person who collects the bets in Filipino cockfights, named for his outstretched hands. Attaching knives to the cocks' legs has long been a common feature of Filipino cockfighting.

CHAPTER 13: OF WHITE CITIES AND BRONZE MEDALS

1. The winners of the medals, including the Dabdoub brothers, are recorded in the list of awards for the exhibition held at the Chicago History Museum, Research Center: "Dadboub [sic] Bros.,- Bethelem [sic]. Carvings in mother of pearl." See List of Awards, Foreign Volume, Turkey, Department H, Manufactures, F38MZ /1893.D81, Chicago History Museum Research Center. The quotation giving the reasons for the awarding of the medal is taken from the so-called *Book of the Fair* produced by the Chicago exhibition organizers, which explained what the medals looked like, how they were awarded, and the composition of the judging panels. See Hubert Howe Bancroft, ed., *The Book of the Fair: An Historical and Descriptive Presentation of the World's Science, Art and Industry, as Viewed through the Columbian Exposition at Chicago in 1893* (Chicago: Bancroft, 1895), chap. 27.

2. The legend of the medal is still known in Bethlehem and is often embellished to make the medal seem more significant. I have imagined this scene in Bab al-Dayr as a way to capture the sense of mystique that would have surrounded the brothers when they returned with such an object.

3. There is no evidence Jubrail read the article, but there would certainly have been awareness and pride that the authors of such reports had visited the booth and were including it in their publications. The quote here is included in the book that was later compiled from Kunz's reports for the US Commission of Fish and Fisheries. See George F. Kunz, *Pearls; Their Occurrence in the United States, Etc.* (Washington, 1900), 452.

4. For the Ottoman government contract with Souhami Sadullah and Company, see Başbakanlık Osmanlı Arşivleri (Ottoman Archives of the Prime Minister's Office, Istanbul, hereafter BOA), Y.A. Res 58/33, 25 Şevval 1309, May 24, 1892.

5. The agreement between the Dabdoub brothers and Souhami Sadullah and Company is detailed in correspondence between the grand vizier to the governor of Jerusalem. See BOA, Documents of the Record Office of the Ministry of Interior (DH.MKT), 2015/22, 6 Rebiyülahir 1310, October 28, 1892. My thanks to Yasemin Avçi for translating this document.

6. As documented in the correspondence between the Ministry of Interior and the Ministry of Public Works and Trade. See BOA, DH.MKT, 2019/59, 20 Rebiyülahir 1310, November 11, 1892; and BOA, DH.MKT, 2030/77, 23 Cemaziyelevvel 1310, December 13, 1892. My thanks to Yasemin Avçi for translating these documents.

7. The *saraya* was the Ottoman government building constructed in Bab al-Dayr (Manger Square) during the days of Jubrail's childhood.

8. This is an English translation of a verse form an Arabic poem attributed to the poet and intellectual Suleiman al-Bustani, who was appointed as Ottoman commissioner to the World's Columbian Exposition of 1893 in Chicago and published the monthly Turkish-language newspaper there. The lines were translated by Adele Younis, who describes how they became one of the "memory gems" learned by heart by many of the Arabic-speaking participants of the Chicago exhibition whom she interviewed. See Adele L. Younis, "The Coming of the Arabic-Speaking People to the United States" (PhD diss., Boston University, 1961), 189–90.

9. Jubrail and Jadallah appear on the passenger list of the SS *La Touraine*, which arrived in New York from Le Havre on March 21, 1893. They were listed as merchants traveling in the second-class compartment of the ship alongside many other merchants from Bilad al-Sham. See "Passenger Lists of Vessels Arriving at New York, 1820–1897," M237, 675, Records of the US Customs Service, Record Group 36, National Archives, Washington, DC. La Touraine was the fifth largest steamship in the world at the time, measuring about 518 feet in length and 8,893 tons in

weight. See N. R. P. Bonsor, *North Atlantic Seaway*, vol. 2 (Jersey: Brookside Publications, 1978), 629.

10. The employment of Bethlehem stonemasons to cut a path for the railway through the hills around Jerusalem is detailed in the 1893 reports of the American vice consul in Jerusalem, Selah Merrill, as cited in Nadi Abusaada, "Building Urban Palestine: Jaffa and Nablus, 1870–1930" (PhD diss., University of Cambridge, 2021), 73–74.

11. The details of the opening ceremony are based on the descriptions in Anthony Travis, *On Chariots with Horses of Fire and Iron: The Excursionists and the Narrow Gauge Railroad from Jaffa to Jerusalem* (Jerusalem: Hebrew University Magnes Press, 2008), 6, 61–63; and Vincent Lemire, *Jerusalem 1900: The Holy City in the Age of Possibilities* (Chicago: University of Chicago Press, 2017), 94–97.

12. This wording is a reference to Travis's *On Chariots*.

13. Dovid Rossof writes, "While the train puffed up the steep mountains towards Jerusalem, agile passengers would hop off, pick some flowers, and climb back on the moving train." See Dovid Rossof, *Where Heaven Touches Earth: Jewish Life in Jerusalem from Medieval Times to the Present* (New York: Feldheim, 2001), 351.

14. Ruth Kark discusses the effect of the railway on increasing the flow of imports into Jerusalem from Jaffa in *Jaffa: A City in Evolution, 1799–1917* (Jerusalem: Yad Ben Zvi, 1990), 238.

15. The Canawati family from Bethlehem appears to have been one of the families specializing in the import of mother-of-pearl with offices in Jerusalem, as recorded in *Palestine Gazette* 1071 (January 9, 1941), 31–32.

16. Travis describes the negative effect of the new railway on the preexisting transportation services in the Jerusalem area but also explains how some of these services reinvented themselves as "branch lines" of the railway. See Travis, *On Chariots*, 234.

17. From the Arabic proverb إذا كان الصبر أمّ فعاقبته حلوة

18. Arabic speakers made up a large component of the exhibitors in Chicago. Their colorful appearance has been widely documented in both the official and unofficial publications produced at the exhibition, as well as in a wide range of secondary literature. All these sources testify the extent to which Middle Easterners and North Africans "dressed up" to pander to Americans' sense of the "exotic Orient." Adele Younis's detailed study of the Arabic-speaking presence at the Chicago exhibition summarizes: "The streets overflowed with Arabians in flowing gowns—some turbaned while others wore the familiar red fez—and an abundant array of 'Oriental splendor' shone in the gold, silver, copper, and bronze manufactures prominently displayed." See Younis, "Coming of the Arabic-Speaking People," 192. For examples of photographic albums produced at the fair, see F. W. Putnam, *Portrait Types of the Midway Plaisance* (St. Louis, MO: N. D. Thomp-

son, 1894); *The World's Fair Album* (Chicago: Rand McNally and Co., 1893); and James W. Shepp, *Shepp's World Fair Photographed* (Chicago: Globe, 1893), 499–518. For discussions of "dressing up" at the fair, see Linda K. Jacobs, "'Playing East': Arabs Play Arabs in Nineteenth Century America," *Mashriq and Mahjar Journal of Middle East Migration Studies* 2 (2014): 79–110; Ray Hanania, *Arabs of Chicagoland* (Chicago: Arcadia, 2005), 9–24; and Eric Davis, "Representations of the Middle East at American World Fairs 1876–1904," in *The United States and the Middle East: Cultural Encounters*, ed. Abbas Amanat and Magnus Bernhardsson (New Haven, CT: Yale University Center for International and Area Studies, 2002), 342–85.

19. The Syrian who organized the troupe of horses was Suleyman Raji Effendi. The Ottoman government was initially reluctant to approve the scheme on the grounds it might trivialize the good name of the empire. But Sultan Abdulhamid II was eventually persuaded by one of his first chamberlains, allowing Raji Effendi to set up the so-called Wild East show at the Chicago World's Fair. The show proved a sensation, paving the way for the formation of the first Arabian Horse Club of Amerka to be formed some years later in 1908. See George H. Conn, *The Arabian Horse in America* (Woodstock, VT: Countryman Press, 1957), 158–72.

20. This is a reference to the Loop District in Chicago, home to the world's first cluster of skyscrapers in the 1880s and early 1890s. The term *skyscraper* was first used in the 1880s to describe the new wave of steel-frame office buildings built in Chicago. See Leslie A. Hudson, *Chicago Skyscrapers in Vintage Postcards* (Chicago: Arcadia, 2004), 7–8. Jubrail and Jadallah would most likely have passed through the Loop en route to the White City. At the time of their arrival, the Masonic Temple Building had just been completed. Standing at twenty-one stories high, it was the tallest skyscraper in the world at that point.

21. For the description of the White City, I have referenced *The World's Fair Album*; and David F. Burg, *Chicago's White City of 1893* (Lexington: University Press of Kentucky, 2015), 286–340.

22. The Venetian gondolas are described in Trumbull White, *The World's Columbian Exposition, Chicago, 1893: A Complete History of the Enterprise* (Chicago: P. W. Ziegler, 1893), 612.

23. The Centennial Wheel, designed by George Ferris Jr., was the first of its kind in the world and the centerpiece of the World's Columbian Exposition. For a description of the wheel's history, see Burg, *Chicago's White City*, 223–34.

24. It has been estimated that the Ferris wheel transported around 38,000 passengers daily. Burg, *Chicago's White City*, 223–34.

25. The Dabdoub booth is described in three specific contemporary sources: First, it is described in documents in the Ottoman archives that mention that Mikhail Dabdoub (Jubrail's brother) and a German named Foster were responsible for transporting mother-of-pearl and olive-tree objects to the Chicago exhibi-

tion. See BOA, DH.MKT, 1987/95. Second, it is described in the Turkish-language newsletter (*Musavver Sikago Sergisi*) produced at the Chicago exhibition, which reads on page 38: "In the Turkish Market there is a booth selling objects made in olive-tree wood and mother-of-pearl produced in Bethlehem, in the district of Jerusalem. This booth belongs to the Syrian company Jacir and Dabdoub and Foster." My thanks to Nicola Verderame for kindly sharing and translating this source for me. Finally, it is described in the report on pearls in the United States. See Kunz, *Pearls*, 452.

26. The descriptions of the Arabic-speaking presence at the Midway Plaisance are based on the following: Zeynep Çelik, *Displaying the Orient: Architecture of Islam at Nineteenth-Century World's Fairs* (Berkeley: University of California Press, 1992), 80–88; Younis, "The Coming," 188–202; Norman Bolotin, *Chicago's Grand Midway: A Walk around the World at the Columbian Exposition* (Chicago: University of Illinois Press, 2017); Shepp, *Shepp's World Fair*; Jacobs, "'Playing East'"; Burg, *Chicago's White City*; and Davis, "Representations," 362–72.

27. For a study of how the period immediately preceding the Chicago exhibition had witnessed the emergence of Christmas as the most popular and commercialized Christian festival in the US, and for the role played by Christmas cards and carols, see Penne L. Restad, *Christmas in America: A History* (Oxford: Oxford University Press, 1996), especially chap. 9.

28. For descriptions and photographs of Cairo Street, see Younis, "The Coming," 196–200; and Çelik, *Displaying the Orient*, 83–85.

29. بعيد عن السامعين Literally, "Far be it from the listeners!" This is a standard verbal flourish in the Palestinian *khurāfiyya* oral folk tale tradition, used to warn listeners that a socially odious subject is coming. See Ibrahim Muhawi and Sharif Kanaana, *Speak, Bird, Speak Again: Palestinian Arab Folktales* (Berkeley: University of California Press, 1989), 6.

30. The sensation caused by the belly dancers at the exhibition is documented in Burg, *Chicago's White City*, 221–23.

CHAPTER 14: OF FERTILITY POTIONS AND THE DIZZYING HEIGHTS OF SUCCESS

1. The Dabdoubs' participation in these exhibitions and their various earnings are mentioned in the unpublished memoir of Jubrail's cousin. See Ibrahim Yuhanna Dabdoub, "Mukhtasar tarikh 'ilat al-marhum Yuhanna Yaqoub al-Dabdoub" (unpublished memoir, 1923, private collection of Anton Shukri Dabdoub), 8–9.

2. This Arabic appellation for Paris (*'arūs mudun al-'ālim*) is used in Nagib T. Abdou, *Dr. Abdou's Travels in America and Commercial Directory of the Arabic Speaking People of the World* (Raleigh, NC: Moise A. Khayrallah Center for Lebanese Diaspora Studies Archive), 428, accessed August 21, 2018, https://lebanesestudies.omeka.chass.ncsu.edu/items/show/13912.

3. Variants of this phrase are used several times in the memoir of Jubrail's cousin Ibrahim Yuhanna Dabdoub, reflecting the perceived connection for that generation of merchants between piety and business success. See Dabdoub, "Mukhtasar," 11, 16.

4. In 1886 a group of Bethlehemite merchants initiated the campaign to have an Arabic church consecrated in Paris for the first time by sending a petition to the French Foreign Ministry on behalf of the wider Syrian community in Paris. These merchants were Yaqub Kattan, Giries (Georges) Kattan, Yaqub Abu Zaʿrur, and Yaqub Giacaman. Following much deliberation between the Foreign Ministry, the Interior Ministry, and the Paris Police Prefecture, the Syrians were eventually granted their church in 1889 at Saint-Julien-le-Pauvre, and a Melkite (or Greek Catholic) priest was appointed accordingly. See Archives Nationales (AN), Pierrefitte-sur-Seine, Paris, F/19/5590, Ministère de l'Instruction Publique to Prefecture de Police, May 15, 1886; Prefecture de Police to Ministre de l'Instruction Publique, June 24, 1886; Ministre de l'Interieur to Ministre de la Justice et des Cultes, August 26, 1888; and Ministre des Affaires Étrangères to Ministre de la Justice, October 5, 1892.

5. In its deliberations over the request for an Arabic church at Saint-Julien-le-Pauvre, the Paris Police Prefecture listed the addresses of the Bethlehemite signatories of the petition. Their residences were all in the Temple District, clustered around the Boulevard de Strasbourg. See AN, F/19/5590, Ministère de l'Instruction Publique to Prefecture de Police, May 15, 1886. I have come across a number of other Bethlehemite businesses located on or around Boulevard de Strasbourg in this period. These include Jaʿar, Daccarett and Company (39 Boulevard de Strasbourg) and Suleiman Jacir et Frères (6 Boulevard de Strasbourg), both listed in Nagib Abdou's 1907 directory of Arab businesses around the world. See Abdou, *Dr. Abdou's Travels*, 428.

6. The relocation of Hanna and Mikhail Dabdoub to this address in New York is documented in numerous sources. These include the family letters reproduced in Peter Dabdoub, *The Little Bear: Origins of the Dabdoub Family*, (Mexico City: Endora, 2009), 80–84, especially the letter from Hanna and Mikhail Dabdoub to "Uncle Ibrahim," New York, March 22, 1910; and Abdou, *Dr. Abdou's Travels*, 165, which lists Hanna and Mikhail as commission merchants at 39 Broadway (the street number is possibly an error).

7. The prevailing narrative of the Syrians' movement from Lower Manhattan to Brooklyn in the late nineteenth and early twentieth centuries is one of upward mobility, assimilation, and greater permanence. Recent research carried out at the Moise A. Khayrallah Center for Lebanese Diaspora Studies, however, suggests this to be overly simplistic and that the communities in Brooklyn were much more varied than previously assumed and included poorer, recently arrived immigrants as well as the longer-standing residents of New York. Meanwhile, Washington

Street continued to be a hub for Syrian businesses well into the 1920s. See "Syrians in New York: Mapping Movement, 1900–1930," Moise A. Khayrallah Center for Lebanese Diaspora Studies, accessed April 8, 2019, https://ncsu.maps.arcgis.com/apps/MapJournal/index.html?appid=ddofd4568704465fac9cea7476869ebf. See also Linda K. Jacobs, *Strangers in the West: The Syrian Colony of New York City, 1880–1900* (New York: Kalimah Press, 2015).

8. The Dabdoub brothers' maintenance of a commercial address at 35 Broadway alongside a residential address on Wyckoff Street in Brooklyn is documented in the New York City Business Directory of 1910–11. See *Trows General Directory of the Boroughs of Manhattan and Bronx, City of New York*, vol. 124 (New York: Trow, 1911), 323. Previous editions of the directory only mention the brothers' Broadway address, starting with their first mention in the 1908–9 edition, suggesting a lag between the brothers establishing properties and paying to be included in the directory. We know from other sources that they first set up the business on Broadway around 1895. See "Mukhtasar," 8–9. This was confirmed to me in interviews with Dr. Michel Abdallah Dabdoub (grandson of Mikhail Dabdoub) on March 15 and 17, 2011.

9. Yaqoub was the brother of Ibrahim Yuhanna Dabdoub, who chronicled Yaqoub's death in his memoir. The memoir uses the phrase "He moved to the mercy of his Lord on the twentieth day of Tammuz." See Dabdoub, "Mukhtasar," 7.

10. This particular imagery is borrowed from the fifteenth-century account of Suriano, who recorded that women who drank such potions would have "paps and breasts like two fountains." Francesco Suriano, *Treatise on the Holy Land*, trans. Theophilus Bellorini and Eugene Hoade (Jerusalem: Franciscan Printing Press, 1983), 137.

11. The Franciscan chapel was built in 1871–72. A number of renovations and modifications have been made since, including the construction of a second chapel, built into the back of the caves in 2007.

12. Several sources attest to the Franciscan practice of stamping the Jerusalem Cross (a five-fold cross associated with the Crusader Kingdom and later with the Latin Patriarchate of Jerusalem) onto packages of the Milk Grotto powder. See, for example, Corneille le Bruyn, *A Voyage to the Levant: Or, Travels in the Principal Parts of Asia Minor*, trans. W. J (London: Jacob Tonson, 1702), 200.

13. This ritual of prayer when drinking the mixture from the Milk Grotto is still practiced today. See "Milk Grotto Church of the Virgin Mary in Bethlehem," Hazboun, accessed January 15, 2018, http://www.hazboun.org/arthur/milkgrotto/milkgrot.html. Extracting powder from the cave walls to mix with water has been practiced by both Christian and Muslim women in the town for centuries. Travelers' descriptions from the seventeenth and eighteenth centuries describe how the powder was made into small cakes, both for local consumption and for sale to

pilgrims. See Le Bruyn, *Voyage to the Levant*, 200; and S. Kosmopolites, *A Series of Letters, Addressed to Sir William Fordyce, containing a Voyage and Journey from England to Smyrna*, vol. 2 (London: Payne and Son, 1788), 198–99.

14. This specific ritual is based on the instructions in a leaflet provided today by the Franciscan custodians of the shrine. They claim the ritual is based on long-standing customs.

15. Moral outrage at the intermingling of the sexes in public spaces was a common reaction among Syrian and Palestinian migrant men in the United States in the early twentieth century. It was often used to justify preventing women from migrating overseas. One famous example, upon which I have based this description, can be found in Khalil Sakakini's diaries. See Akram Musallam, ed., *Yawmiyyat Khalil al-Sakakini: Yawmiyyat—rasa'il—ta'ammulat. Al-kitab al-awwal: New York, Sultana, Jerusalem, 1907–1912* (Ramallah: Markaz Khalil al-Sakakini al-thaqafi, Mu'assasat al-dirasat al-qudsiyya, 2003), 278.

CHAPTER 15: OF WEEPING ICONS, GHOSTLY ARMIES, AND VISIONS OF THE VIRGIN

1. The descriptions of Marie-Alphonsine's early life are based on a handful of hagiographies of Marie-Alphonsine written either by members of the Congregation of the Rosary Sisters or scholars associated with the Latin Patriarchate in Jerusalem. In particular, I have used Sister Praxede Sweidan's account, which also reproduces Marie-Alphonsine's own notebooks dating from her later life. See Sister Praxede Sweidan, *Kalimat al-'adhra' al-mukarrama al-umm Marie-Alphonsine Danil Ghattas* (Jerusalem: Latin Patriarchate Press, 2004). Other sources I have used are Benedict Stolz, *A Handmaid of the Holy Rosary: Mother Mary Alphonsus of the Rosary, First Foundress of an Arab Congregation, 1843–1927*, trans. Natalie Bevenot (New York: Benziger Brothers, 1938); and Pierre Duvignau, in *Mother Marie-Alphonsine and the Congregation of the Rosary*, trans. Vincent F. Gottwald (Amman: Economic Press, 1987).

2. These were well-known practices at that time among Jerusalemites whose previous children had died. See H. H. Spoer and A. M. Spoer, "Sickness and Death among the Arabs of Palestine," *Folklore* 38, no. 2 (1927): 141.

3. These details about Danil Ghattas were recorded in the hagiography of Marie-Alphonsine by Pierre Duvignau, a French priest of the Sacred Heart of Jesus. See Duvignau, *Mother Marie-Alphonsine*, 9–11.

4. These are all miracles reported to have happened to Danil Ghattas as a result of his devotion to the Virgin. The miracle of the weeping icon is reported by Franciscan scholar Benedict Stolz, who carried out research in the 1930s on Marie-Alphonsine's life. See Stolz, *Handmaid of the Holy Rosary*, 28. Reports of icons of the Virgin Mary "sweating" oil that cured the sick were common in Palestine and

Syria at that time. See, for example, James Grehan, *Twilight of the Saints: Everyday Religion in Ottoman Syria and Palestine* (Oxford: Oxford University Press, 2016), 155. Meanwhile, the lost souls of purgatory guiding Danil to safety are described in Duvignau, *Mother Marie-Alphonsine*, 11–12.

5. This description of Danil Ghattas eventually granting permission to his daughter to enter the religious life is based on Duvignau's account in *Mother Marie-Alphonsine*, 24–25.

6. The descriptions here of Marie-Alphonsine's visions are based on her own account provided in her notebooks (all translations from Arabic are my own). The notebooks are divided into two manuscripts, the first of which describes the numerous visions and dreams she experienced of the Virgin Mary, while the second details her work with the Rosary Sisters and the various miracles she performed. Both manuscripts are reproduced in full (both in the original handwriting and transcribed) in Sweidan, *Kalimat al-ʿadhra'*. In the notebooks, Marie-Alphonsine repeatedly states her inability to describe in words the beauty of her visions, particularly the first one. See Marie-Alphonsine, first manuscript, 2–5, in Sweidan, *Kalimat al-ʿadhra'*, 105–6.

7. Her alienation and withdrawal from the French nuns in the Order of Saint Joseph is described in Duvignau, *Mother Marie-Alphonsine*, 106–7.

8. Marie-Alphonsine describes this vision in her first manuscript, 2–5, in Sweidan, *Kalimat al-ʿadhra'*, 105–6.

9. "Lowly servant" translates to *ʿabda ḥaqīra* in the original Arabic. The word *ḥaqīra* can be translated variously as "wretched" or even "despicable." In a religious context, *ʿabda* usually carries connotations of being a servant of God, although it literally means "female slave."

10. Many of Mariam's meetings with the Virgin Mary seem to contain sexual undertones. In one example, she writes: "I stayed for a while with her until I quenched the burning thirst of my desire [*ghalīl ashwaqi*] for the sweetness of her delights [*ʿudhubat bahjatha*]." In another passage, she writes: "The Virgin used to approach me amid a radiant light, in her hand something round and luminous, and would enter into me. I felt as though I were having holy communion with the taste of honey [*ḥalāwa ʿasaliyya*] in my mouth, which I kept inside me as long as I could without eating any food." Marie-Alphonsine, first manuscript, 8, 38, in Sweidan, *Kalimat al-ʿadhra'*, 108, 123. This mirrors the sexuality described in other analyses of female Christian mystics in the region, such as Akram Khater's study of the eighteenth-century Maronite nun Hindiyya al-ʿUjaimi. See Akram Khater, *Embracing the Divine: Passion and Politics in the Christian Middle East* (Syracuse, NY: Syracuse University Press, 2011), 173–82.

11. The ritual is discussed in Grehan, *Twilight of the Saints*, 155. Although the effigy was usually named Umm al-Ghayth (Mother of the Rain), Grehan stresses

the overlap with the Muslim cult of the Virgin Mary, as well as with older pagan practices.

12. Spoer and Spoer, "Sickness and Death," 18.

13. These examples are taken from stories in oral tradition that were collected by the ethnographer and folklorist Issa Massou and reproduced in the online archive Palestine-Family.net. See "Bethlehem Folklore and the Virgin Mary," https://palestine-family.net/bethlehem-folklore-and-the-virgin-mary/.

14. Palestine-Family.net, "Bethlehem Folklore and the Virgin Mary," https://palestine-family.net/bethlehem-folklore-and-the-virgin-mary/.

15. These visions are described by Marie-Alphonsine in the first manuscript, 17–18, in Sweidan, *Kalimat al-'adhra'*, 112–13.

16. The appearance of a brilliant white light is a regular feature in Marie-Alphonsine's notebooks. She writes that the Virgin accompanied her "in the form of a beautiful star" and that "she kept something miraculously imprinted in my eye, a Marian light, about which I had to remain silent because it cannot be explained in words." Marie-Alphonsine, first manuscript, 12–3, Sweidan, *Kalimat al-'adhra'*, 110.

17. The Arabic phrase Marie-Alphonsine uses for self-mortification (or mortification of the flesh, as it is often called in Catholic theology) is *imaataat jasadiyya*. Marie-Alphonsine, first manuscript, 40, Sweidan, *Kalimat al-'adhra'*, 124.

18. Marie-Alphonsine, first manuscript, 50, Sweidan, *Kalimat al-'adhra'*, 129.

CHAPTER 16: OF THE ENCHANTED PALACES OF BETHLEHEM

1. The description of the primus stove and Eddison phonograph is based on the account provided by Wasif Jawhariyyeh (1897–1972), who recalls the sensation caused by these inventions in Jerusalem. Although he does not provide exact dates, these scenes take place during the early stages of the Ottoman section of the memoir, meaning that they can be dated to the first decade of the twentieth century. See Wasif Jawhariyyeh, *Al-Quds al-'uthmaniyah fi al-mudhakkarat al-jawhariyah: Al-kitab al-awwal min mudhakkarat al-musiqi Wasif Jawhariyyeh, 1904–1917*, ed. Salim Tamari and Issam Nassar (Beirut: Institute for Palestine Studies, 2003), 49–51. The story of Hanna Mansour's motorcar was told to me by Anton Mansour, the great-great-grandson of Hanna Mansour. The story was told to Anton by his grandfather, Victor Georges Mansour (grandson of Hanna Mansour). Again, this is thought to have occurred at some point during the first decade of the twentieth century.

2. In his memoir, Wasif Jawhariyyeh describes his trip to Bethlehem to look at the famous gas lamp hanging from the church and the reactions of wonder it inspired: "The town was amazed [*qad duhishat al-madina*] when it witnessed this new invention for the first time." He then goes on to describe how this was outdone by the new electric lamps run from generators that began to be used by the wealthy

families of Jerusalem and Bethlehem shortly after: "We were astonished by this process [wa-ta'ajjabna jiddan min mushahadat hadha al-'amaliyyah] . . . and said that it was indeed greater than the [gas] lantern." See Jawhariyyeh, *Al-Quds*, 31.

3. The principal building material that spurred the construction boom in Bethlehem in the early twentieth century was dolomite limestone quarried from the rich deposits found in the hills between Bethlehem and Hebron. Meanwhile, lime mortar and aggregates of sand and gravel were used as binders. See Mumen Abuarkub, "Traditional Building Materials and Techniques in Palestine," *Prostor* 25, no. 1 (2017): 143. Because of the proximity of the limestone deposits, Bethlehem stonemasons were renowned all over Palestine for their expertise in cutting and dressing the stones. Most of the new houses in Jerusalem in the early twentieth century were built by Bethlehem stonemasons, as reported in Yehoshua Ben-Arieh, *Jerusalem in the Nineteenth Century: The Emergence of the New City* (New York: St. Martin's Press, 1986), 400; and Ruth Kark and Michal Oren-Nordheim, *Jerusalem and Its Environs: Quarters, Neighborhoods, Villages, 1800–1948* (Detroit, MI: Wayne State University Press, 2001), 126. It was only in the 1920s that cement became widely used in Palestinian construction, as described in Nimrod Ben Zeev's discussion of the "cement wars" between the Zionist and Arab communities in Mandatory Palestine. See Nimrod Ben Zeev, "Building to Survive: The Politics of Cement in Mandate Palestine," *Jerusalem Quarterly*, no. 79 (Autumn 2019): 39–62. See also Andrew Ross, *Stone Men: The Palestinians Who Built Israel* (New York: Verso, 2019), 55–93.

The older generations in Bethlehem today relate how it was often the women who supervised the construction of new houses while the men were away on business trips abroad. This was also the case in Ramallah, one of the towns that followed in Bethlehem's footsteps with high rates of emigration in the early twentieth century. See Nazmi al-Ju'beh and Khaldun Bshara, *Ramallah 'imarah wa-tarikh* (Ramallah: Riwaq, 2002).

4. *Mizzi ahmar* is a type of golden-pink limestone that was used in much of the building boom that took place in Bethlehem in the early twentieth century as a result of remittances sent from abroad.

5. Some of the architectural features of the new wave of Bethlehem mansions are discussed in Diala Khasawneh, *Memoirs Engraved in Stone: Palestinian Urban Mansions* (Jerusalem: RIWAQ, 2001), 23–28.

6. This assessment was made by a journalist from the Jaffa-based Arabic newspaper *Falastin* in 1913. See *Falastin*, August 27, 1913, 2. For a discussion of the Bethlehemites as the "nouveaux riches" of Palestine in the early twentieth century, see Jacob Norris, "Return Migration and the Rise of the Palestinian *Nouveaux Riches*, 1870–1925," *Journal of Palestine Studies* 46, no. 2 (Winter 2017): 60–75.

7. Some of the villages that experienced the highest rates of emigration after

Bethlehem were Ramallah, al-Bireh, Beit Jala, and Beit Sahour. For a discussion of emigration from the Muslim village of al-Bireh and its impact on the local economy, see Saleh Abdel Jawad, "Landed Property, Palestinian Migration to America and the Emergence of a New Local Leadership: Al-Bireh, 1919–1947," *Jerusalem Quarterly*, no. 36 (2009): 13–33.

8. This is a reference to the 1908 Constitutional Revolution that occurred across the Ottoman Empire and was enthusiastically received in Palestinian cities such as Jerusalem and Jaffa. For a study of the revolutionary slogans adopted in Jerusalem, and particularly the new meanings attached to freedom (*huriyya*), see Michelle Campos, *Ottoman Brothers: Muslims, Christians, and Jews in Early Twentieth-Century Palestine* (Stanford, CA: Stanford University Press, 2010), 20–58.

9. For a discussion of the explosion of new newspapers in Palestine in the wake of the 1908 Constitutional Revolution and their promulgation of nationalist and secularist ideologies, see Rashid Khalidi, *Palestinian Identity: The Construction of Modern National Consciousness* (New York: Columbia University Press, 1997), 53–59. The first Bethlehem newspaper was not established until 1919, and the first printing press was not established until 1925.

10. The tensions in Bethlehem between the clergy and the younger generation of secular and nationalist intellectuals erupted in 1921 when the town's first newspaper, *Bayta Lahm*, was shut down by the Latin Patriarchate because of its publication of a novel written by its editor, Yuhanna Dakkarat, named *Asl al-Shaqa'* (The origin of misery), which expressed anticlerical views. The Latin Patriarchate sued Dakkarat for libel at the Court of First Instance in Jerusalem, although this decision was later overturned. See Adnan Musallam, *Folded Pages from Local Palestinian History in the 20th Century: Developments in Politics, Society, Press and Thought in Bethlehem in the British Era, 1917–1948* (Bethlehem: WIAM, 2002), 86–87. This dispute clearly had a longer backstory, as the church printing presses had previously enjoyed a monopoly over the circulation of printed materials in Bethlehem. When Jubrail Dabdoub returned to Bethlehem in 1909, tensions would already have been apparent, as secular newspapers founded after the 1908 Constitutional Revolution were arriving in the town.

11. The boycott of the Christmas procession to Bethlehem as part of the so-called Orthodox Renaissance is documented in Campos, *Ottoman Brothers*, 52–55.

12. All the descriptions of palaces in this chapter are based on my own visits to the houses, carried out between 2014 and 2019. The Morcos Nassar mansion was built around the year 1900. It was renovated in 2014 by the Centre for Cultural Heritage Preservation in Bethlehem. Information on the renovation can be found on the website of the Centre for Cultural Heritage Preservation (CCHP), "Rehabilitation of Dar Morcos Nassar," last modified February 19, 2014, www.cchp.ps/new/en/about-us/item/376-rehabilitation-of-dar-morcos-nassar.

13. The close relationship between Jubrail Dabdoub and Suleiman Handal is evidenced by the fact that Jubrail's second son, Yousef, married Suleiman's daughter Afifeh in 1922. Afifeh was born in New York in 1908. She was just fourteen when she married, while Yousef was twenty-eight.

14. The rags-to-riches story of Saleh and Giries (later Hispanicized as "Pacifico" and "Jorge") Hirmas in Chile is related in the autobiography of Saleh's daughter Victoria. The story includes an episode in which the former Chilean president, José Manuel Balmaceda, saw the brothers hawking rosaries in Santiago outside the Cathedral in Plaza de las Armas and decided to rent them a store. See Victoria Kattan de Hirmas, *Mis 100 años de vida: Chileña nacida en Belen* (Santiago de Chile: A&V Comunicaciones), 50–51.

15. The details of the Jacir family's application for a building permit to the Ottoman government are provided on the website of today's Jacir Palace Hotel, "History," accessed May 11, 2019, http://www.jacirpalace.ps/index.php/layout/2014-07-24-15-48-16 (site discontinued).

16. Jacir Palace Hotel website, "History," accessed May 11, 2019, http://www.jacirpalace.ps/index.php/layout/2014-07-24-15-48-16 (site discontinued).

17. For a discussion of how newspapers were read aloud in cafés and public squares in early twentieth-century Palestine, see Ami Ayalon, *Reading Palestine: Printing and Literacy, 1900–1948* (Austin: University of Texas Press, 2004), 103–108, 138–144.

18. The article was published in the newspaper *Falastin*, the most widely circulated Arabic newspaper in Palestine at that time. See *Falastin*, August 27, 1913, 2. The article listed the sum of money spent on each of the palaces, although the Jacir Palace was not yet complete at that point. According to the Jacir Palace website, the building cost 20,000 lira by the time of its completion. See Jacir Palace Hotel website, "History," accessed May 11, 2019, http://www.jacirpalace.ps/index.php/layout/2014-07-24-15-48-16.

CHAPTER 17: OF HYENAS, SERPENTS, AND FRENCH PHILANTHROPISTS

1. The following descriptions of Marie-Alphonsine's life and miracles with the Rosary Sisters is based on her second manuscript, reproduced in Sister Praxede Sweidan, *Kalimat al-ʿadhraʾ al-mukarrama al-umm Marie-Alphonsine Danil Ghattas* (Jerusalem: Latin Patriarchate Press, 2004), 138–70, unless otherwise indicated.

2. Marie-Alphonsine's notebooks state: "I asked her to choose a son of the Arabs from our nation/kind [*min jinsna*]." See Marie-Alphonsine, second manuscript, 49, in Sweidan, *Kalimat al-ʿadhraʾ*, 128.

3. The Congregation of the Rosary Sisters is present today in countries all over the Middle East. Marie-Alphonsine is now widely recognized as the founder of the order and was canonized by the Roman Catholic Church in 2015.

4. Marie-Alphonsine, first manuscript, 58, in Sweidan, *Kalimat al-ʿadhraʾ*, 133.

5. Marie-Alphonsine's posting to al-Salt in 1887 was the result of the founding of a new Catholic mission in al-Salt in 1866 led by the French missionary priest Don Morétain, who began construction of a Catholic church there in 1870. See Eugene Rogan, *Frontiers of the State in the Late Ottoman Empire: Transjordan, 1850–1921* (Cambridge: Cambridge University Press, 2002), 124–27.

6. The details in the following section on Marie-Alphonsine's time in al-Salt are all taken from her notebooks. She describes in detail and with considerable dismay the habits of the local Christian women she encountered, especially those from the Bedouin tribes surrounding al-Salt. See Marie-Alphonsine, second manuscript, 7–10, in Sweidan, *Kalimat al-ʿadhraʾ*, 150–54.

7. A quote from the First Epistle of John in the New Testament (1 Jn 1:5b–10), used today in the catechism of the Catholic Church (1846).

8. These are all examples of things Marie-Alphonsine witnessed or heard about during her time in al-Salt. See Marie-Alphonsine, second manuscript, 7–10, in Sweidan, *Kalimat al-ʿadhraʾ*, 150–54.

9. Marie-Alphonsine describes this scene in detail, writing how the local women believed nuns wore black so they could accept confessions. See Marie-Alphonsine, second manuscript, 9, in Sweidan, *Kalimat al-ʿadhraʾ*, 153.

10. Marie-Alphonsine describes these as "hateful habits" (*al-ʿawayid al-mamqutah*) and writes how the women would "resort to magic and the devil" (*yaltajin ila al-sihr . . . wa yaltajin ila al-shaytan*). Marie-Alphonsine, second manuscript, 10, in Sweidan, *Kalimat al-ʿadhraʾ*, 154.

11. Marie-Alphonsine uses "ya ma Soeur" to describe the way the local women addressed the nuns. She writes this in Arabic as "*yā masīr.*" Marie-Alphonsine, second manuscript, 9, in Sweidan, *Kalimat al-ʿadhraʾ*, 153. *Hjabat* and *tahwitat* are colloquial Arabic terms for amulets.

12. Marie-Alphonsine writes: "When someone was sick they [the local Catholic women] would bring soil from the grotto of a fakir or Muslim dervish, burn incense, and melt the soil for the patient to drink, thinking it would heal him. They would resort to magic by clothing him in magic leaves." Marie-Alphonsine, second manuscript, 10, in Sweidan, *Kalimat al-ʿadhraʾ*, 154.

13. The miracle at Yafet al-Nasrah is described by Marie-Alphonsine in her notebooks. See Marie-Alphonsine, second manuscript, 3–4, in Sweidan, *Kalimat al-ʿadhraʾ*, 142–44. Here I have used the details she provides and imagined how they might be retold once news spread to other towns and villages. Marie-Alphonsine herself describes this event as the "wonder at the well." She also describes how the teacher at the Protestant girls' school in Yafet al-Nasrah promptly converted to the Catholic faith, bringing several of her students with her into the sisterhood of the Rosary and donating the Protestant lands of the village to the Rosary Sisters. From episodes like this, we find that Marie-Alphonsine's reputation for performing mir-

acles became a powerful tool in the struggle of the Catholic Church to contain a rising Protestant presence in Palestine in the late nineteenth century.

14. Marie-Alphonsine's notebooks are ambiguous regarding her own interpretation of her miracles, as she describes them in very matter-of-fact ways. It is clear that her education and service with the French Sisters of Saint Joseph would have imbued her with the official Catholic doctrine on miracles, which insists that supernatural events can only be ordained by God. What is equally clear, however, is that wider society in Palestine held far more heterodox views on the source of miracles. As James Grehan writes in the context of Ottoman Palestine and Syria: "Orthodox jurists insisted that they could bend the laws of nature only with the permission of God, who was the real source of their miracles. Popular opinion did not split such hairs. Saints were hailed—and feared—as miracle-workers who had their own will and acted on their own whims." See James Grehan, *Twilight of the Saints: Everyday Religion in Ottoman Syria and Palestine* (Oxford: Oxford University Press, 2016), 74.

15. Tawfiq Canaan provides a compendium of springs and wells, as well as deep-rooted trees, caves, grottos, and cracks in the ground that were held to be crossing points for jinn and ghouls from the spirit world to the human world. He also documents how particular saints were associated with these sites as guardians or protectors of the crossing points. See Tawfiq Canaan, *Studies in Palestinian Customs and Folklore*, vol. 2, *Haunted Springs and Water Demons in Palestine* (Jerusalem: Palestine Oriental Society, 1922), 18–24.

16. Palestinians have long associated the striped hyena with these demonic traits and practices. For an early academic discussion, see Tawfiq Canaan, *Mohammedan Saints and Sanctuaries in Palestine* (London: Luzac, 1927), 243–45. Striped hyenas still inhabit the Dead Sea wilderness today, albeit in smaller numbers, and continue to be hunted due to their association with evil jinn.

17. This incident occurred in November 1886 and is described by Marie-Alphonsine in the second manuscript, 5, in Sweidan, *Kalimat al-ʿadhra'*, 146.

18. Marie-Alphonsine, second manuscript, 17, in Sweidan, *Kalimat al-ʿadhra'*, 170.

19. Mother Rosalie Nasr is a celebrated figure in the Maronite Church for her role in founding the Congregation of the Maronite Sisters of the Holy Family in Jbeil, Lebanon, in 1895. But in Marie-Alphonsine's, notebooks she appears as a jealous and vindictive figure. As Marie-Alphonsine writes, "Our Lord used her to make me taste a sip from the cup of His holy suffering [*tudhiqni jurʿa min kaʾs alamhu al-muqaddasa*]. She would freely persecute me, saturate me with various insults, and accuse me of things I was unaware of." See Marie-Alphonsine, first manuscript, 59, in Sweidan, *Kalimat al-ʿadhra'*, 133. Duvignau's biography of Marie-Alphonsine attributes Mother Rosalie's actions to jealousy of Marie-Alphonsine's

popularity with Yousef Tannous and the other Rosary Sisters. He states that this eventually caused Tannous to transfer her to Jbeil, where she was beaten to death by a novice. See Pierre Duvignau, *Mother Marie-Alphonsine and the Congregation of the Rosary*, trans. Vincent F. Gottwald (Amman: Economic Press, 1987), 130–44, 187–88.

20. The members of the Picard family were prominent Alsatian Jews who enjoyed great success as jewelers and diamond merchants in nineteenth-century Paris. They held extensive connections with the Bethlehemite merchants in Paris through the 1880s, 1890s, and 1900s. For example, they supplied the Kattan family—as well as the Giacaman family, which was based in Paris in the 1880s—with jewelry for sale in both Paris and Kiev. The mysterious "Madame Picard" was the wife of one of the Picard jewelers. She appears to have been an important sponsor of the Bethlehemites in Paris and the Arabic-speaking Syrian community more generally. In 1888 she was the key facilitator in the appointment of a Syrian priest, Alexis Kateb, as the archimandrite of the first Arab church in Paris, the Melkite Church at Saint-Julien-le-Pauvre. As documented in Paris police reports, Madame Picard even traveled to Syria to persuade Melkite patriarch Gregory to appoint Kateb. All of these connections are documented in Jacob Norris, "Across Confessional Borders: A Microhistory of Ottoman Christians and Their Migratory Paths," in *Minorities and the Modern Arab World: New Perspectives*, ed. Laura Robson (Syracuse, NY: Syracuse University Press, 2016), 39–60.

21. The donation is described in Marie-Alphonsine, second manuscript, 13, in Sweidan, *Kalimat al-'adhra'*, 162.

22. Marie-Alphonsine describes her reluctance in Marie-Alphonsine, second manuscript, 13–14, in Sweidan, *Kalimat al-'adhra'*, 162.

23. Described in Duvignau, *Mother Marie-Alphonsine*, 201.

24. Marie-Alphonsine mentions these specific merchants in her second manuscript, 13, in Sweidan, *Kalimat al-'adhra'*, 162.

25. Duvignau describes how Madame Picard's donation had been conditional upon the Latin patriarch in Jerusalem helping her gain favor with the Grande Chartreuse Monastery in France. The patriarch eventually refused to comply, causing Madame Picard to withdraw her funding. Duvignau also documents how the French consul was then persuaded to intervene to keep the Rosary Sisters afloat. See Duvignau, *Mother Marie-Alphonsine*, 204. Marie-Alphonsine herself does not seem to have been aware of these negotiations, stating only that the consul came to visit their orphanage and was so impressed he was led to arrange for a stipend from the French government. See Marie-Alphonsine, second manuscript, 15, in Sweidan, *Kalimat al-'adhra'*, 166.

26. Marie-Alphonsine, second manuscript, 13–17, in Sweidan, *Kalimat al-'adhra'*, 162–70.

27. Bethlehem contains a number of monuments and public works from the early twentieth century that bear the names of the most successful merchant families. In 1913, the Jaffa-based newspaper *Falastin* listed "the khawajas, Jacirs, Dabdoubs, Kattans, Hazbuns, and Jadallahs" as among the donors for the electricity and tramway concession bid put together by the Commercial Bank of Palestine. This project was never realized but would have included a tramway that extended to Bethlehem. See *Falastin*, October 25, 1913, 2. Examples of public works still standing today include the statue *Saint George and the Dragon* donated by Anton Dabdoub in 1926 that stands in the entrance of Saint Catherine's Chapel in the Nativity Church complex, as well as the restored Milk Grotto chapel in 1934–35. Its restoration was partly funded by Issa Abdallah Hazboun and included sculptures he provided for the facade.

28. The relationship between Marie-Alphonsine and the khawajas can be understood through the anthropological and sociological literature on patron-client relationships, gift-giving, and miracles. See, for example, Jerome H. Neyrey, "Miracles in Other Words: Social Science Perspectives on Healing," in *Miracles in Jewish and Christian Antiquity*, ed. John C. Cavadini (Notre Dame, IN: University of Notre Dame Press, 1999), 19–56. Scholars of medieval Europe have emphasized the conditional nature of gift-giving to saints, as benefactors expected miracles in return for their gifts. As Aaron Gurevich writes, "When a saint did not respond to the expectations of the believers [i.e., no miracles were produced], they regarded his inactivity as a violation of the principle of reciprocity." In this context, Marie-Alphonsine appears as a "broker" between patron (the khawajas) and client (the Virgin Mary), producing an expectation among the khawajas that miracles would occur to their benefit. See Aaron Ya. Gurevich, "A Gift Awaits an Answer: A Page from the Cultural History of Society," in *The Man of Many Devices, Who Wandered Full Many Ways: Festschrift in Honour of János M. Bak*, ed. Balazs Nagy and Marcell Sebok (Vienna: Central European University Press, 1999), 333–39. It is often assumed that the Counter-Reformation produced a break in this client-patron view of miracles as the Catholic Church sought to impose a more rationalized understanding of supernatural events. But recent work is showing how these practices persisted in Catholic societies well into the early modern and even modern periods. See, for example, Mary Laven's work on ex-votos in "Recording Miracles in Renaissance Italy," *Past and Present* 230, supplement 11 (2016): 191–212. Likewise, James Grehan documents the importance of patronage in producing miracles in late Ottoman Palestine and Syria in *Twilight of the Saints*, 95–96, 73–76.

29. Marie-Alphonsine describes this miracle in Marie-Alphonsine, second manuscript, 14, in Sweidan, *Kalimat al-'adhra'*, 164.

CHAPTER 18: OF THE RESURRECTION OF JUBRAIL DABDOUB

1. At some point in the summer of 1909, Jubrail was held to have been brought back to life by Marie-Alphonsine. In this chapter, I have imagined the scene from Jubrail's perspective using Marie-Alphonsine's own account of the miracle as well as the description provided by Benedict Stolz. See Marie-Alphonsine, second manuscript, 17, reproduced in Sister Praxede Sweidan, *Kalimat al-'adhra' al-mukarrama al-umm Marie-Alphonsine Danil Ghattas* (Jerusalem: Latin Patriarchate Press, 2004), 170; and Benedict Stolz, *A Handmaid of the Holy Rosary: Mother Mary Alphonsus of the Rosary, First Foundress of an Arab Congregation, 1843–1927*, trans. Natalie Bevenot (New York: Benziger Brothers, 1968), 97. Both of these accounts mention how Jubrail's sister Sara tore her dress upon realizing Jubrail was dead. This custom of tearing the dress and later sewing it up with wide stitches as a sign of mourning is described in H. H. Spoer and A. M. Spoer, "Sickness and Death among the Arabs of Palestine," *Folklore* 38, no. 2 (1927): 135.

2. Based on interviews with Jubrail's sister Sara, Stolz states that Jubrail had contracted typhoid fever. See Stolz, *Handmaid of the Holy Rosary*, 97. Typhoid fever was widespread in Palestine at the time, especially during the summer months when bacteria could spread more easily through flies feasting on the contaminated water that passed through open sewage pipes. S. Peller, "Typhoid Fever in Palestine," *Epidemiology and Infection* 28, no. 3 (December 1928): 318–23. See also Salim Tamari's discussion of the uncovered sewage pipes in Jerusalem in *The Great War and the Remaking of Palestine* (Berkeley: University of California Press, 2017), 59–60. There is also a vivid description of the spread of typhoid fever in Bethlehem during World War I, and the way herbal medicines were used to treat it, in the Bethlehem University Oral History collections of the Planet Bethlehem Archive. See "Woman from Bethlehem Discussing the Ottoman Period and World War I" Bethlehem University Oral History collections, Ottoman Empire and World War I, http://planetbethlehem.org/.

3. Both Christians and Muslims in Palestine frequently attributed the contraction of diseases such as typhoid fever to malignant spirits, or jinn. Christian belief in jinn was not only the product of folk culture but was also transmitted through the most widely read Arabic Bible, the so-called Van Dyck translation (completed 1865), which used the collective plural of jinn, *al-jann*, on a number of occasions to denote what is usually translated in English as "spirits." For examples, see Van Dyck, Arabic edition, *Al-Lawiyin* (Leviticus) 19:31, 20:6, and *Samu'il al-awwal* (1 Samuel), 28:3, 28:9. Jubrail Dabdoub and Marie-Alphonsine most likely grew up reading this version of the Arabic Bible, although as Catholics they may have later switched to the Jesuit Arabic Bible, translated by Augustin Rodet and Ibrahim al-Yaziji and first published in 1880, which also used the term *al-jann*, in line with the Van Dyck version.

4. This is the final prayer commonly said by Catholic priests during the last rites, before the sick person is invited to consume the Eucharist. Catholic last rites involve three stages: confession, anointing of the sick, and a special communion called *viaticum*. These rites are followed by Roman Catholics in Bethlehem and are usually performed in Arabic.

5. This sentence is adapted from Salman Rushdie's description of Azrael, angel of death, in his magical realist novel *The Satanic Verses* (London: Viking, 1988), 416. In Rushdie's novel, Azrael appears in a vision experienced by the character Saladin, which Saladin interprets as a warning against pursuing the character Mishal.

6. Azrael is often described as a specifically Muslim angel of death who separates the soul from the body at the moment of death. But he was also known in the same terms among Arabic-speaking Christians and Jews in early twentieth-century Palestine. For examples, see Spoer and Spoer, "Sickness and Death," 116–17; and J. E. Hanauer, *Folklore of the Holy Land* (London: Duckworth, 1910), 166–175.

7. Azrael is commonly described as holding a scroll with the names of people who have been called to death by God. See Jane Smith and Yvonne Yazbeck Haddad, *Islamic Understanding of Death and Resurrection* (Albany: State University of New York Press, 1981), 35.

8. Azrael was seen as a messenger of God, not the arbiter of a person's death. See Spoer and Spoer, "Sickness and Death," 116–17. The phrase "Lord of the two worlds" (referring to God) comes from the memoir of Jubrail's cousin. See Ibrahim Yuhanna Dabdoub, "Mukhtasar tarikh 'ilat al-marhum Yuhanna Yaqoub al-Dabdoub" (unpublished memoir, 1923, private collection of Anton Shukri Dabdoub), 19.

9. There are various local legends associating Azrael with the caves in Wadi al-Nar. See, for example, Hanauer, *Folklore*, 169, and the myths and legends from the wider Bethlehem area collected by ethnographer and folklorist Toine Van Teeffelen, "Wadi Nar: A Story," Palestine-Family.net, accessed March 28, 2020, https://palestine-family.net/wadi-nar-a-story/. Van Teeffelen relates the story of Azrael's cave in Wadi al-Nar, where the burning candles represent the lives of every person on Earth.

10. Comparative research on near-death experiences by the likes of Kellehear, Pasricha, and Corazza has suggested the phenomenon of the "life-review" in near-death experiences is a cultural function of specifically Western notions of the interior self and linear notions of time deriving from the monotheism of Christianity. But these characterizations tend to overlook the existence of non-Western forms of monotheism (Islamic, Christian, Jewish, etc.) that also espouse linear notions of time. As a Palestinian Roman Catholic who spent his life moving between Asia, Europe, and the Americas, Jubrail defied divisions of "Western" and "Eastern," and I have therefore included a form of life-review in his near-death expe-

rience, albeit in jumbled, surreal form that does not conform neatly to the classic "Western" model. Some of the key publications on near-death experiences include Allan Kellehear, *Experiences of Near Death: Beyond Medicine and Religion* (Oxford: Oxford University Press, 1996), 28, 33; Satwant Pasricha, "A Systematic Survey of Near-Death Experiences in South Asia," *Journal of Scientific Exploration* 7, no. 2 (1993): 161–71; and Ornella Corazza, "Exploring Space-Consciousness and Other Dissociative Experiences," *Journal of Consciousness Studies* 17, no. 7/8 (January 2010): 173–90.

11. In 1927 (the year of Mariam Ghattas's death), H. H. Spoer wrote that she had once met a nun from the Rosary Sisters who had expressed the belief that severe illnesses were produced by jinn and that a large crowd could help disperse the illness. See Spoer and Spoer, "Sickness and Death," 119.

12. Marie-Alphonsine describes how she dipped her rosary beads in water, sprinkled the drops on Jubrail's head, and prayed the Rosary. She would most likely have recited the Glorious Mysteries of the Rosary, which requires ten Hail Marys to be said while meditating on Jesus's resurrection. See Marie-Alphonsine, second manuscript, 17, in Sweidan, *Kalimat al-ʿadhraʾ*.

13. Marie-Alphonsine writes: "I asked for something that I could try to give him to eat, and they brought quince jam [*maraba safarjal*], which I gave him, and he started eating very slowly until he came back to life [*rajaʿa lil-hayaah*] through the intercession of the Lady of the Rosary [*bi-shafaaʿat sultanat al-wardiyya*]." See Marie-Alphonsine, second manuscript, 17, in Sweidan, *Kalimat al-ʿadhraʾ*, 170.

14. Marie-Alphonsine emphasizes the family's gratitude to the Virgin Mary the moment Jubrail displayed signs of life: "Everyone present thanked the Virgin Mary, Mother of God [Mariam al-Batūl, umm Allah] and increased their fervency [*al-ḥarāra*] in worshipping the Rosary." See Marie-Alphonsine, second manuscript, 17, in Sweidan, *Kalimat al-ʿadhraʾ*, 170.

15. Benedict Stolz, who interviewed members of Jubrail's family about the miracle in the 1930s, writes: "From that day Gabril Dabdub lived without any further illness until death overtook him in 1931 in his seventieth year. His wife and son are still alive. In their eyes Mother Mary Alphonsus is a great saint." See Stolz, *Handmaid of the Holy Rosary*, 97.

16. Nabʿ al-ʿadhraʾ (the Spring of the Virgin) is located in a valley to the south of the village of Ein Karem. Tradition holds that Mary drank from the spring before climbing the hill to meet Elizabeth, mother of John the Baptist. Numerous legends tell of the Virgin's frequent appearance at this site.

17. As described in Duvignau's hagiography of Marie-Alphonsine. See Pierre Duvignau, *Mother Marie-Alphonsine and the Congregation of the Rosary*, trans. Vincent F. Gottwald (Amman: Economic Press, 1987), 130–34.

18. Only the first of Marie-Alphonsine's two manuscripts (describing her vi-

sions of the Virgin Mary) was burned. The second manuscript (describing her work with the Rosary Sisters and the miracles she performed) still survives in its original form. The discovery of the notebooks and the attempts of the Nazarene faction of the Rosary Sisters to destroy them is recounted by Sister Praxede Sweidan in *Kalimat al-ʿadhra*ʾ, 99–100.

19. Marie-Alphonsine, second manuscript, 17 in Sweidan, *Kalimat al-ʿadhra*ʾ, 170.

EPILOGUE

1. The house still stands today and is occupied by the Bethlehem Bible College. During my visits to the building, the guesthouse manager, Jihan Qanawati al-Aʿma, explained how the tiles date back to the original flooring laid by artisans from Istanbul.

2. As specified in League of Nations reports, the collapse of these countries' economies after 1929 was due largely to their dependence on exports to the United States (copper and nitrates in Chile, tin in Bolivia). See C. H. Lee, "The Effects of the Depression on Primary Producing Countries," *Journal of Contemporary History* 4, no. 4 (1969): 139–55.

3. Paulo Drinot, introduction to *The Great Depression in Latin America*, ed. Paulo Drinot and Alan Knight (Durham, NC: Duke University Press, 2004), 12–23.

4. Details of the collapse of the Dabdoub family business have been gleaned from numerous sources. Their pleas to partners in Bolivia and Chile to pay back their debts is documented in a series of letters written by Jubrail from Paris between January and May 1930, held in the private collection of Peter Dabdoub. My thanks to Peter for sharing these letters with me. Other details were provided by Jubrail's granddaughter, Alice-Madelaine Siman (daughter of Yusef Dabdoub), who now lives in El Salvador. My thanks to Alice's son Jose Eduardo Siman for sharing his mother's memories with me.

5. Numerous stories are told in Bethlehem of Suleiman Jacir's bankruptcy and the anger it inspired in those to whom he owed money. This particular story was shared with me by Anton Mansour, great-great-grandson of Bethlehem's first mayor, Hanna Mansour.

6. This story was told to me by Paulette Tissaire Dabdoub, who was married to the grandson of Jubrail's brother Mikhail. Interview in Bethlehem, August 14, 2015.

7. The story of Hanna Kawas buying up the Jacir and Hirmas mansions comes from two separate sources: oral tradition shared with me by Anton Mansour and from Ghadeer Najjar, *Bethlehem: The Historic Center and Bethlehemites in Jerusalem* (Bethlehem: Diyar, 2017), 103.

8. This description of Hosh Dabdoub is based on the description given in the

childhood autobiography of the celebrated writer Jabra Ibrahim Jabra, who grew up in Bethlehem in the 1920s and early 1930s. Jabra came from a poor Syriac family and lived in the hosh as a young boy in the late 1920s when the Dabdoub family was renting it out. See Jabra Ibrahim Jabra, *Al-bi'r al-ula: fusul min sirah dhatiyah* (Beirut: al-mu'assisah al-'arabiyah lil-dirasat wa al-nashr, 2001), 84.

9. My thanks to Edgar and Emilio Batarse (grandson and great-grandson of Wardeh Dabdoub) for sharing with me copies of Wardeh's passport, which shows her arriving in El Salvador via Cuba and Guatemala, on November 10, 1930.

10. These details have been pieced together using the Bethlehem Latin Parish Archive (which records births and deaths overseas when known) and surviving business letters Jubrail exchanged with relatives in South America.

11. Stories of having to sift through animal dung to find scraps of barley to eat is a common feature of interviews recorded with people from Bethlehem who lived through World War I. These interviews, carried out by Bethlehem University under the direction of Adnan Musallam, have been digitized in the Planet Bethlehem Archive. For examples, see interviews with Wadie Salah, Zakhariya Abu Aita, and Hanna Abdallah Giacaman in Bethlehem University Oral History collections, Ottoman Empire and World War I, http://planetbethlehem.org/.

12. This description is based on numerous recordings of interviews with Bethlehemites who lived through the locust plague housed in digitized form in the Planet Bethlehem Archive. See Bethlehem University Oral History collections, Ottoman Empire and World War I, http://planetbethlehem.org/.

13. This is adapted from Khalil Sakakini's diary entry on April 1915, in which he describes the humiliation of Christian men being rounded up as rubbish collectors and how the women cried as they watched from their windows. Sakakini ends the passage by writing, "There is no doubt that this is the ultimate humiliation.... And yet the Muslims still expect the Christians to love this state." See Akram Musallam, ed., *Yawmiyyat Khalil al-Sakakini: Yawmiyyat—rasa'il—ta'ammulat. Al-kitab al-thani* (Ramallah: Markaz Khalil al-Sakakini al-thaqafi, Mu'assasat al-dirasat al-qudsiyya, 2003), March 28–April 4, 1915.

14. I am grateful to Antonio Dabdoub Escobar, great-grandson of Sara Dabdoub, for sharing this story of Sara's hair with me. According to the story, Sara and her second husband, Ibrahim Odeh, visited the Tomb of the Patriarchs in Hebron to ask for a son (Ibrahim already had seven daughters from a previous marriage). Sara pledged to grow her hair for twelve years and name their son Isaac in honor of Patriarch Ibrahim's son if their wish was granted. She subsequently gave birth to a boy, whom she named Ishaaq (Isaac in Arabic), and let her hair grow for twelve years. The story is also recounted on Antonio Dabdoub Escobar's website: accessed May 19, 2020, http://losdabdoub.blogspot.com/.

15. This story is recounted in more detail in chapter 14.

16. My thanks to Antonio Dabdoub Escobar, great-grandson of Sara, for sharing this story with me.

17. Jubrail's mansion still stands today in Bethlehem on Hebron Road, bearing his name in Arabic and his initials in Latin characters on the front gates. Today the building is owned by the Bethlehem Bible College. His brother Mikhail's mansion also still stands around three hundred feet down the road and is owned by the Latin Patriarchate.

18. These are widely recounted legends in Bethlehem and Beit Jala today. They feature among the examples collected by Palestinian folklorist Issa Massou and displayed in the online archive Palestine-Family.net. See "Bethlehem Folklore and the Virgin Mary," Palestine-Family.net, accessed May 18, 2020, https://palestine-family.net/bethlehem-folklore-and-the-virgin-mary/.

19. I have seen elderly people in Bethlehem using these local plants to treat bad coughs and fever. They are also recorded in Nidal Jaradat's study, "Medical Plants Utilized in Palestinian Folk Medicine for Treatment of Diabetes Mellitus and Cardiac Diseases," *Journal of al-Aqsa University* 9 (2005): 1–28.

20. Mariam continued to live in the house after Jubrail's death, until she herself died in 1938. Alice-Madelaine Siman (granddaughter of Jubrail and Mariam) recounted to me how she visited her grandmother there around 1936.

21. My thanks to Anton Mansour, great-great-grandson of Hanna Mansour, for sharing the story of the first car in Bethlehem, which is said to have arrived at some point in the late 1890s or early 1900s. The story was told to Anton by his grandfather Victor Georges Mansour (grandson of Hanna Mansour).

22. In Toine Van Teeffelen's story of Azrael's cave in Wadi al-Nar, a visitor accidentally knocks his candle to the ground in an effort to stop it from extinguishing, then instantly dies, representing the futility of trying to change one's destiny. See "Wadi Nar: A Story," Palestine-Family.net, accessed March 28, 2020, https://palestine-family.net/wadi-nar-a-story/.

AUTHOR'S COMMENTARY

1. Hayden White, *The Content of the Form: Narrative Discourse and Historical Representation* (Baltimore: Johns Hopkins University Press, 1987), 1.

2. Walter Benjamin, *The Arcades Project*, trans. Howard Eiland and Kevin McLaughlin (Cambridge, MA: Harvard University Press, 1999), 460.

3. See Hayden White, "Tears in the Fabric of the Past: New Theories of Narrative and History," panel discussion, October 30, 2014, University of California, Berkeley, https://www.youtube.com/watch?v=Mr5DgDv1two.

4. Among the historical anthropologists to explore nonlinear ways of writing is Richard Price, whose writing on modern Caribbean history has seen him "searching out or even inventing a literary form ... in order to effectively evoke that partic-

ular society, or that particular historical moment." In his book *The Convict and the Colonel* (Durham, NC: Duke University Press, 2018), he experimented with various narrative techniques such as "temporal shunts, flash-backs and cuts forward, a wide range of photos that punctuate the text and accentuate rhythm." For a discussion of writing, see Richard Price, "Practices of Historical Narrative," *Rethinking History* 5, no. 3 (2001): 361. For examples of writing by literary anthropologists, see Anand Pandian and Stuart J. McLean, eds., *Crumpled Paper Boat: Experiments in Ethnographic Writing* (Durham, NC: Duke University Press, 2017).

5. For examples of these historians' work, see Natalie Zemon Davis, *Women on the Margins: Three Seventeenth-Century Lives* (Cambridge, MA: Harvard University Press, 1995); Jonathan Walker, "Antonio Foscarini in the City of Crossed Destinies," *Rethinking History* 5, no. 2 (2001): 305–34; and Sarah Knott, *Mother Is a Verb: An Unconventional History* (London: Picador, 2020). For a discussion of how academic historiography tends to use a nineteenth-century realist style of writing, see Daniel Fulda, "Historiographic Narration," in *The Living Handbook of Narratology*, ed. Peter Hühn, John Pier, Wolf Schmid, and Jörg Schönert, last updated March 25, 2014, https://www.lhn.uni-hamburg.de/node/123.html.

6. Robert Shanafelt, "Magic, Miracle, and Marvel in Anthropology," *Ethnos* 69, no. 3 (2004): 336.

7. For a key formulation of the recent "ontological turn" in anthropology, see Martin Holbraad and Morten Axel Pedersen, *The Ontological Turn: An Anthropological Exposition* (Cambridge: Cambridge University Press, 2017). This work builds on earlier interventions, such as those of Eduardo Viveiros de Castro, "Cosmological Deixis and Amerindian Perspectivism," *Journal of the Royal Anthropological Institute* 4, no. 3 (1998): 469–88; and Marilyn Strathern, *The Gender of the Gift: Problems with Women and Problems with Society in Melanesia* (Berkeley: University of California Press, 1988).

8. Viveiros de Castro, "Perspectival Anthropology and the Method of Controlled Equivocation," *Tipití: Journal of the Society for the Anthropology of Lowland South America* 2, no. 1 (2004): 6.

9. Natalie Zemon Davis, *Trickster Travels: A Sixteenth-Century Muslim between Worlds* (London: Faber, 2007), 12–13.

10. Bryant Simon, "Narrating a Southern Tragedy: Historical Facts and Historical Fictions," *Rethinking History* 1, no. 2 (1997): 165–87.

11. Walker, "Antonio Foscarini," 325.

12. James Grehan, *Twilight of the Saints: Everyday Religion in Ottoman Syria and Palestine* (Oxford: Oxford University Press, 2016).

13. Michael Wood, "In Reality," *Janus Head*, special issue, *Magical Realism* 5, no. 2 (2002): 9–14.

14. The presupposition of faith on the part of the reader was observed by Alejo

Carpentier, the writer who did the most to define Latin American magical realism through his concept of "lo real meravilliso americano." See Alejo Carpentier, "De lo real maravilloso americano," in *Tientos y diferencias* (Montevideo: Arca, 1967), 96–112.

15. Seymour Menton, *Magic Realism Rediscovered, 1918–1981* (Philadelphia, PA: Art Alliance Press, 1983), 13–14.

16. Marjorie Becker, "When I Was a Child, I Danced as a Child, but Now That I Am Old, I Think about Salvation: Concepción González and a Past That Would Not Stay Put," *Journal of Theory and Practice* 1, no. 3 (1997): 343–55.

17. Jubrail Dabdoub to Anton Dabdoub, Paris, February 10, 1930, private collection of Peter Dabdoub.

18. Ibrahim Muhawi and Sharif Kanaana, *Speak, Bird, Speak Again: Palestinian Arab Folktales* (Berkeley: University of California Press, 1989), 5–6, 18–20, 46.

19. Issa Basil al-Bandak, *Issa Basil Bandak: Hayatuhu, aʿmaluhu, mudhakkaratuhu, 1898–1984*, ed. Adnan Musallam (Bethlehem: Diyar, 2013), 48–49.

20. Jabra Ibrahim Jabra, *Al-biʾr al-ula: fusul min sirah dhatiyah* (Beirut: al-muʾassisah al-ʿarabiyah lil-dirasat wa al-nashr, 2001), 109.

21. Emile Habibi, *Saraya, The Ogre's Daughter: A Palestinian Fairy Tale*, trans. Peter Theroux (Jerusalem: Ibis, 2006), 7–9.

22. Emile Habibi, *The Secret Life of Saeed the Pessoptimist*, trans. Salma K. Jayyusi and Trevor LeGassick (1974; repr., London: Arabia Books, 2010), 3.

23. Beshara Doumani, *Family Life in the Ottoman Mediterranean: A Social History* (Cambridge: Cambridge University Press, 2017).

24. The seven clans are the ʿAnatreh, Farahiyyeh, Fawaghreh, Hreizat, Kawawseh, Najajreh, and Tarajmeh clans.

25. Ibrahim Yuhanna Dabdoub, "Mukhtasar tarikh ʿilat al-marhum Yuhanna Yaqoub al-Dabdoub" (unpublished memoir, 1923, private collection of Anton Shukri Dabdoub), 8–9.

26. See Planet Bethlehem Archive, http://planetbethlehem.org/.

27. The Ottoman shariʿa court records document numerous cases from the seventeenth century. For example, in 1679 a tax dispute broke out when the inhabitants of Bethlehem complained that the local *mutawalli* was levying the same tax twice upon them for the local *waqf* fund. The *mutawalli* in turn complained that the Bethlehemites had refused to pay the tax and had rebelled against him and his legion. See Jerusalem Shariʿa Court Sijill, Center for Palestinian Heritage, Abu Dis, Occupied Palestinian Territories, 181, 1090 H/1679 CE, p. 100. Khalil Showkeh relates a similar case from the nineteenth century when the local inhabitants chased a customs officer, Yuhanna Dawud Nasaar al-Armani, out of town in 1860 because of his extortionate collection of taxes. A petition was subsequently put together by men from many of the leading merchant families (including several *mukhtars*

representing their denominational communities) demanding a new officer be appointed. See Khalil Showkeh, *Tarikh bayt lahm fi-1-'ahd al-'uthmani* (Bethlehem, 2005), 267.

28. As explored in Jacob Norris, "Dragomans, Tattooists, Artisans: Palestinian Christians and Their Encounters with Catholic Europe in the 17th and 18th Centuries," *Journal of Global History* 14, no. 1 (2019): 68–86.

✺ WORLDING THE MIDDLE EAST

Emily Gottreich and Daniel Zoughbie, editors

This series investigates the "worlding" of the Middle East and the ever-changing, ever-becoming dynamism of the region. It seeks to capture the ways in which the region is reimagined and unmade through flows of world capital, power, and ideas. Spanning the modern period to the present, Worlding the Middle East showcases critical and innovative books that develop new ways of thinking about the region and the wider world.

Nadim Bawalsa, *Transnational Palestine: Migration and the Right of Return before 1948*
2022

Carel Bertram, *A House in the Homeland: Armenian Pilgrimages to Places of Ancestral Memory*
2022

Susan Gilson Miller, *Years of Glory: Nelly Benatar and the Pursuit of Justice in Wartime North Africa*
2021

Amélie Le Renard, *Western Privilege: Work, Intimacy, and Postcolonial Hierarchies in Dubai*
2021

The authorized representative in the EU for product safety and compliance is:
Mare Nostrum Group
B.V Doelen 72
4831 GR Breda
The Netherlands

www.ingramcontent.com/pod-product-compliance
Lightning Source LLC
Chambersburg PA
CBHW030104170426
43198CB00009B/482